The Jesus Blueprint

Rediscovering His
Original Plan
for Changing the World

DAVE BUEHRING

K. 41

"He was winning and discipling youth in every high school every week, on the Island of Hawaii when he was with YWAM as a young man himself. Decades later, I heartily commend to you Dave Buehring as a personal friend and seasoned spiritual leader, who continues as a disciple-maker. Dave has the experience and spiritual authority to bring you a powerful gift in an easy-to-read book that will inform, inspire, and ignite you to action into one of the greatest missing keys for the transformation of the nation and the world for Jesus and His Kingdom. Jesus said, 'Go, disciple all nations.' Dave writes how in *The Jesus Blueprint*! Let's do it!"

~ **Loren Cunningham**
Founder, Youth With a Mission (YWAM)

"As one who has devoted his life to calling the church to make disciples, this work is a great encouragement. *The Jesus Blueprint* is a clarion call to do what Jesus told us to do by someone who has done it. In other words, Dave Buehring knows what he is talking about, he has practiced it, and now he is evangelizing the church and all of society to be and make disciples."

~ **Bill Hull**
Author and President of Choose the Life Ministries

"The understanding of discipleship has definitely shaped my way of living, leading and looking at life. Today, we are reaping the consequences of a lack of deliberate disciple-making within families, churches and society. In *The Jesus Blueprint*, my friend Dave Buehring challenges and equips us to freshly embrace Jesus' original disciple-making plan – and I couldn't agree with him more! Without it, our championing of justice, our work of transformation, and our empowering of God's people will not survive beyond a generation. However, embracing it allows us to transform generations to come!"

~ **Dr. John Perkins**
Author of Let Justice Roll Down,
*Founder of the Christian Community Development Association (CCDA)
and the John M. Perkins Foundation for Reconciliation & Development*

"I have the highest respect for Dave Buehring. His heart truly beats with a passion to not only make disciples, but disciple-makers. Over one year's time we took 2,500 people in our church through Dave's resource, *A Discipleship Journey*. I'd encourage you to read *The Jesus Blueprint*, follow the plan, and build His kingdom!"

~ **Steve Berger**
Senior Pastor, Grace Chapel in Franklin, TN

"In an age of catastrophic change there is a desperate need for the church to rediscover her true identity and authority. We are called not to be passive bystanders but a force for good, bringing God's kingdom to bear in this present global crisis. In *The Jesus Blueprint*, Dave Buehring provides a compelling case of how God's people can rise up and engage with Him in ushering the greatest move of God the world has ever seen."

~ *Rev. Kathy Giske*
Associate Director, Presbyterian Frontier Fellowship

"I spent my life working with people in power and those without, believing that Jesus Christ is the way. While yielding to Him, studying His building plan, and putting it into practice, it would have been helpful to have Dave Buehring's book *The Jesus Blueprint* handy. No matter what domains we are in, we must be living examples of Jesus' character and ways. History and experience show me that discipleship changes lives when relationships are handled with grace and truth. I've seen it happen in families and communities, and I believe it impacts our political, economic, and belief systems to the benefit of those who are considered the least in our society."

~ *The Honorable Al Quie*
Former State Senator, Congressman and Governor of Minnesota,
Former President and State Director of Prison Fellowship

"*The Jesus Blueprint* resonates with truth, not just because of the content but because Dave Buehring lives his life according to it. For this very reason Dave has had a high level of acceptance and impact within our circle of church leadership. The challenge to impact the 'Dozen Domains' has especially elicited a response to action from our leaders. They long to see discipled followers of Jesus serving in all domains of our society. We are grateful to God for the clarion call that comes through Dave and *The Jesus Blueprint*.

~ *David Wells*
General Superintendent, The Pentecostal Assemblies of Canada

"Dave's heart for disciple-making is inspiring and desperately needed in the church today. I've benefitted from people pouring into my life, and seeing its value in my walk with the Lord, I have a heart to do the same for others. I highly recommend *The Jesus Blueprint* and highly encourage disciple-making!"

~ *Jeremy Camp*
Artist, Leader of Speaking Louder Ministries

"Dave Buehring and I have been friends – no, brothers – for over thirty years, and he has impacted me, my bride, our children, and now our grandchildren. I have been a leader in the church since I was nineteen; now at fifty-eight I can honestly say I know no one who has lived and taught disciple-making more than Dave. *The Jesus Blueprint* is worth reading if you only read the first chapter to find out who will be taking your final exam. I highly recommend this book and my brother to you, but only if you want a changed life that impacts others."

~ *Dr. Samuel M. Huddleston*
Assistant District Superintendent of the Northern California and Nevada Assemblies of God District, Author of Five Years to Life

"David Buehring's passion for making disciples is contagious. His enthusiasm for the Great Commission sparkles in his work on making disciple-makers. In *The Jesus Blueprint*, David explores global principles that hold the seeds for exponential expansion of reproducing faith, one life at a time. You will not be disappointed as you read of the rewarding adventure of making disciples like Jesus."

~ *Woodie J. Stevens*
Global Discipleship Ministries Director, Church of the Nazarene

"In Matthew 13:33, Jesus says the kingdom of God is expanding in the world just like leaven in a lump of dough. But what does that look like? *The Jesus Blueprint* shows us how Jesus expected his kingdom to grow ... through ordinary people who were disciples of Jesus. David Buehring gives us a key to participating in the expansion of God's kingdom: being disciple-makers in all domains of society. Written by a man who is living this message, David brings decades of experience into the poignant principles of this book. I commend it to anyone who seeks to be a partner with God in the advance of His kingdom."

~ *Eddie Broussard*
Associate US Director, Senior Vice President of The Navigators

"At a time in the American church where we are looking for the next 'great program,' Dave Buehring clearly brings us right back to the heart of Jesus and His mandate, 'Go therefore and make disciples of all nations.' *The Jesus Blueprint* will stoke the fire for discipleship in your church and bring you back to where Jesus has called us to live, as disciple-makers."

~ *John Blue*
Retired Pro Hockey Player, Lead Pastor of Pacific Pointe Church (CMA) in Irvine, CA

"For the last seven years, Dave Buehring has been discipling me. I honestly don't know where I'd be had he not walked me through my time on *American Idol*, and the subsequent aftermath of being so vocal about my faith on the show. There is nobody more genuine, equipped, and passionate to speak on the issue of disciple-making. He doesn't just talk it; he walks it."

~ Mandisa
American Idol Finalist, GRAMMY® Nominated Recording Artist

"There are books of information and then there are books of formation; books that inspire and books that are so foundational that they shape peoples' thinking for the rest of their lives. In *The Jesus Blueprint*, Dave Buehring has penned a masterful and paradigm-altering guide aimed at anchoring the Church in her fundamental call: discipling people."

~ Steven Fry
Founder and President, Messenger Fellowship

"*The Jesus Blueprint* spurs on the next generation to take its place in the grand story that God is writing in human history by making disciple-makers in their unique cultural, vocational, and geographical environments. With the wisdom of a father, the discipline of a coach, and the encouragement of a good friend, Dave Buehring shares a contagious vision and practical strategies that fuels the hearts and passions of emerging leaders."

~ Heather Zempel
Author, Discipleship Pastor, National Community Church in Washington DC

"*The Jesus Blueprint* put me on notice that disciple-making is required if I want to transform my culture. Dave Buehring's book will inspire you to rededicate yourself to Jesus' original plan to 'go, make disciples.'"

~ Kevin Mateer
Chaplain (MAJ), US Army

"It has been said that the last command Jesus gave, 'go make disciples in every nation,' has become our least concern. My friend Dave Buehring passionately seeks to change that. In *The Jesus Blueprint* he challenges us to make disciple-makers in every domain of society. A must-read for everyone concerned about changing our world."

~ Dan Sneed
Teacher & Author, Foursquare Church International

"Dave's passion and practical insight in *The Jesus Blueprint* on the last words of Jesus to 'go and make disciples' will stir your heart and reenergize your focus on becoming more like Jesus. An exciting and inspired challenge to be both a hearer *and* a doer of the Word."

*~ **Mary Tomlinson***
18 years with The Walt Disney Company, President of On-Purpose Partners

"As the principal of a school, I have seen first–hand how the 'blueprint' works in the lives of my staff, and therefore in hundreds of our students. In *The Jesus Blueprint*, Dave Buehring makes no bones about this generation being called to be disciple-makers. In this revealing treatise, he lays out the call for aligning to Jesus' last command – of which I'm seeing the results in my domain of education on a daily basis!"

*~ **Mike McAteer***
Principal, Mission Viejo Christian School

"Dave Buehring's teaching of the principles shared in *The Jesus Blueprint* have had a deep impact on the men of North Way Christian Community! The trajectory of my church, men's personal lives, and their families have been radically changed because of this scriptural reminder that the church is the 'disciple-making hub' for every domain of society. I am literally seeing the fruit of men stepping up and making disciple-makers wherever they are planted!"

*~ **Kent Chevalier***
Pastor, North Way Community Church (Wexford Campus) in Pittsburgh, PA

"Dave Buehring beautifully lays out for readers the biblical call for reproducing ourselves. *The Jesus Blueprint* will challenge and excite you about making disciples in your family and may result in a paradigm shift regarding others with whom you journey through life. A must-read for every Jesus follower, no matter what your domain of service may be."

*~ **Paris Goodyear-Brown***
LCSW, RPT-S, Child and Family Therapist, Author and Speaker

"Our Lord's mandate is the basis for *The Jesus Blueprint*. David Buehring's perspective and experience are both inspiring and practically instructive. Through it, Jesus-followers will better understand their call to and the blessing of disciple-making."

*~ **Daniel G. Matthews***
Associate Pastor, Loma Linda University Church of Seventh-day Adventists

"For the Christian veterinary professional, the relationship people have with their animals creates an 'animal bridge' through which a relationship can be established to engage them with the hope of the Gospel. The making of the disciple is birthed in such relationships, opening doors for forming disciples in homes and in the workplace. Through *The Jesus Blueprint*, Dave Buehring challenges us to consider these pillars of the Great Commission."

~ Dr. Kit Flowers
Executive Director, Christian Veterinarian Mission

"Dave Buehring lives what he writes in *The Jesus Blueprint*. He has walked with me as I encounter many challenging situations in the arena of politics and government. No matter what I'm facing, he always points me to the ways and character of God. I see that there can be no separation between what I do and what I believe. As a result, I have come alive and have caught the vision for becoming a disciple-maker of Jesus. If you read this book and apply it to your life, you will too."

~Darren Bearson
Political strategist who has worked at the White House, Congress, and Department of Energy; managed or led political operation in 20 states.

The Jesus Blueprint

Rediscovering His
Original Plan
for Changing the World

The Jesus Blueprint: Rediscovering His Original Plan for Changing the World
by David Buehring

Published by HigherLife Development Services, Inc.
400 Fontana Circle
Building 1 – Suite 105
Oviedo, Florida 32765
(407) 563-4806
www.ahigherlife.com

Unless otherwise identified, Scripture quotations are from the English Standard Version (ESV) of the Bible.

ISBN 13: 978-1-935245-64-3
ISBN 10: 1-935245-64-3

Cover Design: Principle Design Group – David Whitlock
Interior Design: Birdsong Creative | Franklin, TN | www.birdsongcreative.com
Dozen Domain Icons: Corrie Commisso

First Edition
12 13 14 15 – 9 8 7 6 5 4 3 2 1

Printed in the United States of America

Contents

Foreword

All of my Christian life, I have thought about the call of Christ for those who love and follow Him to *make disciples*. Two paradigms have haunted my heart for decades: first, how can we point others to better see, love, and follow the Lord Jesus? And next, by His grace, how can we help them live out forever this momentous eternal shift into the works, ways, and wisdom of God in His great kingdom?

This journey has not been an easy venture for my heart, nor some short trip down an easy-learning lane. I believe that to be true for many. Multitudes who might mentor like Him have. However, like Christian in Bunyan's *Pilgrim's Progress*, whose personal pilgrimage to the Celestial City was met with challenges and loneliness along the way, he found few friendly faces to hold high for him some sign that pointed him in the right direction.

Dave Buehring has done just that for us. *The Jesus Blueprint* is such a signpost, a deeply designed foundational, directional and detailed scriptural sketch, packed with quotables, great stories, and contemporary history. This is one read I can seriously commend not only for us who have walked the way for many years but for so many who will soon make their own entry into the wonderful world of being followers of Jesus.

~ Winkie Pratney
2012 Anno Domini

Acknowledgments

Without the help of the following people, *The Jesus Blueprint* would not be in your hands at this moment. I couldn't have done it without them.

First of all, I want to thank my wife, Cheryl, for her ongoing love, kindness, and sacrifice to bring this book to pass. Through her life and words she has discipled me during our thirty years of marriage to be a better man, husband, father, and follower of Jesus. I dedicate this book to her.

For those who've discipled and poured their life into me—beginning with my dad and mom to those presently speaking in to my life—this book is a reflection of your investment. My continued desire is to steward well what you've passed on to me.

I also want to thank Vicki Campbell, our entire Lionshare Team, and our Intercessors. Thank you for standing with us during this fifteen-month process. I've felt your prayers and have appreciated your expressions of service.

I'm very grateful to my many friends in leadership who have contributed short essays on the role of disciple-making within the Dozen Domains.

Your godly insights and commitment to making disciple-makers is so needed and so appreciated.

Special thanks goes to Susi Harbour for her role in editing the original content. Your hard work, insight, and practical guidance rounded out the rough edges and brought the book together in a way that will aid the reader in more ways than they'll ever know.

I want to honor the HigherLife team that has walked alongside me throughout the entire process. David Welday, thanks for your vision, creativity, and leadership. Wes Harbour, I appreciate you lending me your years of experience and well-earned wisdom. To both of you, thank you for being my friends and doing your best to choose the highest good for the kingdom of God and me. Thank you, Dani Massalone and other members of the HigherLife team, for your role in the development process. I'm grateful for you, Troy Birdsong, one of my disciple-makers, for your layout and design.

A word of gratitude also goes to Jill Wiegand, Dennis and Tammy Garrett, and Al Andrews. Your home in Big Canoe, cabin in Williamson County, and cottage in Franklin came at just the right time, when I needed a fresh place to reflect and write.

To our financial sponsors, whether on the front end as I began writing, as a part of the Sponsorship Team, or via our online campaign: Your willingness to give generously has moved this from vision to reality!

THE JESUS BLUEPRINT

Financial Sponsors

Andrew Coaching, LLC

Bartolomeo, Peggy

Bearson, Sandy

Bearson, Darren & Sonya

Brown, Ray

Buron, Doug & Debbie

Cain, Leslie

Cannon, Bill & Teasi

Chevalier, Kent & Erica

Colvis, Erin

Cornacchione, Mark

Counts, Rusty & Tamara

Crawford, David A

Crosspointe Church

Daltorio, Joe & Janice

Davis, Rick & Jeanie

Dollar, Jeff

Drennan, Leon

Dunning Graves, Dawn

Eaton, Jim & Maureen

Fleece, Angelo & Kim

Flowers, Lois

Freeburg, Jonathan

Frey, Laurie

Fullmer, Bob

Garrett, Jason

Gilmore Becky

Giske, Steve & Kathy

Gooch, Patrick & Sherrill

Goodman, Rob

Gorrell, Paul

Gorrell, Todd

Gueffroy, Lisa

Gustafson,
  Mike & Caroline

Hammond, Dan & Cherie

Hargis, Heather

Harrill, Doc

Hendrickson, Emily

Holland, Sean

Huddleston, Samuel

Hudson, Darren & Erin

Johnson, Carol

Kerr, Autumn

Koenig, Bob

McCoy, Allison

Mello, Tish

Neola, Stephen

Packer, Kirk & Nikki

Park, David & Sunita

Phillips, Caleb & Amy

Ranzau, Matt

Ronhovde, Heather

Salciccioli, Greg & Dianna

Saunders III, R Scott

Sawyer Family

Schenk, Chris & Judy

Seaman, Cory

Smith, Gabriel

Smith, Greg & Darla

Snelgrove, Annie

Song, Shin Young (Gloria)

Stein, Robert A

Strazzer, Gene

Templin, Hal & Esther

Vengala, Chris & Megan

Wallace, Guy & Cindy

Whitley, Brett & Rebecca

Whitman, Bob & Dar

Winston, Karin

Woodbridge, Keith

Woodsmall, Dennis

Wray, Alberta

Young, Jim

Zemple, Ryan & Heather

Introduction

While writing this book, I've had the privilege of teaching and discipling some of our "Ironmen" at our home church, Grace Chapel. We've been exploring the Scriptures together, examining Jesus' practice of making disciples, while also looking at the impact of disciple-making on society. In the process, we've realized that we are reaping the lack of intentional disciple-making both within the church and within society as a whole.

How often do we get frustrated and angry with those in government, the media, the education system, the world of the arts, entertainment, and sports? We rant and rave about the negative effects that the leaders within them—and their choices—are having on our children, our society, and us. Yet have we ever once stopped and realized that we have contributed to the problem by not reproducing disciples Jesus can raise up to serve society? Indeed, we are reaping what we've sown.

If we are not deliberately obeying the command of Jesus to make disciples, as recorded in Matthew 28:18-20, then He has no Davids, Nehemiahs, Esthers, or Daniels to place in leadership roles throughout society to represent His character, ways, and mission!

Greg, a godly man who is a part of our Ironmen group, recently wrote me this insightful email:

Hey Pastor Dave,

After last week's message I've become more acutely aware of how the world "gets it" on this whole discipleship concept while the church lags behind. Just last night, while at a restaurant waiting for my wife to arrive, I grabbed a few minutes of a basketball game on TV. The announcers mentioned how the coach of the one team was a "mentor" to the coach of the other team. They then put up a list on the screen of all this coach's other "DISCIPLES"!!!

Earlier in the week a sports commentator talked of the potential and current football coaches that had come from a professional coach's "coaching tree." Over the past months I've also heard how various politicians were "mentored" by others.

It's seems like everywhere BUT the Church that intentional effort is being given to discipleship.

Thanks for re-awakening me to this important issue. I'm happy to claim I'm a branch on the Buehring tree!

Have a great day!
Greg

He nailed it! What he expressed has challenged me for several decades now. How is it that the world around us seems further along in this truth of Jesus while we, as His Church, find ourselves committed to just about everything else but making disciples? Although I have no way to prove it, I've wondered for years if our lack of cultivating disciple-making communities is one of the main reasons why there has not been a mighty move of God throughout our land. After all, if multiple millions came to Jesus in the span of a month or two, where would He put them—and know with certainty that they would be shaped as reproducible disciple-makers?

We desperately need a disciple-making revival in the Church and a disciple-making movement that can bring real transformation to society! That has been and continues to be my regular prayer. The times we are living in are trying. People are desperate. Nations are desperate. Yet are we desperate enough to realign ourselves to obeying Jesus' last command? If we are, we may find ourselves in the midst of a "ripe" opportunity to see the church reformed, society transformed, and the real needs of people met throughout the world.

As you dive into *The Jesus Blueprint*, you'll notice that the chapters are arranged in three parts:

- *Laying the Groundwork* takes a look at the Scriptures, the life of Jesus, and the fruit of disciple-making in the Book of Acts. I'll share with you some of my own discipleship story and how God develops disciple-makers. I'll also sketch out for you the main theme of this book: the reproducible disciple-making blueprint of Jesus.

- *Windows for Making Disciple-Makers* provides you with the understanding of making disciple-makers within the Dozen Domains of society and snapshots of each of the domains. You'll glean much from some of my domain leader friends who've contributed their experiences and godly insights here as well.

- *A Framework to Build Upon* is all about the "what can I do's?" and "how do I do it's?" It provides a very practical and tangible way for you to prayerfully consider how you can obey

INTRODUCTION

the disciple-making command of Jesus and apply what you've learned in this book to your life and the world around you.

Along with the content in this book, you'll find additional disciple-making essays by godly leaders at www.thejesusblueprint.com. While there, download for free *The Jesus Blueprint* small group facilitator's guide. You'll also be able to link to Lionshare (www.lionshare.org) to sign up for our weekly devotional blog, *The Disciple-Maker*, learn more about our disciple-making network known as *NetDMC*, and obtain our scripturally sound, proven, and practical one-year disciple-making resource, *A Discipleship Journey*.

Now, this is not the be-all, end-all book on disciple-making. As a matter of fact, some of my friends have written wonderful works on this subject that are worthy of your time. As a practitioner, my intent is to simply share what Jesus has taught me in my forty-year journey as His disciple. Much of what you'll read are things I've learned from those who've discipled me along the way. I'm so glad that you'll benefit from their lives as well!

My hope is that you'll encounter Jesus over and over within these pages. My desire is that you'll rediscover His original plan to change the world. My prayer is that you'll obey and co-mission with Him by making disciple-makers where He's appointed you to serve.

Dave Buehring
Easter Weekend 2012
Franklin, Tennessee

PART ONE

Laying the Groundwork

Chapter One

The Acts of the Discipled

It's the first day of class. As students enter the classroom, some are catching up with one another, while others are scurrying about looking for the perfect seat. As the professor moves towards the front of the room, students begin to take their seats. Because this class has never been offered before, everyone is interested in learning more about it.

After welcoming them, the professor dives into a thorough overview of all that will be covered throughout the semester. He provides each person with a handout of his lecture topics, along with what books will be required reading.

To the delight of the entire class, he also communicates in his opening presentation that there will be no pop quizzes, no weekly tests, no research papers, and no mid-term exam! Once the volume of the sudden mass frenzy dies down, he goes on, saying,

> *"I want you to get everything you possibly can out of my class, so you must listen very carefully to what I am about to say. To do well, you must attend all of my lectures each week and make sure that*

you read the books I've assigned to you. It is the content contained in these that will be on the final exam on your final day of class. One other thing: I'd like you to find one person outside of this class with whom you'll share what you're learning each week. Do these things well, and I can assure you that you're on your way to receiving a great grade for your work."

Following these words, he dismissed the class—nearly 30 minutes early! Heading out the door, people were heard saying to one another, "What a no-brainer" and "This class will be an easy A." Others were so overjoyed they were making up lyrics and singing, "Ship's leaving the harbor…it's cruising time, it's party time!"

Just as the professor had promised, there were no quizzes, tests, or papers that had to be written throughout that entire semester. Most of the students showed up for his three weekly lectures and, on various levels, digested the assigned reading material.

During the last class of each week, as was his habit, the professor led them in a conversational review of the material, answered everyone's questions, and then summarized the key takeaways for the week. On top of that, he also regularly spent time with students who requested extra help.

Fast forward to the end of the semester.

During the class prior to the day of the final exam, the professor spent the entire hour rehearsing the key takeaways from the previous fifteen weeks while answering questions along the way. In the concluding moments, he then addressed his students:

"It's been a privilege to teach you this semester. I've done everything I can to help you learn this material. Now, remember on our first day

*together I asked you to find one person outside of this class that you would share what you're learning with. When you leave here today, please make sure you communicate with that person the time of your final exam so they can be sure to be here. You see, they'll be taking your final for you and **their grade will be your final grade."***

The last words of Jesus in Matthew are:

> "All authority in heaven and on earth has been given to me. **Go therefore and make disciples** of all nations, baptizing them in the name of the Father and of the Son and of the Holy Spirit, teaching them to observe all that I have commanded you. And behold, I am with you always, to the end of the age."

— MATHEW 28:18–20

When applying this story to the mandate of Jesus to make disciples, who have you poured into that could take your final exam? And if you could name one or some, have you discipled them deliberately, so that you'd be assured of a passing grade? My Wife

Obviously, disciple-making is not about "final grades"—but you get the point. The last thing Jesus commissioned His disciples to do was to reproduce what He'd invested in them in others, who in turn would do the same. How are you really doing on this front?

This disciple-making assignment was not a last-minute idea thrown in by Jesus at the end of His life. Rather, it was the summation of how He had lived among His disciples for three years. He taught the multitudes, but His primary focus was on investing in twelve. Disciple-making was, is, and will remain His blueprint for changing the world!

While reflecting on this Matthew 28 passage, among other things, I find it interesting that this disciple-making commission is sandwiched between noteworthy bookends. It opens with "All *authority* in heaven and on earth has been given to me. Go therefore and make disciples..." Can I just say that's an unimaginable amount of weight, influence, power, and clout! It emanates from the throneroom of heaven through the risen, living Son of God into the ears of His disciples. Of all things He could of said, He told them to make disciples! He lived and modeled it for them every day for three years, and now He's asking them to do the same. It was to be the beginning of a never-ending chain of His followers who reproduce followers, who reproduce followers right up to today!

The corresponding bookend is found at the end of this passage: "And behold, *I am with you always*..." The promise of His presence! He knew that once He was gone that they would feel incapable to do what He had done for them. That they would wrestle with their own weaknesses and insecurities. Yet He assures them that He would be with them every step of the way. Ultimately, He knew where each one would need to grow, mend, be equipped, and transformed. I wonder how many times those words *"I am with you always"* came back to their hearts and minds?

Authority | Disciple-Making Commission | Presence

Throughout the four decades of my own discipleship journey I have watched the *authority* and *presence* of Jesus flow in and through those committed to obey His disciple-making mandate. I have seen godly offspring reproduced as an expression of God's heart as a father. Jesus reproduced the ways of the kingdom in the Twelve. And the Holy Spirit empowered His disciples to obey Jesus' blueprint in the Book of Acts.

Speaking of Acts...

Jesus was not ascending into heaven in Acts 1 with His fingers crossed hoping that His disciples "got the hint" on disciple-making. Nor were the disciples wondering among themselves as He passed through the clouds, "What in the world did He mean by making disciples?" The stakes were way too high for that! After all, this was His team that would advance His kingdom and launch His Church! Therefore He was very intentional about disciple-making from the very beginning—*who* He invested in, *what* He passed on, and *how* He went about doing it. In the end, His disciples knew exactly what He had asked them to do. He had taught, demonstrated, and replicated His disciple-making blueprint so thoroughly that it resided *within* them!

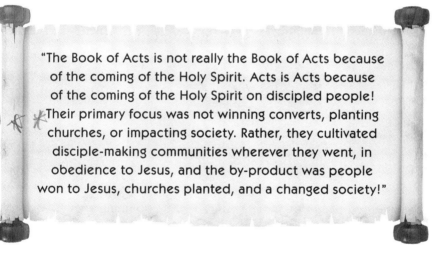

"The Book of Acts is not really the Book of Acts because of the coming of the Holy Spirit. Acts is Acts because of the coming of the Holy Spirit on discipled people! Their primary focus was not winning converts, planting churches, or impacting society. Rather, they cultivated disciple-making communities wherever they went, in obedience to Jesus, and the by-product was people won to Jesus, churches planted, and a changed society!"

We see how deeply engrained this blueprint was within them as Acts plays out. This little band of Jesus followers numbered around 120 on the day before Pentecost. After the empowering of the Holy Spirit and Peter's bold preaching, they grew to number about 3,120 the day after! What did they do with all these new Jesus followers? They did what Jesus had prepared them to do. They made disciples!

7

Look with me in Acts:

> And they devoted themselves to the apostles' teaching and
> the fellowship, to the breaking of bread and the prayers. And
> awe came upon every soul, and many wonders and signs
> were being done through the apostles. And all who believed
> were together and had all things in common. And they were
> selling their possessions and belongings and distributing the
> proceeds to all, as any had need. And day by day, attending
> the temple together and breaking bread in their homes, they
> received their food with glad and generous hearts, praising
> God and having favor with all the people. And the Lord add-
> ed to their number day by day those who were being saved.
>
> — ACTS 2:42–47

These new followers devoted themselves to be taught by the disciples
Jesus had walked with (also known as apostles, by virtue of their gifted-
ness). They also walked together in the context of everyday life, relating
well with one another while enjoying food and times of prayer. It appears that the disciples simply included these new followers in the same
activities that they'd had participated in with Jesus.

So, what were the disciples teaching? We can lean here on our previous passage from Matthew 28: "teaching them to observe all that I have
commanded you." They were passing on the commands and words of
Jesus, His teaching on God's character, ways, and mission.

It's important to note here that these second generation disciples weren't
just being "taught," but like Jesus had done with the twelve, they were
being taught to observe, or obey. In other words, they were learning to
apply the knowledge they were gaining and to express it through their
lives. Obedience to Jesus is what brings about real and lasting change
in the lives of His followers and impacts those around them.

Disciples are followers of Jesus, not in name only, but in the very real ways in which they live their lives. Disciples actually *follow* Jesus—doing what He shows them to do and saying what He shows them to say. They need to be in constant fellowship with Him so they know what He's doing and can follow His lead. *Not just when we feel like it or when convenient*

We live in a culture where taking initiative and being the leader is what is highly prized and sought after. Yet Jesus' invitation to be His disciple has nothing to do with either of these. Instead, throughout the Gospels He called people to leave everything—relationships, possessions, opportunities, and agendas—to *follow*:

> And he said to them, "**Follow** me, and I will make you fishers of men." Immediately they left their nets and **followed** him.
> — MATTHEW 4:19–20

> And he said to him, "Teacher, all these I have kept from my youth." And Jesus, looking at him, loved him, and said to him, "You lack one thing: go, sell all that you have and give to the poor, and you will have treasure in heaven; and come, **follow** me." Disheartened by the saying, he went away sorrowful, for he had great possessions.
> — MARK 10:20–22

> After this he went out and saw a tax collector named Levi, sitting at the tax booth. And he said to him, "**Follow** me." And leaving everything, he rose and **followed** him.
> — LUKE 5:27–28

> And he said to all, "If anyone would come after me, let him deny himself and take up his cross daily and **follow** me. For whoever would save his life will lose it, but whoever loses his life for my sake will save it.
> — LUKE 9:23–24

How did they understand what He meant—He hadn't gone to the cross yet.

CHAPTER ONE : The Acts of the Discipled

*As they were going along the road, someone said to him, "I will **follow** you wherever you go." And Jesus said to him, "Foxes have holes, and birds of the air have nests, but the Son of Man has nowhere to lay his head." To another he said, "**Follow** me." But he said, "Lord, let me first go and bury my father." And Jesus said to him, "Leave the dead to bury their own dead. But as for you, go and proclaim the kingdom of God." Yet another said, "I will **follow** you, Lord, but let me first say farewell to those at my home." Jesus said to him, "No one who puts his hand to the plow and looks back is fit for the kingdom of God."*

— LUKE 9:57–62

*When he has brought out all his own, he goes before them, and the sheep **follow** him, for they know his voice...My sheep hear my voice, and I know them, and they **follow** me.*

— JOHN 10:4, 27

*"If anyone serves me, he must **follow** me; and where I am, there will my servant be also. If anyone serves me, the Father will honor him."*

— JOHN 12:26

*Peter turned and saw the disciple whom Jesus loved... When Peter saw him, he said to Jesus, "Lord, what about this man?" Jesus said to him, "If it is my will that he remain until I come, what is that to you? You **follow** me!"*

— JOHN 21:20–22

Following Jesus means just that—*following* Jesus. We die to self to live for His kingdom purposes. He leads; we have the privilege of serving. He initiates; we implement. Yet even as we serve and implement, we do so according to His ways, reflecting His character and with His mission always in mind. Do we do Jesus' work His way or our way?

It is important to understand that we can *only produce followers if we are followers.* If we weren't discipled to follow Jesus, we're not going to reproduce followers of Jesus! We might reproduce someone who says he is a follower, but, ultimately, his life will reveal something contrary.

As these followers in Acts simply obey and walk in the Jesus blueprint, they multiply disciples. Acts 6:7 states, "And the word of God continued to increase, *and the number of the disciples multiplied greatly* in Jerusalem, and a great many of the priests became obedient to the faith" (emphasis added). Consider for a moment with me the kind of transformational community that was emerging among these disciple-makers in Acts:

> *A Presence Community.* There was a very real and tangible sense of Jesus being with them as they gathered (2:14), reached out (2:5–41), interacted (5:1–13), and did what He did (5:12–16), even in the midst of persecution (7:54–60).
>
> *A Praying Community.* They prayed in one accord (1:14); they were devoted to prayer (2:42); the leadership was committed to prayer (6:4); they prayed in the midst of persecution (12:1–17); their prayers launched the missionary movement (13:1-3); and they prayed while detained in prison (16:25–34).
>
> *An Empowered Community.* Not only did they pray regularly, but God's power and direction was often demonstrated in direct answer to their prayers: believers were emboldened (4:31); healings and miracles manifested (9:40); vision was imparted (10:9–48); angelic deliverance occurred (12:6–19); a jailor and his family were converted (16:25–34).
>
> *An Ever-Expanding Community.* The newly formed church continued to grow and be added to (2:41,48), with men and women

CHAPTER ONE : The Acts of the Discipled

coming to Jesus (5:14), not only in Jerusalem (6:7) but also in Judea and Samaria (9:31) and beyond (11:19–26).

A One-Heart, One-Mind Community. They expressed unity by operating in oneness of heart and mind (1:14), sharing life together (2:42–48), while gladly and generously meeting each other's needs (4:32–34).

An Obedient Community. They referenced God's ways in the Scriptures (1:15-26) and did what Jesus had taught them to do while daily following the lead of the Holy Spirit (8:26–40; 10:9–48).

A Fearing-God Community. A sense of awe fell upon them (2:43) as they reverenced God above all else (5:1–13), walking in the Fear of the Lord (9:11) and not giving in to the fear of man (5:29).

A Missional Community. This band of Jesus followers continued to extend His kingdom from Jerusalem to Judea and Samaria, and to the ends of the earth (Chapters 1–8: Jerusalem; 8–12: Judea & Samaria; 13–28: the ends of the earth).

A Society-Impacting Community. Along with "turning the world upside down" (17:6), meeting the needs of the needy (4:34–35; 11:27–29) and healing the sick (5:16; 8:7; 9:34), the disciples participated in a relational transformation between Jews and Gentiles (15:1–35).

A Sacrificial, Enduring Community. The disciples endured great persecution (4:1–31; 5:17–42), as Jesus had said they would; this was soon followed by the deaths of Stephen (6:8-8:1) and James (12:1–3) and the imprisonments of Peter (12:6–19) and Paul (16:16–40; 24:26–27; 28:17–31).

A Jesus-Glorifying Community. The Name of Jesus was exalted (2:21; 3:15–17; 4:10; 5:39–41) and glorified through the lives and

THE JESUS BLUEPRINT : PART ONE

sacrifices of His disciples (7:55–56; 11:15–18; 12:21–24; 13:46–49; 21:17–20).

A Disciple-Making Community. Their mission was to simply obey the mandate Jesus gave them to make disciple-makers, and they multiplied greatly (2:42–47; 5:42; 6:7; 15:35; 18:11; 28:31).

What Jesus follower wouldn't love being a part of a community like this—and what pastor wouldn't love leading one? Talk about impact! In the midst of obeying Jesus and loving one another well, they served God's purposes in their generation while laying the groundwork through disciple-making to make a mark on future ones as well.

A Few Observations from Acts on Disciple-Making

First, I've come to realize that the Book of Acts is not really the Book of Acts because of the coming of the Holy Spirit. *Acts is Acts because of the coming of the Holy Spirit on discipled people!* Three years of deliberate discipling by Jesus infused by the power of the Holy Spirit provides an accurate picture of why Acts is what it is. I like referring to Acts as "The Acts of the Discipled."

Second, we learn from Acts that first-generation disciples were intent on obeying the commission of Jesus to "make disciples." Their primary focus was not winning converts, planting churches, or impacting society. Rather, they cultivated disciple-making communities wherever they went, in obedience to Jesus, and the by-product was people won to Jesus, churches planted, and a changed society! Because they had personally experienced being a part of a disciple-making community with Jesus for three years, they (super) naturally reproduced them!

13

Third, in light of Jesus' disciple-making mandate, the primary existence of the church in a given locale was to serve as a "disciple-making hub." It functioned as a "spiritual hot house" where followers of Jesus were re-produced. They grew in knowing His character, were developed around His ways, and equipped to partner with Him in His mission. We see this not only in Jerusalem, but also in Antioch and in the various cities Paul visits, where he later continues to disciple through his letters.

Fourth, the goal of the disciples was not about making a disciple here or there; it was *reproducing disciple-makers*. Through them was launched a multiplying disciple-making movement. The disciple-making seed that had been planted in them by Jesus, when fully grown, would pro-duce more reproducible seeds that were to multiply disciple-makers for generations to come. Each generation is to "own" their generation by taking responsibility to disciple those who are currently on the planet with them—in every tribe, tongue, people, and nation. In doing so, they also pass it forward to the next generation.

Are you reproducing *disciple-makers*? If this blueprint of Jesus is to advance, expand, and multiply His kingdom on Earth, what does that mean for you and me? Pause just for a moment and consider the follow-ing four questions before we move ahead:

- Have I ever really been discipled? No
- What am I really reproducing?
- Are those that I've discipled now reproducing disciple-makers?
- Am I currently taking responsibility to make disciples within my relationships and within the domain of society were Jesus has appointed me to serve?

Current Hindrances to Disciple-Making

Have you ever considered why something that seems so clear and simple and also produces multi-generational spiritual fruit appears to be beyond our grasp? Might it be that the enemy of our soul recognizes disciple-making as a seismic threat and does whatever he can to bring disruption to this Jesus-initiated and Jesus-commissioned chain of multiplication?

In the late 1990s, while pursuing a master's degree, I had the privilege of meeting Tim Elmore[1] who was teaching on mentoring in a class I was taking. Since then we have become comrades in investing the kingdom of Jesus within others. He was the first to provoke me to think about hindrances to disciple-making. How did we get here, where disciple-making is no longer the norm?

My desire in relaying the following observations is to enable each of us to find a "starting place" so we know which direction to head for the purpose of reengaging Jesus' disciple-making mandate. I love Jesus and His bride, the Church. Nothing would thrill me more than to see a disciple-making revival in the church that would spill over into the other domains of society! It is with that end in mind that I share these thoughts with you.

Disciple-Making Illiteracy. While talking together recently, my good friend Randy Young of the Agora Group,[2] said, "It seems like Jesus' last command has become our least concern." Cal Thomas, a syndicated columnist and social commentator, challenged Jesus-followers to take a look at the root behind cultural problems when he said, "The problem in our culture...isn't the abortionists. It isn't the pornographers or drug dealers or criminals. It is the undisciplined, undiscipled, disobedient and Biblically ignorant Church of Jesus Christ."[3] I can't even begin to tell you how many people—pastors and spiritual leaders included—have said to me, "I have never been discipled" or "Why have I not learned about this before?"

I'm constantly amazed at how many people have never been taught about the key role that disciple-making plays in the kingdom of God and in the lives of followers of Jesus. I wonder, at times, whether we've omitted disciple-making altogether. I offer these words from Dallas Willard because they pinpoint the problem perfectly: "We need to emphasize that the Great Omission from the Great Commission is not obedience to Christ, but discipleship, apprenticeship to Him.

In conversations with leaders from various "tribes" throughout the Body of Christ, we have agreed that actual disciple-making churches are few and far between. We all have found it rare to find a group of people whose primary mission, next to loving Jesus with all their heart, soul, mind, and strength and their neighbor as themselves, is disciple-making. However, it is very encouraging in these days to see what Jesus is doing to cultivate disciple-making communities throughout the Earth!

Building Our Empires Instead of His Kingdom. There is something deep within us that wants to be recognized for what we have done. Part of that is right and appropriate, as we need to actively honor those to whom honor is due (Romans 13:7). What we sometimes fail to realize, however, is that there is a fine line between what is honorable and what is within us that is downright idolatrous.

Not unlike Lucifer himself, who wanted to ascend and be like the Most High (Isaiah 14:12–17), the focus of our hearts can become captivated with our own visions, plans, and accomplishments. That sort of focus was expressed by those building the Tower of Babel when they spoke, "Come, let us build ourselves a city and a tower with its top in the heavens, and let us make a name for ourselves..." (Genesis 11:4). We know how that line of thinking worked out! All of us are vulnerable to building our own empires, whether we are growing a church, involved in entrepreneurial endeavors, making new discoveries, writing a Top Ten song, or winning an election. We are all tempted to reroute our energies into things revolving around our personal agendas instead of into Jesus' mandate of disciple-making.

Take a moment and consider the things you're involved with now. How much of that have you instigated and how much of that was born out of God's initiation? Are we building corporations, clients, careers, and denominations for our agendas or His? Are they being made in our image or are they reproducing His?

Creating Cultures of Religion vs. Cultures of Obeying Jesus. Have you noticed that we've often created a culture within our churches where people are very devout and conscientious about showing up at a certain place on a certain day at a certain time each week? They are faithful to be present at two to four services a month, drop a little pocket cash in the offering basket when it's passed, and occasionally volunteer a little of their time "for God." The problem? No doubt they are great people, but they are often placed in a system that produces religiosity—not obedience to Jesus.

Jesus discipled His followers to walk in obedience. Throughout His teachings, Jesus conveyed that obedience is a primary expression through which they would experience God and live their lives. As we understand the lives of Jesus-followers in the New Testament, they seemed to reference what they'd already been taught by Jesus while asking, "What's the Lord saying to us now?" They heard from God and responded in obedience. They cultivated their inner lives so that they were sensitive to His leading and guiding.

They walked in community with one another, where they could hear His voice and discern the will and way of Jesus for that moment together.

Willard points to the central focus of obedience in the lives of Jesus followers: "Christian spirituality is supernatural because obedience to Christ is supernatural and cannot be accomplished except in the power of a life from above. The will to obey is the engine that pulls the train of spirituality in Christ."[5]

Sometimes when we encourage people to obey what they believe Jesus is showing them to do, it gets a little messy. Learning to hear from Jesus and follow Him is a process, and no one does it perfectly. Even so, wouldn't we rather deal with having to do a bit of cleanup knowing that people are truly experiencing God moving in and through their lives?

The Pastor/Flock Distinction. The changes in the church brought about by Emperor Constantine's issuing of the Edict of Milan in 313 A.D. are well documented. I don't need to say much about this except that it significantly altered how Jesus-followers practiced their walk of faith. One notable change that Constantine implemented was exalting the "clergy," providing them, through various expressions, with a special class status.[6] This division between "clergy" and "laity" has continued to today. Why is it important to note here? Because many within the church continue to believe it is solely the pastor's responsibility to make disciples, because, after all, "it's their job!"

Yes, we need church leaders, especially discipled ones, that reflect the character, ways, and mission of Jesus, to actively engage in making disciples! But we seem to have lost the fact that disciple-making belongs to *all* who call themselves followers of Jesus. We have strayed from Ephesians 4:12–13, which tells us that those God places in roles of servant

leadership are to "equip the saints for the work of the ministry, for building up the body of Christ, until we all attain to the unity of the faith and
of the knowledge of the Son of God, to mature manhood, to the measure
of the stature of the fullness of Christ…" Did you catch that? Leaders are
to equip Jesus-followers to do the work of the ministry: to build up, helping all attain the unity of the faith and the knowledge of the Son of God
to the point of maturity and fullness. Sounds like disciple-making to me!

The Poisoning of the Well. Because disciple-making is a common theme
in my life, I tend to get all kinds of feedback about it from all kinds of
people. There are a couple of familiar phrases I hear that spring from
the same well. One goes like this: "Discipleship—that wrecked my life!

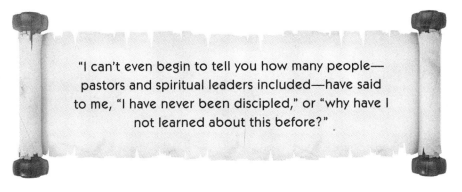

"I can't even begin to tell you how many people—
pastors and spiritual leaders included—have said
to me, "I have never been discipled," or "why have I
not learned about this before?"

Never again will I submit to some manipulative leader who tries to control every aspect of what I do." The other comment is: "I went through
a six-week discipleship class years ago—I've already been discipled."
These two trains of thought represent poisoned places in the disciple-
making well. Both bring sadness to my soul.

Regarding the first, manipulation and control have nothing to do with
the kingdom of God—ever—especially within the context of disciple-
making. For those who have labored in such an atmosphere for years,
please know that many of my friends who are leaders would join me in

offering a deep and sincere apology. Please forgive leaders for not modeling the heart and life of Jesus to you. You are greatly valued and genuinely loved by Jesus. He has given you unique gifts and callings, some of which remain to be fulfilled. When the time is right, know that we need you to reproduce the life of Jesus, which resides in you, within others.

For those who have been taught that discipleship is simply a short-term class you go through, please forgive the lack of personal involvement and pick up where you've left off. Ask Jesus to bring disciple-makers your way that will meet you where you are and equip you to pour what Jesus has invested in you into others.

The Hebrew vs. Greek Model of Learning. There is much that has been and can be said about the differences between the values and emphases of the Hebraic and Hellenistic cultures in biblical times.[7] The Greeks value individualism; the Hebrews, a body of people following God together. The Greeks dwell in rationale and reason while the Hebrews' reliance is on the Scriptures and revelation. The Greek mind seeks the holiness of beauty, where the pursuit of the Hebrew is the beauty of holiness.[8] For our disciple-making purposes here, I'd like to highlight one essential difference.

 Western civilization is often referred to as Judeo-Christian, but in terms of how we learn, we have defaulted closer to a Greek model. The Greek asks, "What are you learning?" and "Why must I do it?" while the Hebrew asks, "Who are you learning from?" and "What must I do?" One values philosophy and the intellect; the other, the investment in others and practical wisdom of the heart.[9] The Scriptures teach that we are to love God with our heart, soul, mind, and strength (Luke 10:27), so we can certainly glean from both perspectives.

With that said, many of our models of transmitting spiritual truths have relied much more on what we are learning (Greek) than who we are learning from (Hebrew). The Jesus blueprint is definitely weighted on the side of who is investing in our lives. Words, actions, wisdom, and advice represent the overflow of what's in one's heart and life, so the source from which we are drawing from becomes important. Are we learning from sources that spring from the character and ways of God, exuding His holiness and integrity, truth and justice, grace and peace? Does this source demonstrate what it looks like to live a God-honoring life?

Disciple-making involves a hands-on approach: people teaching and investing, modeling and demonstrating, replicating and reproducing. It spawns new and renewed motivations of the heart, wise decisions and habits, and helping hands ready to come to the aid of others in need. Yes, loving God with our minds is very important, but it must be in tandem with the transformation of our hearts.

A Maintenance vs. Missional Mentality. As long as we see people participating in the programs and activities we're providing, our bills are getting paid, and conflicts are kept to a minimum, then life is good. Right? Left to ourselves, we tend to default to what's easiest. Often, it's easier just to settle and maintain where we're at. Yet Jesus has commissioned us to a mission that often requires some sacrifices of our time, energy, and resources.

The consumer mentality of our times also cuts against the grain of our disciple-making mission. People often jump from church to church depending on what they like and don't like. It results in church-goers who maintain where they're at spiritually. They often do not stick around long enough to let others speak to the real issues in their lives that would actually cause them to grow, mature, and engage with Jesus in His mission.

The mandate of Jesus is clear: "Go, make disciples of all nations..." Until every follower of Jesus owns that mandate, and every person within every domain of society within every nation has been discipled in the character, ways, and mission of Jesus, we've still got a job to do! Where we have allowed apathy, a settling for the status quo, or a maintenance mentality to consume our lives—or the soul of our church—we must repent and ask Jesus to re-energize our vision for His disciple-making, kingdom-advancing mission.

The Pride of the Human Heart. Finally, and maybe the most subtle obstacle of all, the pride of our own hearts hinders us from producing the fruit of disciple-making. I'm reminded of Jeremiah 17:9–10 that states: "The heart is deceitful above all things, and desperately sick; who can understand it? I the Lord search the heart and test the mind, to give every man according to his ways, according to the fruit of his deeds." Our inclination towards deception and pride makes us believe that we have a better way to change the world than what Jesus demonstrated for us and asked us to do.

We often go from latest thing to latest thing trying to make something happen for God. Or we rely on the strengths of our own gifts to grow God's work. We need to learn to ask whether a work will endure when our involvement comes to an end. Have we laid a foundation and set the trajectory in such a way that it will expand to reach people and places we could have only dreamt of impacting? A disciple-making work carries on when we are gone because it has been firmly rooted in His blueprint.

To counter pride, we purposely need to place around us people who we have asked to speak honestly into our lives. Without their loving insights we become islands, standing alone and unable to see ourselves for who we really are. I've discovered in my own life that I'm so deceived I don't even know where I'm deceived—until Jesus shines the light on it through scripture and an honest friend! I like how Bill Hull puts it when he says, "A disciple is someone who submits to at least one other person in a healthy and appropriate way as a means of support and accountability to develop fully as a follower of Jesus." How many of us have this in place or should we do this in our group

Reaping and Sowing

We are reaping today from what we have sown. We are currently left extremely shorthanded when it comes to active disciple-makers.

Recently, a group of godly young professionals said to me, "We have many peers that we can share life with; however, we are having a difficult time finding people who are further along in the things of God who are willing to disciple us." The only way I knew how to respond was to humbly ask them to forgive me—and us—for our failure to pursue making disciples. I then offered to help.

Speaking of godly young leaders, consider what George Barna found in his Top Trends of 2011 research: "84% of Christian 18 to 29-year-olds admit that they have no idea how the Bible applies to their field or professional interests. For example, young adults who are interested in creative or science-oriented careers often disconnect from their faith or from the church. On the creative side, this includes young musicians, artists, writers, designers, and actors. On the science-oriented side, young engineers, medical students, and science and math majors frequently struggle to see how the Bible relates to their life's calling. The

Barna study showed that faith communities can become more effective in working with the next generation by linking vocation and faith."[10]

Jesus followers are called to reap good fruit in the area of disciple-making. Now is the time to rediscover and "sow" the Jesus blueprint into the very fabric of our lives, our churches, the domains of society—and in the next generation.

As we move forward, I want you to consider with me how we are to measure fruitfulness in and through our lives. And how does God go about growing and developing a disciple-maker?

Chapter Two

The Fruitfulness Factor

Measuring Fruitfulness

Have you ever been "ruined for the ordinary" by something someone said—a passing comment—an unusual insight or words spoken directly to you that resonated deep inside and marked your life? I had such an occurrence—a divine moment that shaped my life—at 40,000 feet in the air between Los Angeles and Washington, DC, in April of 1980.

At the time, I was twenty years old, living in Kona, Hawaii, and serving with Youth With a Mission (YWAM).[1] My day-to-day responsibilities (and part of my own discipleship) involved leading a youth ministry known as "Acts 2." I had the privilege of leading a team of very capable young adults that engaged in weekly ministry on eight high school campuses around the Big Island. To fuel what we were doing on the campuses, we hosted quarterly "advances" that allowed us to bring students from all of our lunchtime campus clubs together for weekends of discipleship. Each summer, we also hosted several Acts 2 Discipleship Camps where we spent eight hours each day for twelve days discipling students and their youth pastors in the ways of God. It was exciting for me and my team to watch Jesus touch and transform so many lives as youth groups gathered for these discipleship intensives in Hawaii and other locations on the US mainland.

One day in the early spring of 1980, I was approached by Peter Jordan, a godly friend from Canada, who served as the personal assistant to YWAM's founder, Loren Cunningham. He wondered if I would be open to praying about doing some traveling with Loren on an upcoming trip that would take him from Dallas to Los Angeles and then on to Washington, DC. I understood that my role on the trip would be very simple: be available to help Loren when called upon and anticipate ways to serve. It was an honor to be asked, and I committed to Peter to seek the Lord about it and get back to him shortly. As you might imagine, it didn't take me long to get a green light from Jesus on this one!

We began in Dallas where Loren taught for the week at the Christ for the Nations Institute. I was to be available to talk with CFNI students who wanted to learn more about serving as missionaries with YWAM, among other things. Loren's plate was full with teaching, interviews, and meetings with leaders. I had the opportunity to glean some good insight as he graciously shared some things he had learned over his years with me during breaks at our apartment and while traveling in the car.

Then we flew to Los Angeles where Loren and his wife, Darlene, hosted an evening television show. The following morning the two of us were off to our nation's capital where Loren was among those addressing some 750,000 people who were gathering to seek the Lord in prayer for our nation at "Washington for Jesus."[2] This gathering had been called in an election year by godly leaders who were concerned about where our nation was headed. At that time, the US was in the midst of the Cold War with the Soviet Union, memories of Vietnam and Watergate still lingered in the American consciousness, and we were currently entangled in a crisis with Iran where fifty-two Americans were being held hostage at the U.S. embassy in Tehran.

While still in Los Angeles, we learned that a rescue attempt of the hostages in Iran had just been tried by our military but had failed.[3] We felt that this news would only add a greater dimension of desperation to those assembling in Washington to seek the face of Jesus. I looked forward to being a part of what would be an historical prayer gathering.

While having a conversation with Loren that next morning on the flight, he asked me a question: "Dave, what do you think your spiritual gifts are?" To be honest, at twenty years of age, I was still in the process of figuring that out for myself! I hemmed and hawed a bit, taking my best shot at it based on what I knew and understood at the time.

Loren had observed me leading our youth ministry in Kona for several years. In light of that, he began to share with me what he thought my gifts were and some practical ways to grow and develop them. Then, he spoke the following words, and with them came my "ruined for the ordinary" moment:

Loren's words

"You know, Dave, it really isn't important how big the organizations are that you will lead, or the size of the groups that you will teach. The way that God will measure the fruitfulness of your life is how you invested to the third and fourth generations."

He'd already had my attention but now I was really locked in! He began to explain to me that he was not speaking of generations usually divided in to forty-year increments, but rather, the generations referred to in 2 Timothy:

27

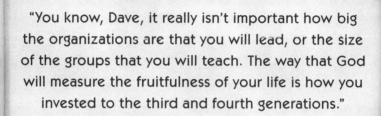

"You know, Dave, it really isn't important how big the organizations are that you will lead, or the size of the groups that you will teach. The way that God will measure the fruitfulness of your life is how you invested to the third and fourth generations."

"...and what you have heard from me in the presence of many witnesses entrust to faithful men who will be able to teach others also."

— 2 TIMOTHY 2:2

In other words, Paul (1st generation) discipled Timothy (2nd generation) who was to invest in faithful men (3rd generation), who then could pass on what they received to others (4th generation). Not fully realizing it at the moment, I had just been envisioned with a *four-generational model of disciple-making*, and along with that had received a practical way of how Jesus would measure the fruitfulness of my life and ministry. Talk about a game-changer!

From that moment in time until this present one, those words from Jesus through Loren have significantly shaped my life. Reproducing disciples who reproduce others is my primary reference point for fruitfulness. Am I (1st generation) so discipling Stan (2nd generation) that the truths he is learning are being fully incarnated within his own life? Is he, in turn, pouring the same into Marty (3rd generation), who then invests in Barry (4th generation)?

THE JESUS BLUEPRINT : PART ONE

On and on it goes, as each one disciples another: impacting people, families, domains of society, entire nations, and multiple generations, in perpetuity! The Jesus blueprint is simple. It's disciples deliberately reproducing followers of Jesus. It's the primary way He intended His kingdom ways and mission to be imparted and reproduced. It's what He's commissioned us to do until we see Him face-to-face!

That coast-to-coast conversation provided me with a lifelong reference point for measuring fruitfulness. Another key experience that came years later afforded me the opportunity to understand how God goes about growing and developing a disciple over a lifetime for the purpose of fruitfulness—and finishing well.

Growing a Disciple-Maker: God's Developmental Process

Growing a reproducing, fruit-bearing tree is a process. It takes the right soil, sunshine and rain, fertilizer, a nurturing hand, some pruning, and time. When these elements are added together, a tree grows deep roots, sprouts shoots, and produces healthy fruit. The root system below the ground absorbs water and nutrients, enabling the tree to survive, keeping it firmly grounded and upright. The shoot system consists of the parts above the ground such as the stem (trunk), leaves, buds, flowers, and fruit. And within each piece of fruit are seeds that reproduce more of its kind—whether apples, oranges, papayas, pears, or cherries!

In God's creation, healthy things reproduce, so a healthy expression of being a disciple is reproducing more of them! We are to reproduce much fruit so that God is glorified (John 15:8). Fruit is God knowing, God loving, God fearing men that live like Jesus - By living this way God is glorified and God then uses us to show his glory through works and miracles as well - But we must first must be fruitful.

Along with the lesson on measuring fruitfulness, another game-changing moment in my life occurred when I learned how Jesus develops us over an entire lifetime. This second moment took place when I had the opportunity to learn from Dr. Bobby Clinton[4] and his research. While pursuing my Master's Degree at Regent University, I took a one-week modular class that he taught called "Leadership Development Theory," which was followed by a three-month project on how it applied to my life: past, present, and future.

From the moment Bobby walked into the classroom, he had my attention. He asked the fifty or so of us present to number off by threes and then asked all the "twos" to stand. As they stood, he started the class with, "In my research since 1983 of the 1200+ leaders from Scripture, church history, and today, I've found that only one in three finishes well."[5] Those words plus the visual of two-thirds of us still remaining in our seats spoke volumes!

He then began to outline for us, over the next five days, through a "generalized timeline"[6] how one goes about cooperating with God within their "seasons of life" for the purpose of leading a life that finishes well. This was resonating loudly within me—both personally and as a disciple-maker.

Following the module, I launched into the project with instructions on how it was to be done. It contained nine core components that we needed to discover in our lives and then catalogue in a very specific way. It all revolved around a personal timeline that contained developmental phases, separated by boundaries (or thresholds) that move us from one season of life to another. I was learning that, typically, for someone who lived into his seventies and beyond, a timeline would contain five developmental phases. Tied to the timeline, the other components included: character checks; life and leadership insights; destiny processing; the blend of one's abilities, skills and gifts displayed on a Venn Diagram; life purpose and one's ultimate contribution (or godly kingdom legacy) left behind.

Sensing the weight of how this would impact my life, when I returned home I took a three-month sabbatical from my pastorate (except for preaching on Sunday mornings) so I could focus on what Jesus wanted to reveal to me through this material. At the time I didn't realize the insights I was gleaning for my own life through this process would also provide me with a grid for understanding disciple-making in the context of one's season of life. This would help me better cooperate with what the Holy Spirit wanted to do as He develops disciple-makers.

My Storyline

9/14/14

As I jumped headlong in to this three-month project, I began to see the hand of Jesus developing me as His disciple throughout my entire life. With it came numerous "aha" moments accompanied by the need for further reflection. I gained a deep sense of gratitude from seeing God's intervening hand in some tender places in my heart. He revealed my missteps and gave me a fresh perspective on them. I read the articles Bobby provided, pulled on writings in my old journals, and had conversations with my wife, Cheryl, which added greatly to what I was learning.

Probably like yours, my story contains the norms of everyday life along with some stretches of struggle and some divine interventions. It has been sprinkled throughout with wonderful joys and surprises as well as with severe disappointments. It includes people who helped, harmed, and healed as well as plenty of opportunities to grow, share, and serve. My story, like yours, is unique—not better or worse, not ideal, but very real.

CHAPTER TWO : The Fruitfulness Factor

As I put pen to pad, I discovered patterns that marked my storyline, places where Jesus was working in me over time. Things like: walking more in obedience to Jesus and in the Fear of the Lord; attempts to die to self to live more selflessly; endeavoring to wait on the Lord before rushing in to do what I think is best; forming new habits of referencing God's character and ways in Scripture in the midst of life and leadership choices; and learning to relate well with those around me. In some instances I hit the mark, while in others I missed it significantly. I was finding that this journey of discipleship really does last a lifetime and that God's greatest aim is to conform me into the image of His Son (Romans 8:28–30). No wonder it seems like it's taking so long!

Doing this exercise reminded me that no one is born a disciple-maker; disciple-makers are deliberately developed. Jesus uses the events and people in our lives to shape us to have His character and to teach us His ways. He sovereignly positions us to strategically participate in His mission and to prepare us for it. He redeems and restores where sin has ravaged us, equipping us for noble purposes that glorify Him and bet-

> We must learn that the process of being developed to bring forth fruit is just as valuable to Jesus as the fruit itself. Living within a performance-oriented culture, we often miss this, as we only have the end in mind. We need to recongnize the developmental seasons that Jesus has us in, fully embrace them, and see it as valuable in and of itself.

ter the lives of those around us. To accomplish these things, however, He uses disciple-makers who will deliberately teach, demonstrate, and replicate these realities in the lives of His followers.

My Storyline: Sovereign Foundations Phase

The first developmental phase of Bobby's generalized timeline is referred to as "Sovereign Foundations."[7] It's that time from birth to somewhere between your late teens and early twenties where much of what comes your way has been decided for you: your eye color, first and last name, where you live, where you go to school, who your neighbors are, etc. For some, these years end up being a solid jumping off place while for others they are laden with hurt that Jesus wants to heal. The older you get the more clearly you see the hand of the Lord in this phase of your life as unique preparation and/or incredible redemption that serves to bless the lives of others. This particular phase is where your roots are to grow deep, basic character and personality are developed, and where underlying godly values are shaped. Some hints of God-given destiny may emerge but usually are not recognized as such until later on.

For me, this season began in my home as a boy. Dad and Mom were regulars on Sundays at the Lutheran church, and my younger brother, Tom, and I were always in tow. Dad grew up Lutheran in Duluth, Minnesota, on the shores of Lake Superior, and Mom grew up in the Presbyterian church as a part of a farming family in the Northwest corner of the state. Looking back, I'm grateful for my spiritual heritage bleeding through my parents.

I remember having devotions each morning at the breakfast table before leaving for school. Even when Dad traveled on business, Mom was faithful to make sure we took in a piece of truth and were prayed for. As

CHAPTER TWO : The Fruitfulness Factor

long as I can remember, she rose early each morning to pray for Dad, her two sons, and the world around her. She was also very active in local women's Bible studies and national prayer groups.

When I was 12–13 years of age and living in Southern California, my Dad was having deep stirrings in his spiritual life. With his growing hunger for Jesus, he was found hanging out more at the beach reading the Scriptures than he was making his sales calls! I remember going on some early morning jogs with him along the golf cart paths in Rancho Bernardo, where we lived, pausing for a few minutes along the way to read and reflect on a portion of Scripture together.

God used my parents to point me to Jesus. They put me in environments to ground me in spiritual things. That included bringing Tom and I along to their weekly Wednesday night adult Bible studies which cultivated godly habits and attitudes within us. It was during this time that I gave my life to Jesus while laying in bed one night.

While living in Rancho Bernardo, we were a part of a church in a community just a few miles south of us. Pastor Ernest Karsten,[8] who had served years before as a chaplain in the US Army during World War II, had recently planted a budding congregation. Tom and I were invited to participate in a Lutheran process called "Confirmation" where we were instructed in such things as the life of Jesus, the Scriptures, the Ten Commandments, the Lord's Prayer, and the Apostle's Creed. Pastor Karsten led us through the process, meeting regularly with us over several months. We were being prepared for a time of public confession and confirmation of our faith in Jesus, while also preparing to receive our first communion.

My commitment to Jesus led me to digging into the Scriptures. I was invited to do some teaching at our little youth group, made up of young teens around my age. I was doing the same at school as an 8th grader, hosting a once-a-week Bible study during lunch with the help of a godly math teacher.

This season also marked my first real "Lordship" moment of my life. A year earlier I had been selected to represent my community as a part of a basketball all-star team in a regional tournament. In light of this, I was really looking forward to the upcoming season. As the coaches drafted their teams for the new season, I landed on a team with several friends of mine with whom I'd played previously—things were looking good!

We held several practices each week as a team preparing for the season. As the first Saturday game grew closer, our coach announced that our practices from here on out would be held on Wednesday nights and Sunday mornings. As a new follower of Jesus, I had commitments on Wednesday nights and Sunday mornings! After explaining this to my coach, the result was a lack of playing time during our games.

As I sought the Lord one Saturday evening following a night of frustration while watching most of the game from the sidelines, He revealed to me from the Scriptures what He desired for me to do. He wanted me to lay down basketball so that I could continue my pursuit of Him. While difficult, I remember that when I yielded to what Jesus asked me to do, I sensed a very real peace. Shortly after, I communicated with my coach what I was going to do.

Needless to say, this was a huge step in my spiritual growth. It was Jesus developing His values within me. It taught me that following Him meant

What does this look like for each of us?

CHAPTER TWO : The Fruitfulness Factor

sacrificing my will for His, trusting Him in obedience while knowing that He always has my highest good in mind. ⟨handwritten⟩

Shortly after this experience, my Dad's growing spiritual hunger led to a major move for our family from California to Minnesota so he could attend Northwestern Bible College in a St. Paul suburb. This move would mean that he would leave his job and Mom would go back to work as a receptionist/secretary. Nowadays it is not so unusual for a man in his late thirties to go back to school, but at the time Dad was only one of two men in the whole student body of that age! All of this required obedience and sacrifice for both Dad and Mom—and in smaller ways for Tom and me.

Throughout my high school years in Arden Hills, Minnesota, my spiritual appetite grew and was being fueled through others that Jesus brought in to my life: youth leaders at North Heights Lutheran Church, godly friends at school, and visiting missionaries that stayed in our home. While wrestling with all the inner dynamics as a typical teen, the spiritual disciplines of being in the Scriptures, prayer, fellowship, and serving others helped me continue to mature in the things of the Lord.

The events of this season cultivated a spiritual disposition in me and provided a kind of "Velcro" that would allow the ways of God I was about to learn stick better as I headed into my young adult years.

My Storyline: Early Developmental Phase

From Bobby's research, I began to understand that building on the "Sovereign Foundations Phase" was what he called the "Early Developmental Phase".[9] This is a season, generally in one's twenties and thirties, where character continues to be formed, lots of learning through doing

---

THE JESUS BLUEPRINT : PART ONE

is experienced, and some leadership is exercised. Indications of gifted-ness and life purpose also emerge. *This may be at a later stage of one's life depending on maturity and willingness*

You may have already noticed that Bobby's developmental phases provide a very different picture, for most of us, of how lives and leaders are developed. Most of us grew up thinking that by the time we graduated from college, or certainly by the time we hit thirty, we should be "hitting our strides." The picture that Bobby paints is vastly different. In his research of over a thousand godly leaders, he found this "early phase"—the second in his timeline—is all about Jesus transforming us on the inside, receiving tools and unique methodologies, and discovering His real life purpose for us. The key, I was learning, was not chasing after positions by "climbing the ladder" or pushing for opportunities, but rather cooperating with what He was building inside me. I was seeing it: Jesus' aim in this season is building His character and ways *within* me so that later I can sustain what He wants to do *through* me.

Just as shoots begin to appear in the form of branches on a tree, the "branching out" time of my life began after high school. Jesus used the next seven years of my life in YWAM to build on the good foundation in my life, to mature my walk with Him, and to give me a vision and tools that would help me discover and fulfill God's call on my life. God brought many seasoned leaders, teachers, and disciple-makers into my life that imparted the ways of God to me. Their lives spoke volumes to me about loving Jesus, commitment, sacrifice, obedience—and being fruitful disciple-makers! *To be a disciple we must be open to the Holy Spirit - to be transformed to be able to "fulfill God's call on our lives"*

In my twenties, I was learning more about God's character and responding to Him in worship. I was growing in my responses to the leading of the Lord. I found that God's grace, Jesus' death on the cross, and truly

CHAPTER TWO : The Fruitfulness Factor

living daily as His disciple was becoming more real to me. I began to value other kinds of spiritual disciplines, like waiting on God and fasting. I gained a greater understanding of the Fear of the Lord and what it meant to walk in obedience. I realized that this disciple-making process was extending into all areas of my life!

At the same time, the Lord opened doors for me to practice what I was learning in reaching out to others. Working on high school campuses throughout Hawaii allowed me to share Jesus with those who didn't know Him, and it provided me multiple opportunities each week to exercise an emerging preaching/teaching gift that I'd had hints of during my youth group years. It also trained me in things like hearing God's voice, waging spiritual warfare, and trusting God. Living in Hawaii taught me the value and beauty of various cultures and how to receive from them and relate to them in a godly way. In the midst of all of this activity, I practiced making disciples—reproducing in others what I had received.

Along the way I was also exposed to God's heart for the nations when I made trips to Brazil and Australia. In Brazil, I had the privilege of teaming with others to impact the lives of teenagers of diplomats from around the world. In several cities in Australia, we partnered with friends to teach and disciple youth and young adults.

During this same period of time is when I met a beautiful young woman from Washington, Cheryl Buma, who several years later became my bride! I not only became a husband, but, in time, the father of two wonderful children, Ryan and Malia. I was indeed growing shoots in many ways, yet the deep inward work of Jesus continued in my life.

Following YWAM, we moved to Northern Minnesota where we helped

THE JESUS BLUEPRINT : PART ONE

my dad, mom, and others pioneer a church. In my late twenties, I twice co-led a three-month discipleship/missions training school in the middle of winter for farmers and people in the community, followed by a two-week international outreach. At the same time I poured into the two youth in our youth group! While very much enjoying my friendships, this season taught me much about dying to self and my vision and provided me with a real love for the local church.

Several years later, the Lord then took our young family to San Jose, California, where I served with Messenger International (now Messenger Fellowship).[10] God was continuing to form His character and ways in me as He combined my missions and local church experiences to equip local church teams for major missions thrusts in Krasnodar, Russia, when God flung the doors open there in 1991. Jesus had used Communist leaders—without them knowing it—to prepare a way, using the high literacy rate to invade that land with the Gospel through relationships and written materials! Never have I seen such a ripe harvest field!

As I mentioned earlier, this season of life is more about what God is building in us than what He is doing through us. Now, that does not mean I shouldn't expect to be mightily used by the Lord, but above and beyond that, it's a crucial season of paying attention to the ways of God that I was learning. After all, what I am learning and what God is building within me is what I carry forward for the rest of my life!

After my full-time stint with Messenger, the next decade-and-a-half was spent pastoring two churches in the Nashville, Tennessee, area. God used these roles to continue the refining process inside me while allowing me to exercise my gifts of leadership, preaching, and teaching. I served as the senior pastor of a wonderful church plant and as the equipping pastor of a large congregation that we merged with. Each gave me the opportunity to be significantly stretched. Both experiences added to my life, and I had the privilege of adding to the lives of those who were a part of those congregations. Joy! MATT 25:21

While attempting to cultivate disciple-making cultures in both settings, I ran into opportunities and obstacles. I was afforded the opportunity to create a deliberate one-year discipleship process that would lead to greater spiritual maturity and also equip each one to obey Jesus' disciple-making command. I also encountered obstacles in the form of leaders who didn't carry Jesus' disciple-making mandate in their hearts. Through this experience I learned an important lesson: when leaders don't "own" Jesus' command to make disciples, it is significantly more difficult to move disciple-making forward as a whole within that setting. (But not impossible)

I also took away from those challenging circumstances that there are always "hungry hearts" to disciple in all situations. It's important to focus on finding the willing learners and sow well there, knowing that as others see the lives of those being transformed, they'll want to get in on it too!

As I worked away over several months on my timeline, I saw how the Lord accomplished a couple of things at once throughout this phase. He continued shaping me internally to have more of His character and ways while he developed in me the gift sets I would need to accomplish what He's called me to do. Sometimes the "vocational formation" seemed to be the tip of the arrow, while at other times it was the internal "spiritual formation." I learned to pay more attention to God and His work, both in and through me, which really aided my overall development.

In this phase the Lord also used such things as conflict and crisis to reveal leadership and authority insights to me. He taught me the value of relational leadership, how to only engage in what He initiates, and the

THE JESUS BLUEPRINT : PART ONE

process of regularly seeking Him on specifics in prayer with my wife or leadership team. I grew more secure in my own skin—who I was and was not in my personality, gifts, and calling. And the beauty of it all was as I learned to yield to His work in me, I had more to pass on to those I was discipling.

My Storyline: Middle Developmental Phase

As I continued to chip away at my project, I recognized that I was transitioning into the third phase of Bobby's generalized timeline known as the "Middle Developmental Phase."[11] Most enter this phase somewhere in their thirties, with it often lasting into the late-forties to mid-fifties. In the latter portion of this season, most firm up their life purpose, are functioning maturely in their gifts, and are moving towards their "major role."

A major role may or may not have a title attached to it, but everyone around them recognizes the godly weight and authority that they're walking in. When a leader emerges in their major role, it often brings with it great leadership challenges and, at times, backlash from followers. As I mentioned earlier, the pressures of this particular season will reflect how much character work one allowed Jesus to do within him during the earlier developmental phases!

In creating my personal timeline based on Bobby's generalized one, I was learning how unique our developmental timeframes can be, even though this process may be fairly common for all of us. I also was seeing that because this is God's work within us, we really can't speed up the process. We'll emerge either spiritually "weighty" or "thin" as we hit later phases, depending on our cooperation with God and obedient responses to Him, or lack of them, in earlier phases.

While in my mid-forties, the Lord used some very difficult circumstances to cause me to be open to step into something I might not have otherwise felt quite ready to consider. Bobby calls this "negative preparation." Honestly, because I had this teaching under my belt when this event occurred it saved me from potential bitterness and dwelling in the land of disappointment. Because I understood these phases, I was able to move forward into what Jesus had for me next without carrying a lot of baggage.

At that time, I was experiencing what Bobby refers to as "boundaries,"[12] or thresholds, through which one leaves one season of life and enters into another. I was learning in the articles I was reading that these transitions can last anywhere from about six months up to six years! They are often marked by significant change and confusion, either internally and/or externally. They tend to follow a course of *looking back* at what's transpired, then *looking upward* to God for understanding and direction, and then *looking forward* into a new season.

Boundaries are a space in time that God uses to prepare us for what He wants to do in and through us next. If we're not careful, we can miss what He may be doing in us because we are solely focused on surviving what's in front of us. As we encounter boundaries in our late thirties and into our forties, I wonder how many have mistaken what really is a "boundary" for a "mid-life crisis"? Boundaries are God's gracious way of taking away from us and adding to us so we are ready to run the next leg of the race He's called us to.

Walking towards the very end of this Middle Phase (the season I'm in while writing this book at fifty-two years of age) it seems as if what I'm called to is falling more into place. I'm functioning in stronger levels in my gifts and seeing more clearly than ever my life's purpose. I've also noticed that taking the territory God intends for me to have frequently only comes through serious contending. The enemy of my soul, and yours, attempts to do everything he can to hinder, hassle and cause hiccups along the way to fulfilling our God-given assignments. I can't even begin to tell you how grateful I am for the many disciplers and leaders around me who stressed godly character first in my Early Phase. I don't know if I would have made it through some of the challenges I've faced over the last decade if they had not helped me build up my inner man.

During the Middle Phase, God sets many faith challenges before us as we apply what we've learned, flexing our spiritual muscles for the purpose of spiritual breakthroughs in the areas where we serve. As we learn how to gain ground via spiritual warfare, God uniquely uses these periods of contending to bring each of us back to another round of inner "spiritual formation" and shoring up issues of the heart.

Other hallmarks of this phase include functioning efficiently, or doing things right, and Jesus moving us more from "doing" to "being," where what we do flows freely out of who we are.

My current storyline ends here. I want to briefly share with you, however, what I'm anticipating in upcoming phases from what I've learned from Bobby and by watching the lives of godly men and women who are further down the road than me.

Latter Developmental Phase

Those living in the "Latter Development Phase"[13] clearly see their God-given destinies and are deliberately moving towards fulfilling it. Their actions come through the convergence of a mature character, seasoned gifts and through identification of a God-given sphere of influence.

Generally speaking, they begin this season somewhere in their fifties and continue in it through their sixties. They "hit their stride" during this season, obeying God and significantly advancing the kingdom for God's glory.

It's in this phase where efficiency (doing things right) yields to effectiveness (doing the right things). It's where "vocational formation" fades and "strategic formation" comes into play. In this season, while being very strategic in all that's done, the inner work of the Spirit to shape us in the image of Jesus continues.

This is what you've been born for, what God's been developing you for. Your aim is clear, your steps are deliberate, your life's purpose is unfolding. Although you've been fruitful in making disciples throughout your journey, the fullness of fruitfulness in making disciple-makers is at hand!

While here, let me divert us for a moment to Moses. As you may remember his storyline, his first forty years were spent in Egypt where he was provided with the best education of his day. The next forty, following a flight from Egypt, were spent in the wilderness where he was shaped into a man of God through trials and lots of time with sheep. His next forty years, following a transition which started with a burning bush, were spent delivering the people of Israel from Egypt and preparing them to enter their Promised Land.

That's three forty-year segments. If you do the math, you find that two-thirds of Moses' life were lived in preparation for the last one-third. You'll find Bobby's math, based on his observations of 1,200+ leaders, to be about the same. If the average lifespan is seventy-five years, that means our first fifty years or so are all about God preparing us for what He wants to do through us in the final twenty-five! Something to think about.

Another character from Scripture that I think a lot about, in light of how God is the one who places us *where* He wants us to be *when* He wants us to be there, is Joseph. You can read his full story in Genesis 37–50. It is worth reading and reflecting on. My point here is: Joseph, who was (falsely) accused of raping an Egyptian noblewoman, was promoted from prison to second-in-command of the whole land of Egypt in a day! How often do we wrestle and jockey for position, striving with everything within us to make something happen? God's way is focusing on the preparation of our inner man, knowing He can put us *where* He wants us *when* He wants us there! Trust and obey—it's still Jesus' way!

Finishing Well Phase 5th phase

Bobby calls the final phase the "Finishing Well Phase."[14] Generally speaking, we arrive here around our late sixties to early seventies. This phase reflects a sense of fulfilling what you were born to be and do while reaping the fruit of a lifetime of faithfulness. Your focus is now more on your ultimate contribution[15]—a godly legacy that you are to leave behind in people, resources, and accomplishments for kingdom purposes. This season is best spent investing godly wisdom in younger leaders, using the ways of God you've gleaned from your life's journey.

According to Bobby's years of homework, the six characteristics of someone finishing well are:[16]

- They preserve a *personal vibrant relationship with God* right up until the end.
- They maintain a *learning posture,* learning from all kinds of sources.
- They display *Christ-like character,* evidenced by the fruit of the Spirit.
- They *live in the truth they've learned,* demonstrating to others that the convictions and promises of God are real.
- They leave behind one or more *ultimate contributions* as a lasting kingdom legacy.
- They walk in a *growing awareness of fulfilling their God-given destiny,* in part or full.

Do you remember me telling you at the beginning of Bobby's class his first words were: "In my research since 1983 of 1200+ leaders from Scripture, church history, and today, I've found that only one in three finishes well"? One in three. One in three! What happened to the two-thirds?

Watching over the years, I've seen all kinds of things take people out of the race. Chief among them are:

Be Aware of These & others

- Seduction of sin (selfishness, immorality, etc.)
- Rabbit trails of woundedness, bitterness, and disappointment
- Pride that causes them to go it alone, hindering them from hearing and learning from others and enjoying relationships
- Power grabs and control around position, fame, and/or finances

- Giving place to fear and/or passivity
- The pursuit of perceived success (note: biblical success is obeying God)
- Choosing to walk in disobedience to what Jesus has asked them to do

Are you on the path to finishing well? If not, why not? In light of what you've learned about developmental phases, or seasons of life, what can you do today to start strong, to enhance mid-life, or to finish well?

Obviously, so much more could be said on this entire topic. Bobby's research is amazingly thorough and detailed—a true gift to the body of Christ. I'd highly commend it to you.[17] I've referenced it in my life for a decade-and-a-half now. With Bobby's gracious permission, I've modified portions of his material into a format that I use to disciple Jesus-followers in how to cooperate with Him as He develops them as His disciples and as godly leaders.

Fruit in Season

We must learn that the *process* of being developed to bring forth fruit is just as valuable to Jesus as the fruit itself. Living within a performance-oriented culture, we often miss this as we only have the end in mind. Think about it: A tree's fruit-developing (ripening) process usually produces fruit that is less green, softer to the touch, sweeter to the taste, and contains within it seeds of reproduction. We need to recognize the developmental seasons that Jesus has us in, fully embrace it, and see it as valuable in and of itself.

In one season of your life it may be all about growing your character—

this is a "win" in Jesus' eyes. Another season may be about flexing muscles in regards to your gifts. Still another may be about learning to relate well to others, becoming more whole, or transitioning well from one season to another. What is Jesus trying to develop within you in this current season of your life? As you focus on the present place of His development in your life—or in the lives of those you're discipling—over time, you will reap healthy and reproducible fruit!

As we journey into the next two chapters, we're going to take a closer look at the Jesus blueprint, observing a scriptural pattern and a cultural paradigm that we can learn from to make disciple-makers today. We'll also dive deeper into Jesus' life as a follower of His Father, allowing us to see more clearly what our own lives and leadership are really reproducing.

Chapter Three

The Jesus Blueprint

Over the years I've had the opportunity to be a part of a number of start-up works. Each one begins with a dream of the heart or a picture within one's mind of something that needs to be created, changed, or accomplished. Regardless of what it is, at some point it gets translated into a working plan to move it from idea or desire into reality.

A blueprint is necessary when building a home, university campus, church facility, stadium, or sprawling new office complex. A blueprint is a design, pattern, model, guide, or prototype—the reference point for how that building needs to be built. Among other things, the blueprint must factor in exterior surroundings, the foundation, inner wall locations, and structural design. It considers the necessary cooperation of the mechanical, electrical, and plumbing trades. Some of the blueprints that I've seen are architectural pieces of art! They give a preview of the finished product and instruct each builder involved with what he needs to know to complete his part in constructing it. A good blueprint results in a structure that fulfills the purposes for which it was designed and built.

While writing this book, I've been watching the new equipping center being built on our church campus. Not too long ago this space was simply a parking lot. Then one day a friend emailed me pictures of the foundation being poured. The building had begun! Soon after, the structure began to emerge as beams were put in place defining where the various rooms would be. Next, I noticed even larger beams constructed where the roof would be located. As I drove up to the site, after being gone for a few weeks, it was amazing to see that the walls and roof were already in place! This structure that began as a blueprint will soon become a building used to equip and disciple thousands of Jesus followers for His kingdom purposes!

In the Scriptures, Jesus spoke about laying a good foundation (Luke 6:46–49) and the necessity of building on that foundation to finish what was started (Luke 14:27–33). Although you cannot build anything without a solid foundation, no one builds just a foundation. It's always laid so something can be built on it!

If we desire to participate in the mandate of Jesus to make disciples, we must rediscover how He approached it.

A Pattern and Paradigm

Years ago, when I was creating a one-year formational framework for disciple-making in a local church, I began to discover a pattern from the life of Jesus. At the same time, while pursuing further education, I had the opportunity to explore a cultural paradigm that Jesus and His disciples would have functioned within and been influenced by. Both helped me better understand the Jesus blueprint—His disciple-making emphasis, process, and aims.

As you will see, these stand in contrast to our maturing and multiplying methods of today that more often than not revolve only around classroom settings. I've frequently thought that if classroom settings alone produced disciples (note our shelves full of notebooks of information we've received from church services, Wednesday night studies, and seminary classes), we should have had revival and reformation in the church, along with societal transformation, a hundred times over by now!

Now, don't get me wrong. The passing on of the ways of God through teaching truth is one of several key ingredients to growing disciples. We have, however, repeatedly exalted gaining knowledge and information over the practice of *applying* what we've been taught in obedience to Jesus! The intention of disciple-making is becoming more like Jesus— not only the gaining of more information. Knowledge by itself puffs up; obeying Jesus grows us up. One leads to pride and independence; the other, to humility and dependence. Discipleship is not about gaining information—it's really about life transformation!

Just a quick note as we walk this path together. Please do not reduce what is shared here to a formula or consider it the latest method to grow one's church or sphere of influence. Instead, take it for what it is: a blueprint—a model, guide, prototype—that you can reference as you seek Jesus about applying disciple-making within the context of where you live and lead.

> We have, however, repeatedly exalted gaining knowledge and information over the practice of applying what we've been taught in obedience to Jesus! The intention of disciple-making is becoming more like Jesus—not only the gaining of more information.

The Matthew Pattern

While navigating the New Testament's book of Matthew, I observed a simple pattern containing key ingredients in the disciple-making dynamics of Jesus and the Twelve. I also see these same ingredients in the way His disciples related to the next generation of disciples in the Book of Acts (i.e., Acts 2:42–47):

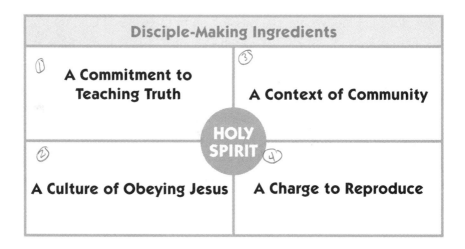

This pattern in Matthew, in brief, looks like this: Jesus begins to *teach the truth* about His character, ways, and mission (i.e., the Semon on the Mount in Matthew 5–7), while inviting them to walk in *community* with Him (beginning in Matthew 4:18–22). As they walk alongside and minister with Him, He looks for them to be responsive to Him by their *obedience* (i.e., being sent out in Matthew 10, feeding the 5,000, and Peter's walk on the water in Matthew 14). After His death and resurrection, He commissions them to *reproduce* in others what He had taught them to obey (Matthew 28:18–20). Let's take a little closer look at each of these.

A Commitment to Teaching Truth

Jesus was referred to as "Rabbi" or "Teacher" by the disciples. He was the source of their truth and wisdom during their three years together. Although they surely didn't understand it at the time, Jesus was fully aware that He was laying the groundwork, through these disciples, for the largest and most powerful movement the world will ever know—His kingdom expressed through His church! What He taught, why He taught what He did, and how He passed on truth to them so that they owned it and could reproduce it is of great significance. Jesus made sure they really caught what He was teaching as He expected them to later do the same for others.

Teaching can be done both formally and informally, in large groups, small groups, and one-on-one. Often, our idea of teaching conjures up images of one standing up in front of a class. That's certainly one way, but a read through the Gospels reveals that Jesus used all kinds of opportunities, settings, and means to pass truth on to His disciples.

Through my three-and-a-half decades in ministry I have run across some who've said something to this effect: "It is only my responsibility to teach, it is the hearer's responsibility to apply what I've taught." Although I absolutely agree that it is up to the learner to steward and apply what he has been given, I do differ with the perspective of this kind of teacher, based on the approach of Jesus.

A true teacher desires truth to be made real in the life of the one he is teaching. In other words, a teacher helps the learner understand, digest and apply what he is learning to his life. This approach reflects the maxim, "if the student hasn't learned, the teacher hasn't taught". With kingdom truths that Jesus taught being of utmost importance, how can we do anything less than our very best to see those truths made real in the lives of those we disciple?

Jesus transformed lives with the truths of His kingdom. He did so through the pattern of *teach—demonstrate—replicate* as he taught to the point of understanding, demonstrated what it looked like, and then asked the disciples to replicate it in front of Him.

We see an example of this in Matthew 14. When the disciples see the massive amount of people present as the meal time approached, they ask Jesus to send them away to nearby villages to buy food. However, Jesus responds with "you give them something to eat." They'd heard Him numerous times teaching about faith, and now it seems He wants to stretch theirs by *demonstrating* His. They collect five loaves and two fish. Jesus blesses the meal and multiplies it to feed everyone present. And just to make the point sharper, there are twelve baskets worth leftover, one for each of them!

In the next scene, in the same chapter, Jesus, the "Teacher," moves from *demonstration* to *replication*. While on a boat in the midst of a storm, Jesus comes walking to the disciples on the water! Jesus invites Peter to join Him on the water and Peter does! Peter replicates the faith Jesus had taught and that he had just seen demonstrated. Yes, we all know that fear later got the best of Peter, but his faith got exercised and he actually walked on the water!

We'll take a further look at the paradigm of *teach—demonstrate—replicate* when we discuss some practical aspects of making disciple-makers later on.

Without teaching in the context of disciple-making, it leaves followers of Jesus adrift from the truth of Scripture. Doing so produces shallow people that can be very vulnerable to deception and who follow after every teaching that tickles their ears.

A Context of Community why?

Disciple-making takes place in the context of relationships. Jesus chose a small band to "be with Him" (Mark 3:14), a dozen men that He spent significant amounts of time with. Together for three years, they experienced the ups-and-downs and in-and-outs of life!

Think about a group of people that you've spent three years of your life with. It could be in college, in the military, on the job, as neighbors, as a ball team or band, or in a small group. Not only does an experience like this meld you together, but you also rub off on each other! You come to a place of valuing this environment of community where you are cared for, challenged, and encouraged. _Love!_

This little community of Jewish men that Jesus brought together—including fishermen, a tax collector, a zealot—made for a unique community. Although they probably had similar upbringings, they all had different passions, skill sets, interests, and life experiences that they brought to the table. No doubt Jesus knew walking together would expose their hearts, creating opportunities for Him to equip and empower them.

In community Jesus showed them what love looks like. What it means for someone to lay down their lives for another. What it's like to know someone will be with you always, through thick and thin. He also demonstrated how important it is to forgive those who'd sinned against them. And how to view people and life through His set of lenses.

We've already seen the fruit of godly community as we took a brief look at the Book of Acts. No one in Acts is seen "going it alone" when it comes to their spiritual development through discipleship. Rather, there is a constant togetherness, whether in large groups, small groups, or traveling teams. It seems that everyone was always walking alongside someone else.

One of the dangers of doing discipleship outside of relational community is that it tends to produce poor relaters and breeds an attitude of independence. In its extreme form, I've run across "solo flyers" who come off very super-spiritual, yet lack the authenticity of walking in healthy, accountable relationships. Interdependence and encouragement are necessary components in a healthy walk with Jesus and occur in the context of community.

A Culture of Obeying Jesus

We arrive at what I believe is often the key missing piece in our attempts to cultivate disciples: obeying Jesus. As we stated earlier, following Jesus actually means *following* Jesus!

We need to ask ourselves whether we're obeying Jesus out of a loving relationship with Him, or whether we are just religious about doing certain things. In John 14:15, Jesus said, "If you love me you'll obey my commands." We obey Jesus as an expression of our love for Him. Obeying is not a "got to" but rather a "get to." Richard Foster[1] in his great book, *Celebration of Discipline*, states, "In the spiritual life only one thing produces genuine joy and that is obedience." — *Obedience isn't always easy or fun!*

Jesus modeled obedience for His disciples. He followed when the Spirit led Him into the wilderness. Throughout His life He consistently did what the Father asked Him to do. In the Book of Acts, we see His disciples obeying Him and following the lead of the Holy Spirit. Here are a few examples:

THE JESUS BLUEPRINT : PART ONE

- Jesus told them to wait in Jerusalem to be empowered by the Holy Spirit—they did!

- Jesus told them to lay hands on the sick—they did!

- Jesus taught them to pray—they did!

- Jesus taught them to fear God not man—they did!

- Jesus told them to preach the Gospel throughout the whole world—they did!

- Jesus taught them to operate in faith—they did!

- Philip was led by the Spirit to the chariot to speak to the Ethiopian eunuch—he followed!

- Peter was told by the Spirit to go to Cornelius' home—he did!

- Paul was asked by Jesus to carry His name to the Gentiles, kings, and children of Israel—he did!

- Jesus commanded His disciples to make disciples—they did!

Obedience begins when we do what the Scriptures say and continues as we obey the promptings of the Holy Spirit in the midst of everyday life. Sometimes, obedience requires us to hurdle our own fears and step outside of our comfort zones. There are times that we'll miss it and we'll need to humbly acknowledge it, while learning for next time. When we get it right and lives are impacted—wow, talk about growing and being encouraged! When we obey God, we experience Him—team up with Him—to fulfill His purposes!

Maybe you've noticed when the Lord reveals a truth and we don't act on it by applying it, we become less pliable and more paralyzed in that part of our lives. On the other hand, when we obey Him, our lives, and those around us, are transformed. Indeed, obedience is the engine of transformation!

lisciples of Jesus, it is crucial that we foster within our disciple-cing communities a culture of obeying God. Often leaders won't fan the flames of hearing from and obeying Jesus. I'd submit several reasons why they don't. First, we haven't deliberately discipled them, so we neither trust what they might "hear" nor how they'll "obey." Second, we don't have the ability to add anything to our already overburdened structures and systems. We're often so overwhelmed by the strain of what's already going on that we're not open to anything else, even if it might be Jesus initiating it. And, third, often if we can't control it, we don't want any part of it.

One other thing. Obedience to Jesus costs us something. When persecution and difficult times arose in the lives of the disciples in Acts, they continued to faithfully obey Him. G. Campbell Morgan said, "Our faith is one that will require persecution. Does our current discipleship prepare us for this?"[2] His words, perhaps, are more appropriate today than ever.

A lack of cultivating obedience to Jesus results in the lack of real transformation. In a church, this may result in inflexible and immovable systems and structures that look like they cannot be changed. On a personal level, a lack of obedience can produce a spiritual blindness with the outcome being a puffed-up head and a hard heart towards God and people.

> The danger of not reproducing disciples...well, it's what we're seeing today: spiritually "thin" people who believe obeying Jesus and reproducing disciple-makers is optional. Before us is a generation looking to be discipled and yet there are not enough willing or equipped to do so!

A Charge to Reproduce

We arrive at what I would call the most neglected of these four disciple-making ingredients. A.W. Tozer said, "Only a disciple can make a disciple."[3] Jesus intended for the kingdom of God to be advanced through disciples reproducing disciples. *How does Sunday sermon accomplish this? (mega church)*

We're already aware of Jesus discipling the Twelve in the Scriptures and the continued focus and fruit of reproducing disciples in Acts. Regardless of our age, gender, or nationality, if we are disciples of Jesus, we have been commissioned by Jesus with reproducing disciple-makers. Irrespective of our call to the various domains of society, we have been commanded by the One we love to be His disciple-makers. It does not matter if we're relational kinds of people or taskers; if we are disciples of Jesus we have been commanded to make disciples. Embracing disciple-making changes the way we live our lives, the way we run our churches, and the way we lead within our vocations.

The "Great Commission" in Matthew 28 is not the "Great Recommendation"! The feel of "go and make disciples" in the original language is "as you are going, make disciples." In other words, as you are living life, make disciples. In the course of all that you're doing, make disciples. As breathing, eating, and sleeping is a regular part of our lives, so should disciple-making be.

We tend to emulate what's been modeled for us. We also only reproduce, with authority, what we've integrated into our lives. This brings us to a healthy question that we all must ponder: *what am I really reproducing?* It's a question worth reflecting on. (We'll address this topic thoroughly as we look at the life of Jesus in the next chapter.)

The danger of not reproducing disciples…well, it's what we're seeing today: spiritually "thin" people who believe obeying Jesus and reproducing disciple-makers is optional. Before us is a generation looking to be discipled and yet there are not enough willing or equipped to do so! Another place of reaping is the current lack of godly men and women who actually fear God and reference His character and ways while leading within society's domains.

Referencing a Cultural Paradigm

Along with this pattern in Matthew, we'd do well to explore the Rabbinic prototype that Jesus and His disciples would have followed, along with the Greek idea of imitation that was culturally prevalent in New Testament times. My intention here, in brief, is to help us understand how the paradigm of the time also impacted disciple-making, while providing us with some insights and principles that can be applied today.

At the time of Jesus and His disciples, the word "disciple" was a term for a student of a teacher or philosopher. This term, and the social realities of it, was familiar to both Jewish and Greek societies: "The Jewish institution of discipleship shows many similarities with the form of discipleship in early Christianity. There are, however, considerable differences, especially in regard to questions concerning the substance of teaching and the person of the teacher. The rabbinic scholar is bound to the Law, which is, in principle, supreme over the teachings of any individual rabbi, while Jesus' disciples are connected to the person of Jesus in a particular way. Students choose their rabbis, while Jesus takes for Himself the initiative to call those He chooses. In Greek culture, the teacher-student relationship took varying forms, but generally discipleship involved adherence to a great teacher and his particular way of life. The early Christian form of discipleship, with its emphasis on the person of Jesus, comes closer to the individualistic Hellenistic teacher-disciple relationship."[4]

It goes without saying that relationships between teachers and followers existed among people for centuries before the disciple-making of Jesus. Among Jews in the Old Testament we find examples such as: Jethro and Moses, Moses and Joshua, Elijah and Elisha, Naomi and Ruth, Ezra and his followers, and Mordecai and Esther. There is also a mention of disciples by Isaiah (Isaiah 8:16).

As we know, Jesus was referred to as "Rabbi," a term with meanings ranging from respect to "teacher/role model." It's evident from the Scriptures that the latter describes how His disciples related to Him. Several passages in John (13:34; 17:18,23; 20:21) reinforce Jesus as the teacher and role model via the expression, "As I…so you." We also see this in John 13:15, where Jesus states, "For I have given you an example, that you also should do just as I have done to you."[5]

Examining Jesus' role more closely reveals the depth of this teacher-follower relationship, which goes beyond Him being just an example to Him deliberately reproducing. To provide a framework of understanding, consider these five facets of rabbinical tradition that formed first-century discipleship, highlighted by Bill Hull in his great book, *The Complete Book of Discipleship: On Being and Making Followers of Christ*:

1. *A decision to follow a teacher.* The disciple of first-century Judaism learned everything from his teachers: their stories, life habits, keeping the Sabbath his way, and his interpretations of the Torah. A disciple's commitment to follow his teacher lies at the heart of the transformational process.

Once accepted as a disciple, a young man started as a talmidh, or beginner, who sat in the back of the room and could not speak. Then he became a distinguished student, who took an independent line in his approach or questioning. At the next level, he became a disciple-associate, who sat immediately behind the rabbi during prayer time. Finally he achieved the highest level, a disciple of the wise, and was recognized as the intellectual equal of his rabbi.

2. *The memorization of the teacher's words.* Oral tradition provided the basic way of studying. Disciples learned the teacher's words verbatim, to pass along to the next person. Often disciples learned as many as four interpretations of each major passage in the Torah.

3. *The disciple learns the teacher's way of ministry.* A disciple learned how his teacher kept God's commands, including how he practiced the Sabbath, fasted, prayed, and said blessings in ceremonial situations. He would also learn his rabbi's teaching methods and the many traditions his master followed.

4. *The imitation of the teacher's life and character.* Jesus said that when a disciple is fully taught, he "will be like his teacher" (Luke 6:40). The highest calling of a disciple was to imitate his teacher. Paul called on Timothy to follow his example (2 Timothy 3:10–14), and he didn't hesitate to call on all believers to do the same (see 1 Corinthians 4:14–16; 11:1; Philippians 4:9). One story in ancient tradition tells of a rabbinical student so devoted to his teacher that he hid in the teacher's bedchamber to discover the mentor's sexual technique! Although this is inordinately extreme, such an action demonstrates the high level of commitment required to be a disciple.

5. *The disciple raises his own disciples.* When a disciple finished his training, he was expected to reproduce what he'd learned

by finding and training his own apprentices. He would start his own school and name it after himself.

Now, we must note that Jesus made a distinction here. His disciples were not to raise up new disciples for themselves. The disciples of Jesus were never to take the role of master (Matthew 23:8–10). Both then and now, Jesus commands his disciples to raise up more disciples *for Him*. Yes, we'll have teachers, mentors, and leaders, but they'll never become our masters. Yes, we submit to authority, but it's voluntary and an act of love and humility. As disciples today, just as in the first century, we're called to follow Jesus and to raise up others to be *His* disciples.

These five facets were the expression of discipleship as practiced in the first century. Jesus used these practices with His closest followers. When He called on them to make disciples, He expected them to find others who would make the five commitments. When he said, "Teach them to obey everything I have commanded you" (Matthew 28:20), they knew the task would require the kind of dedication found in these five commitments.[6]

Rabbi Jason Sobel,[7] who ministers throughout the Los Angeles area and beyond, passed on some wise precepts to me, which reinforced the centrality of rabbis reproducing disciples. The first was:

> *"They [the Men of the Great Assembly] would always say these three things: Be cautious in judgment. Establish many disciples/pupils. And make a safety fence around the Torah."*
>
> AVOT 1:1

The second was:

> *"There are three things every person must seek for themselves, a spiritual mentor and teacher (a rabbi), a spiritual*

63

CHAPTER THREE : The Jesus Blueprint

friend (chaver) who one can learn and grow together with, and a spouse to establish a family in which godly children can be raised in fulfillment of the first command in the Bible, "Be fruitful and multiply and fill the earth." As the Rabbis teach, "Joshua the son of Perachiah said: "Acquire for yourself a teacher; find a friend; and judge everyone favorably."

ETHICS OF THE FATHERS 1:6

In Jewish tradition contemporary with Jesus, as well as in the New Testament itself, disciples desired to replicate every detail of their teacher's life. "Ben Sirach (175 BC) cites the goal of a rabbi is to train his student to such an extent that 'when his father [teacher] dies, it is as though he is not dead. For he leaves behind him one like himself.'"[8]

In the Greek world, the teacher-student relationship "is predominantly characterized by the concept of *mimesis*. Teachers and students are bound together by a certain teaching and practice of life, and the student is recognizable in his imitation of the teachings and life of the teacher."[9]

Along with the above mentioned contributions, one of my Regent professors, Dr. Jon Ruthven, found in his research that the Greek *mimesis* or "imitation" theme is quite significant in the New Testament. He found that although there are only five words in the immediate family of *mimesis*, some forty-two words or word groups appear in the semantic field: words like guide, discipline, follow; twenty-six expressions for teach, instruct; and a sizeable number of references to such activities as following, obeying, repeating, and instructing. He also discovered the field of words related to "knowing", "contains a strong Semitic overtone of "knowing by interaction with someone" as opposed to knowing by detached observance or by deriving knowledge from abstract principles."[10]

THE JESUS BLUEPRINT : PART ONE

Both the Jewish and Greek paradigms are brought to bear in the life of the Apostle Paul. Having both a rabbinic education and broad exposure to Greek thought and culture,[11] he speaks of his role as a spiritual father among the Corinthians (1 Corinthians 4:14–17), urging them to be "imitators of me." He exhorts them to imitation in several other passages as well (1 Corinthians 11:1; Ephesians 5:1; Philippians 3:17; 1 Thessalonians 1:6; 2 Thessalonians 3:7, 9), reinforcing this in the hearts and minds of those being discipled.

Some Observations to Consider

So, why is this pattern and paradigm significant? What are some observations that might help us in making disciple-makers today?

Now, I am *not* saying that we are to do disciple-making exactly like the cultural paradigms of 2000 years ago. However, I *am* saying that there are some substantial takeaways here, worthy of prayerful consideration and application for our day.

First, if the Twelve embraced the five characteristics of rabbinical tradition that formed first-century discipleship, *they knew exactly* what Jesus was commissioning them to do in Matthew 28:18–20. They knew they were to reproduce in others what had been replicated in them. This reaffirms our earlier view of Acts as a portrait of what can happen through discipled people who are committed to making disciples!

Second, the process of disciple-making was very deliberate on the part of Jesus. Not only did He make disciples, His approach also developed reproducible disciple-makers. We must come to the point in our thinking and emphasis that this is not simply about making a disciple—but rather *disciple-makers!* Reproducing is meant to be a built-in part of being a disciple. Making *disciple-makers* must be our aim. We must invest

CHAPTER THREE : The Jesus Blueprint

in people to such an extent that Jesus' way of life becomes theirs, enabling them to naturally and deliberately invest the same in those God brings to them.

Third, the disciples were spiritually hungry and very deliberate about learning all they possibly could from Jesus. He called and they came. He taught and they obeyed. He modeled and they followed. A follower must be willing to match or exceed the commitment of the one discipling them. These are good qualities to look for in those we are praying about really pouring our lives into.

Fourth, the disciples were a voluntary band of followers. Scriptural disciple-making is always voluntary and has nothing to do with manipulation and control. Godly men and women do not disciple using those methods! They lead lovingly, teach truth patiently, treat others honorably, correct firmly yet gently, and walk with great humility knowing they still have much to learn in their own lives. These are the kind of people you absorb much from!

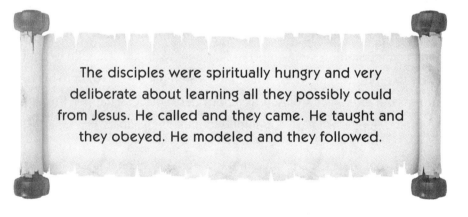

> The disciples were spiritually hungry and very deliberate about learning all they possibly could from Jesus. He called and they came. He taught and they obeyed. He modeled and they followed.

Fifth, disciple-making is always done *for* Jesus and *for* His purposes. It is never about making disciples for ourselves, or in our image. Yes, there will be "thumbprints" of the disciple-maker in the disciple in the way things are done, said, expressed, and reproduced. Yet someone who has been discipled *for* Jesus will ultimately reflect His character, function in His ways, and be focused on His mission.

Because we make disciples *for* Jesus, it means that each disciple belongs to Him. Our role is to encourage each one to respond to and follow His lead at all times. Sometimes, we have the opportunity of discipling people for a season and then we see Jesus relocate them elsewhere to add to what we've invested. We must always hold loosely those God brings our way to disciple. We may have the privilege of stewarding their discipleship for a time, but ultimately they must be available to the call of their Master, the Lord Jesus. A disciple-maker who is trustworthy in this respect will no doubt receive countless disciple-making assignments initiated from above!

Are you currently discipling people *for* Jesus or for your purposes? Is there someone you've been pouring God's ways into that you know you need to release into the next leg of their journey? Is Jesus leading him to another disciple-maker who can add more things to his life or leading him away to accomplish something Jesus has asked him to do?

The ingredients we observed in the pattern in Matthew are *teaching truth, the context of community, obeying Jesus, and reproducing in others*. Together these create a healthy disciple-making environment. Like a good stew, each ingredient is important, and without each one added something is missing. As I mentioned previously, the ingredient I observe that is often missing is a culture of obeying Jesus. Create a context where obeying Jesus becomes the norm is the desired thing to do. We must remember that it's always about *following* Jesus. Also, the most neglected ingredient is reproducing disciple-makers. From the very beginning of your investing in others, help them understand that your godly expectation is that what they receive they are to pass on to others. Help them discover who it is Jesus wants them to disciple, and walk alongside them so they can become proficient in it.

So, who is currently discipling you? When you consider your current settings of influence, do you have a deliberate and reproducible disciple-making game plan in place? Are you actively discipling your family, people in your work place, those in your small group? Next to loving Jesus and others, is making disciples a value and priority for you?

I'd like to encourage you to pause here for just a moment and consider what the Holy Spirit has highlighted for you. What are your key take-aways and obedience points thus far?

A Disciple-Making Definition

We've considered a scriptural pattern and have referenced a cultural paradigm from the time of Jesus. Now it's time to flesh out a practical working definition of disciple-making.

Take a moment to think about your definition of disciple-making. Next, think about how you have gone about hitting that mark—whether deliberately, in a round-about-way, by accident, or not at all. There's no condemnation here for any of us—we're just finding a starting point to see where we've been so we can move towards where we really want to be!

Now, try this definition on for size. It's one I reference regularly after decades of disciple-making:

Reproducing the character, ways, and mission of Jesus in those God brings around you, expecting them to multiply the same in others.

THE JESUS BLUEPRINT : PART ONE

Read it again. Maybe one more time. How does this definition bump up against your past perspective on disciple-making?

Before breaking this definition down, let me first say that the basic reference points for disciple-making are three-fold:

- what the life of Jesus models
- what the Scriptures teach
- the role of the Holy Spirit in the disciple-making process

We've already looked a bit at the life of Jesus, and we'll consider more in the next chapter. We must view the life and approach of Jesus as our primary example. The fruit of His disciple-making has lasted for thousands of years and impacted countless lives, so we need to look to Him as the Master Disciple-Maker.

It is also essential that we are scriptural in all that we do. It is our plumb line for referring to God's character, ways, and mission. With that in mind, we need to be reminded that being transformed as a disciple does not come from how much one knows about the Bible. The devil's been around a long time and he knows what the Bible says quite well. But without yielding to Jesus' Lordship and being obedient to what it says, the Bible leaves him unchanged too! Think about it: we all know people who can quote Scripture like crazy, but the way they live their lives does not reflect Jesus at all! We need a working knowledge of the Scriptures that focuses on following and obeying Jesus in our daily lives—that's what brings about transformation of the heart!

We must continually be sensitive to the role of the Holy Spirit in disciple-making. *Without question, He is the key player in discipling a follower of Jesus!* He knows a person's life journey inside out. He knows their

CHAPTER THREE : The Jesus Blueprint

strengths and gifts, their weaknesses and vulnerabilities. He knows where and how to transform their heart to be more like Jesus. He knows their destiny and the people He wants to add to their life for help along the way. He's the One who empowers them to live a godly life, to serve Jesus and others. Our role in this process is to watch where the Spirit seems to be working in their life and come alongside what He's doing. In reality, we have the privilege of teaming with the Holy Spirit—following His lead—in the disciple-making process!

I want to focus now on the three aspects of our disciple-making definition: the *character, ways, and mission* of Jesus. Reproducing the character of Jesus means developing in His followers *who* God is and what He's really like. The ways of Jesus is about imparting to them *how* He goes about living and leading in life. The mission of Jesus expresses His heart for others through *what* He does. Reproducing the *who, how*, and *what* of Jesus in His followers!

The Character of Jesus

From the moment we respond to Jesus, the Holy Spirit begins conforming us into His likeness—shaping us to reflect His character (Romans 8:29). From Genesis to Revelation, the character of God is put on display! He continuously reveals Himself to His people through His names, titles, and attributes in Scripture, providing us with remarkable portraits of who He really is. We may not see Him with our eyes, but He is in plain view throughout the Scriptures. His character is so awesome that Revelation 4:8 declares that the angels in heaven are endlessly responding to who He is by declaring, "Holy, Holy, Holy is the Lord God Almighty, who was and is and is to come!"

When Philip asked to see the Father, Jesus replied, "Whoever has seen Me has seen the Father"(John 14:8–9). As we behold the life of Jesus we can see what God is like.

- How does Jesus show His heart to the weary? He's the One who can give them rest, revealing God's heart of love and care.

- How does Jesus act towards the woman caught in adultery? He reveals the Father's heart of mercy, forgiveness, and holiness.

- How does Jesus respond to the people He's around? He says they're "like sheep without a shepherd," unveiling God's character as Shepherd.

- How does Jesus relate to the sick and oppressed? He heals them and sets them free, revealing His character as Deliverer.

- How does Jesus act towards the Pharisees caught in their religiosity? He challenges them, revealing Himself as the Truth.

- How does Jesus restore Peter after his denial? By meeting him on his "turf" on the seashore, where He reveals Himself as Redeemer and Restorer. ?? what scripture

The expressions of His character go on and on: justice, kindness, goodness, faithfulness, grace, truth, and compassion, just to mention a few. His names call out His character as well: Abba Father, Advocate, I AM, Almighty God, Ancient of Days, Alpha & Omega, and Author of Life. These are just a few tied to the first letter of the alphabet! Have you ever read through the Scriptures with this set of lenses? It's a life-changer! Recently I decided to mark with purple pencil every name, title, and attribute of God's character that I ran across in my Bible. Now, when I open my Bible, I love that His character draws me in and invites me to know Him more. Have you ever heard the saying, "You become what you behold?" The more we behold who He really is, the more He transforms us in to His image.

CHAPTER THREE : The Jesus Blueprint

We must pay attention to where Jesus is attempting to align us with His character. We usually see it first when He exposes issues of sin and selfishness within us, perhaps through a relational storm, a difficult situation, or challenging circumstances. As we own our issues and respond in repentance, we find ourselves more aligned to His character. In these times, it is wise to look into what the Scriptures say about the matter before us. It is wise to seek counsel and accountability from godly people around us. It is wise to walk in humility while obeying the truth He's revealing to us. As we do, we'll begin to notice ourselves responding differently and reflecting more of the One who dwells within us!

As we get to know His character we grow to trust His leadership and Lordship in our lives, we see that He always has our highest good in mind and the purposes of His kingdom. As we see Him more, we become habitually yielded to His work within us as He forms us into the image of His Son.

How the world desperately needs to see Jesus! We reveal Jesus to the world as He expresses His character through us. Yet, as His followers, we can be the greatest stumbling blocks to people seeing Him for what He's really like! How so? We are stumbling blocks when they bump into our pride and selfishness—often pushing them away from the Jesus we love. Obviously, we're all works in progress so we're not always going to get it right. However, a response of humility to those who have seen us misrepresent Him can go a long way. We must be intentional about cooperating with what the Holy Spirit is doing in us so that He can more consistently express His character through us.

As disciple-makers, are we modeling this process for those we are discipling? Are we pointing them to the character of God? Do we give them the time they need to converse with us about this character transformation process in their lives?

The Ways of Jesus

At the same time God's character is being formed in our lives, we are also learning to walk in God's ways. The Scriptures tell us in Isaiah,

> "For my thoughts are not your thoughts,   *Amen,*
> neither are your ways my ways, declares the Lord.
> For as the heavens are higher than the earth,
> so are my ways higher than your ways
> and my thoughts than your thoughts."

— ISAIAH 55:8–9

In Psalms David said:

> "Make me to know your ways, O Lord;
> teach me your paths."

— PSALM 25:4

Moses cried out to God to show him His ways (Exodus 33:13–14) and we learn in Psalms that He did exactly that:

> "He made known his ways to Moses,
> His acts to the people of Israel."

— PSALM 103:7

Jesus referred to Himself as,

> "...the way, the truth and the life..."

— JOHN 14:6

CHAPTER THREE : The Jesus Blueprint

A practical way to understand the ways of God is that they are His path on a matter. For example: His path on maintaining a healthy marriage; His path on starting a business or planting a church; His path on how to effectively lead people; His path on developing you for your life's purpose; His path on financial matters, dealing with employees, and raising your children. God's ways are how He goes about things. They are how He expresses His heart, His attitudes, and His actions to you and through you.

Like His character, God's ways are revealed in Scripture. Here are a few examples of the ways of Jesus expressed in the midst of real life:

- As a follower of Jesus, how do you go about making an important decision?

  » *When it came time to choose His disciples, Jesus spent the entire night seeking His Father's will. (Luke 6:12–16)*

  » *The ways of God: Referencing God in prayer before making important decisions. Could you imagine if godly leaders actually waited on the Lord before beginning board meetings, getting a feel first for His agenda?*

- *As a follower of Jesus, how am I to relate to others around me?*

  » *Jesus viewed and treated people with genuine love and great value. Romans 12:10 reinforces that truth when it says, "Love one another with brotherly affection. Outdo one another in showing honor."*

  » *The ways of God: We are to walk with people—all people —on the basis of love and honoring them above ourselves.*

- As a follower of Jesus, what am I to do with vision that I am wondering if God put in my heart?

  » *Often we'll do God's work our way. He puts something in our heart and then we "drive it" or "run with it."*

» *The ways of God: A preventative is found in John 12:24 where it says, "…unless a grain of wheat falls into the earth and dies, it remains alone; but if it dies, it bears much fruit." When you're wondering if God has placed something to do in your heart, dig a hole a bury it. That's right! Let it die! If it truly is initiated by God, He'll make sure it rises and lives, clearly letting you know it is "born of Him."*

- As a follower of Jesus, how do I respond when grace is needed to break through a situation or to rectify a broken relationship?

  » *James 4:6 states that "God opposes the proud but gives grace to the humble."*

  » *The ways of God: Showing humility is a choice we can make. It is the willingness to be known for who we really are. When it is expressed with sincerity of heart, it causes an outpouring of grace to bring the breakthroughs needed and healing in relationships.*

- As a follower of Jesus, what's at the core of godly leadership?

  » *Jesus taught that in the world around us, people try to "lord" things over others, jockeying for positions of importance. That is not God's way.*

  » *The ways of God: The kingdom of God is about serving others. Those who are greatest in the kingdom are those who serve others the most (Matthew 20:25–27). And, serving is not a ladder to leadership—serving is what leadership is all about!*

  1 CORINTH 4

The ways of God are revealed all throughout the Scriptures. They are practical, wise, and they work! As we make disciples we must guide them into following God's ways. Let's determine to make a lifelong journey of discovering God's character and ways in the Scriptures!

75

When we do, we will reap the benefits of spiritual health and maturity and reproduce in others what's been deposited in us.

Due to our upbringing, background, experiences, and sinful choices, we are often "stuck" in our ways, following the course of this world (Ephesians 2:1–3). When we become followers of Jesus, we begin to be renewed by the Holy Spirit from the inside out, as we "put off" the old self and "put on" the new self (Ephesians 4:17–32). Life changes come as we pay attention and respond to what the Spirit of God is doing in us, as He changes old habits and establishes Jesus' ways instead.

We must disciple new Jesus-followers to understand that Jesus doesn't save us and then leave us struggling to do our very best to follow "His rules." Instead, Jesus saves us and the Spirit comes and makes us His residence (1 Corinthians 6:19–20; Ephesians 5:18). In the process, He forms the character and ways of Jesus in us, so they overflow through us to touch the world.

As a disciple, what has this discussion of God's ways provoked in you? Do you model walking in the ways of God for those you're pouring into? Do you help them see God's ways in the Scriptures and guide them towards applying them in their lives?

The Mission of Jesus

As disciple-makers, we team with the Holy Spirit to fashion the character and ways of God in the lives of Jesus-followers. We must also develop within them a heart to participate in His mission. When considering this, we often tend to think immediately of the cross, and we are right to do so. As we look at His life in the Scriptures, however, we see that

THE JESUS BLUEPRINT : PART ONE

there are various aspects to His mission that can be reproduced within His disciples.

From my own observations, I see the mission of Jesus as the four wheels of a vehicle. I consider each of these four mission expressions as connected to the others, and they all have the same aim: to get us to join Jesus in what He's doing so that He is glorified through our lives.

Jesus revealed what God is really like. The life of Jesus reveals what God is *really* like. Jesus said, "Whoever has seen me has seen the Father" (John 14:9) and "I have shown you many good works from the Father" (John 10:32). His life on the Earth put God's character on full display! Jesus "fleshed out" God for us to see and experience Him more personally. As we read through the Gospels we are able to see God afresh through the life of Jesus.

The image of God we carry around in our hearts and minds affects the way we live our daily lives. When His image has been tainted in our minds, whether through negative circumstances with authority figures or traumatic life events, the enemy of our souls—the devil—attempts to use that tarnished image to disfigure and destroy the character of God in our thinking.

Part of Jesus' mission through us is to provide people with a fresh and accurate picture of what He's really like. What He looks like with "skin on." That mission requires that we shape those Jesus brings us in His character and ways. When people see Him for who He really is, they can't help but love Him and give their lives to Him!

Jesus reconciled people to God. Another "wheel" in the mission of Jesus is reconciling people to God. Sin has separated us from Him, and

His death on the cross enables that relationship to be restored. Jesus said, referring to Himself in Luke 19:10, "For the Son of Man came to seek and to save the lost."

Jesus pursued those who were not in right relationship with God. He called Matthew to follow Him, and Matthew responded by leaving the tax collector's booth and inviting Jesus to meet his friends at a dinner thrown at his house (Matthew 9:9–13). Throughout the Gospels Jesus converses with people and meets their real needs. He even extends salvation to the criminal hanging next to Him on the cross. As a matter of fact, He spent so much time with needy people that others labeled Him the "friend of sinners" (Matthew 11:19).

We must disciple with hearts of compassion for people, especially as we interact with those who don't know Him. Jesus has given us the ministry of reconciling people to God (2 Corinthians 5:17–21). By the way we live and relate, we should cause people to be drawn to the One we love who has changed our lives. Do you disciple people to live as an ambassador of Jesus to the world around them?

Jesus demonstrated God's kingdom on Earth. The Lord's prayer (Matthew 6:9–11) includes, "Your kingdom come, your will be done on Earth as it is in heaven." Jesus proclaimed the kingdom of God throughout His entire ministry here on Earth. The Sermon on the Mount in Matthew 5–7 is the centerpiece of Jesus' teaching on the kingdom, while Matthew 13 contains numerous kingdom parables that provides further insights into it.

The kingdom is *the arena where Jesus rules and His will is being done.* The kingdom finds expression wherever He is given Lordship. It advances as He brings good news to the poor, binds up the brokenhearted, sets captives free, and replaces mourning with gladness (Isaiah 61:1–3). It

THE JESUS BLUEPRINT : PART ONE

advances as He destroys the works of the devil (1 John 3:8) so people can live their lives to the full (John 10:10). It's expressed as Jesus goes about doing good (Acts 10:38). His kingdom is an everlasting kingdom that will have no end (Psalms 145:13). And, Jesus teaches us to seek it first (Matthew 6:33)!

Regardless of heritage, nationality, or denomination, as followers of Jesus we are all a part of God's kingdom, and we are to participate in its advancement. All of us have key roles to play within it, using our gifts where He's appointed us to serve. We must always make disciples that reflect the advancing of *His* kingdom and not our own. Are you imparting His kingdom vision in those you're discipling?

Jesus reproduced disciple-makers. Let's remember that Jesus taught the crowds but was dedicated to investing in the Twelve. Imagine what you would do if you knew you had three years to deposit everything you could in a few people who would then launch the greatest movement in the history of the world! You would be very selective with whom you spent your time and deliberate about what you would pass on. Your priorities would be crystal clear and your focus firmly fixed.

Disciple-making is the chosen approach of Jesus to make sure that His kingdom mission advances. Gary W. Kuhne provides a good perspective regarding this: "Christ poured three years of His life into the twelve apostles, near the end of this time (approximately six months), He spent nearly all of His time with them. Thus Christ, the master Disciple, felt it necessary to do this to insure the massive multiplication of the Christian church over the following quarter of a century. If there had been a better way, Christ would have used it. You would not have been impressed if you had been an uninvolved bystander at that period of time. There were not more than five hundred followers at the time of Christ's death

CHAPTER THREE : The Jesus Blueprint

and many of these were only peripherally involved. Yet Christ was satisfied with His work, for He saw in His disciples the future multiplication of the Church."[12]

Are you willing to adjust your life to make the four wheels of His mission a higher priority in you life? Will you set your heart to actively disciple those Jesus brings you to fulfill His mission through their lives, so they can do they same for others?

What We've Covered

We've observed a pattern in Matthew, or key ingredients, in Jesus' disciple-making process. These were also used by His disciples to make disciples in Acts:

- A Commitment to Teaching Truth
- A Context of Community
- A Culture of Obeying Jesus
- A Charge to Reproduce

We also referenced a cultural paradigm and made some observations on what may be important as we make disciple-makers today.

Finally, we defined disciple-making as:

> *Reproducing the character, ways, and mission of Jesus in those God brings around you, expecting them to multiply the same in others.*

As we continue to rediscover the Jesus blueprint, I'd like to invite you to reflect with me on Jesus' relationship with His Father as follower and what that reproduced in the lives of His disciples. By doing so, what you're really reproducing will also be revealed.

Chapter Four

What Are You Reproducing?

Not long ago I found myself contemplating Jesus as *follower* of His Father. Jesus said that He did "nothing on [His] own," and His only concern was "the will of Him who sent me" (John 5:30). In reality, Jesus was responding to and following the lead of His Father throughout His life (John 5:19). As followers of Jesus, we look to Him as our central reference point. What if we sought to discover insights from Jesus as a follower while He walked here on Earth? Might that give us some glimpses of what was at the core of His life—and what He asked His followers to imitate and reproduce in others?

I decided exploring this was absolutely worth the pursuit—if for nobody else but me. I've come away with some observations that have begun to serve as my "reproducing reference points": *the priority, focus, means, message, and aim of Jesus.* Attempting to live with these in my own life, I've realized that they serve as two-way reference points for me. First, they align my own life to Jesus and His heart. Second, they shed light on what I'm actually reproducing in those around me.

Can I encourage you to approach this particular chapter with a more contemplative heart? To aid you in doing so, I've placed some life application reflection points at the end of each of the five observations I've made from the life of Jesus.

The Priority of Jesus:
Cultivating Relationship With the Father
OUR priorities should be the same but with Jesus

Imagine the bewildered looks on the faces of Joseph and Mary when they finally track down the "missing Son of God"—their twelve-year-old son—and He [Jesus] says in Luke 2:49, "Did you not know that I must be in my Father's house?" Throughout the Gospels we observe the unique relationship between Jesus and His Father—but in no other book more than John. I remember in my early twenties noticing that relationship and highlighting in blue pencil every mention of it in my pocket New Testament. There are 121 places I marked, which reveal the richness of this relationship. Here are a dozen samplings from John:

- Jesus carried a real concern for His Father's house (John 2:15–17).

- Jesus was loved by His Father (John 3:35).

- Jesus knew what kind of worshippers His Father was looking for (John 4:23).

- Jesus worked with His Father (John 5:17–19).

- Jesus and His Father are one (John 10:30–39).

- Jesus fulfilled His Father's purposes (John 12:27–28).

- Jesus intends to prepare a place in His Father's house for His followers so they can be with Him (John 14:1–3).

- Jesus is the only way to His Father (John 14:6).

- Seeing Jesus is seeing His Father (John 14:9).

- Jesus loves His Father (John 14:31).

- Jesus kept His Father's commands and abides in His love (John 15:10).

- Jesus brought glory to His Father (John 17:1–6).

Returning to our "missing Son of God" story for a moment, have you ever wondered at what moment Jesus realized that He was the Son of God, the Savior of the World? Although the Scriptures don't make this moment plain for us, I've wondered if this story of the twelve-year-old in the Temple may have something to do with it. How I would love to have heard the conversation between Jesus and His parents on the way from Jerusalem to Nazareth! Does Mary share with Jesus about the angelic visitation she experienced and the response of the babe in Elizabeth's womb when she walked into Elizabeth's house? Did Joseph tell Him how the name "Jesus" came to him and about the visit of the shepherds and the wise men? I wonder whether they shared about what Simeon and Anna said in the Temple and what they had been pondering in their hearts. What we do know is that from this time forward, "Jesus increased in wisdom and stature and in favor with God and man" (Luke 2:52). We are reminded here that Jesus learned and grew—just like you and I!

Study this ✱

The Scriptures teach that Jesus "learned obedience" (Hebrews 5:7–8), which would have included cultivating a relationship with His Father, just as we must learn to do! It's apparent that Jesus spent a lot of time in the Scriptures with His Father because He quotes them so often. Jesus continually sought His Father's will in prayer for the daily decisions that needed to be made. Throughout the Gospels we see Jesus relating to and acknowledging His Father in all that He said and did.

Jesus demonstrated what obedience looked like to His disciples, and as we see in the Book of Acts, they caught it! We see them continue to grow in relationship with God as they reference the Scripture—sorting things out in the upper room (Acts 1:15–17); presenting Jesus to others (Acts 8:31–35); and learning daily from them (Acts 17:11). We see them seeking His face in prayer to know His will and ways, literally from the first of Acts (Acts 1:13–15) to the last chapter (Acts 28:8). They prayed for guidance (Acts 1:24); prayed together on a regular basis (Acts 2:42); prayed in the midst of persecution (Acts 4:23–31); prayed to see God's miraculous intervention (Acts 9:40); and prayed to set others apart to what God called them to do (Acts 6:6; 13:3). Like Jesus, they also walked in obedience by following the leading of the Holy Spirit (i.e., Philip in Acts 8:26–27 and Peter in Acts 10:19–23).

I want to clarify here what I mean by "relationship." I realize for some in the Body of Christ, "our position in Christ" (our right standing before God because of the blood of Jesus) and the phrase "relationship with Jesus" are synonymous. Yet, I see them as distinct, although the first certainly lays the foundation for the second. In this context I literally mean relationship, as in connecting, friendship, and sharing life. Jesus calls us friends (John 15:15). As one dear friend said to me, "Just because I am married (my position/standing) doesn't necessarily mean my relationship with my spouse is being cultivated, is healthy and thriving." As a follower of Jesus your position in Christ is secure, but is your day-to-day relationship with Him being cultivated? Is it healthy and thriving?

Absolutely central to the life of Jesus is cultivating relationship with His Father. He made time to be alone with Him. I'm reminded here of Henry Blackaby's words of having regular "unhurried time with God."[1] Jesus listened for His Father's voice and obeyed what He asked Him to do out of a love relationship.

THE JESUS BLUEPRINT : PART ONE

- How are you currently cultivating your relationship with God? Is it honestly central to your life? If not, why not? What hinders you from going deeper in relationship with Him?

- How would you describe your current relationship with Jesus:
  - » *warm/real?*
  - » *hungry/pursuing?*
  - » *formal/distant?*
  - » *master/slave?*
  - » *mechanical?*
  - » *academic?*

- Are your times in the Scriptures deliberate and life giving? Do you actively look to obey and apply what the Lord shows you?

- Do you spend much time ministering to the Lord in thanksgiving, praise, and worship on your own?

- Do you regularly participate in times of quietly waiting on the Lord in prayer, listening for anything He wants to drop into your heart?

- What practical steps can you take today to revive your relationship with God? Whose input, counsel, and prayer might you need to pursue?

- Consider those you influence and disciple. Are you modeling for them what pursuing a relationship with Jesus looks like?

The Focus of Jesus:
Doing What the Father Is Doing

I have witnessed many people attempting to do God's will "in Jesus' name." Some believe if they just do whatever is in their hearts and attach

God's name to it that He will bless it. Others brainstorm and vote on the best idea and then pray for God's hand to be upon them as they "do His will." And still others wait on the Lord for His will, yet never engage in anything He asks them to do. How did Jesus go about doing His Father's will?

In John 5:19, "Jesus said to them, 'Truly, truly, I say to you, the Son can do nothing of his own accord, but only what he sees the Father doing. For whatever the Father does, that the Son does likewise," *Jesus only did what He saw the Father doing.* He operated under this premise throughout His life and ministry as an overflow of His relationship with the Father. Jesus acknowledged the Father in everything He did—seeking first His will and ways. He learned to discern what the Father was doing and aligned His life fully to it.

When it came time to choose the Twelve, Jesus sought what the Father was doing by spending an entire night in prayer (Luke 6:12–16). Those He chose would not only be His followers while on Earth, but the foundation of the newly launched church! Because He wanted to know who the Father would choose, He spent a night seeking His face. As we've seen already, His disciple-making fruit is evidenced in the Book of Acts.

Jesus understood what the Father was doing as He came towards the end of His three-year ministry. He knew it was time to fulfill why He had ultimately come—reconciling people to His Father through the cross. Jesus knew that He must head to Jerusalem where He would be crucified and raised on the third day (Mark 9:31). The Scriptures tell us that when "the days drew near for him to be taken up, He set His face to go to Jerusalem" (Luke 9:51). Not only did Jesus know what the Father was doing, He also cooperated fully with the Father, in spite of the realities of what He would face and how He as "fully human" would respond to it (Luke 22:39–46).

THE JESUS BLUEPRINT : PART ONE

Have you ever considered the great faith employed by Jesus at this time in His life? He completely yielded to what His Father was doing, which meant that He fully entrusted Himself into His Father's hands and to His will while He was:

- arrested, falsely accused, and severely beaten
- abandoned by those closest to Him on earth
- nailed to a cross as the promised Savior for mankind
- placed lifeless in a tomb awaiting a resurrection

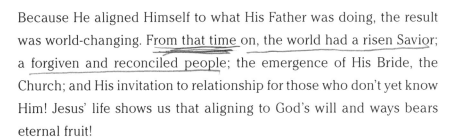

In John 5:19...Jesus only did what He saw the Father doing. When it came time to choose the Twelve, Jesus sought what the Father was doing by spending an entire night in prayer (Luke 6:12–16). Those He chose would not only be His followers while on earth, but the foundation of the newly launched church!

Because He aligned Himself to what His Father was doing, the result was world-changing. From that time on, the world had a risen Savior; a forgiven and reconciled people; the emergence of His Bride, the Church; and His invitation to relationship for those who don't yet know Him! Jesus' life shows us that aligning to God's will and ways bears eternal fruit!

 *What God initiates He perpetuates—what I initiate I have to sustain.* I often draw upon these words as a reminder of aligning myself to God's will and ways. When it's God's idea, when He initiates something and

His purposes are in play, it's like a sailboat coming in line with a strong directional wind. The sailboat then moves almost effortlessly with grace, power, and purpose. On the other hand, when I am initiating something, I'm the one who has to generate all the energy and produce all the outcomes, relying on my own drive and effort. And, it's up to me to sustain it. One is empowering and fruitful, the other exhausting and fruitless. See the difference?

We can see a scriptural foundation for this truth in Genesis 1 and 2, where we observe God's initiation in creation. In the first chapter we meet the repeated phrase, "And God said," where He is speaking or calling things into being that had not been there moments before. In the second chapter, God forms man from the dust of the ground and breathes His very "breath of life" into him, moving him from dust to life!

When we wonder if something is God's will or not, we must train ourselves to ask the question, Is the "breath of God" on it? Is this idea God-generated and am I following His agenda, participating with Him in accomplishing His will? Or is it self-generated, promoting my own agenda? I'll be the first to say that it is not always easy to discern whether a thing is "of God" right away, but if we cultivate a relationship with Him and follow His cues—trusting and obeying like the disciples in Scripture—we'll find ourselves participating in His purposes beyond our wildest imaginations!

Coming in line with this truth of "doing what the Father is doing" requires us to stop initiating and start cooperating! Remember, we are always *followers* of Jesus, meaning we *follow His lead.* He is the Lord, and we are His servants. We see in the Scriptures God initiating and His people obeying, which is accompanied by His blessing. On the other hand, I've yet to find a place in the Scriptures where we initiate "doing things for God" and He pours out His Spirit on it. God doesn't bless acts of the flesh, no matter how good our motives are! We've got to realize that "life" only comes when He initiates and we obey. We cannot accomplish His purposes on our own. We must walk closely to Jesus so we can see what He's doing and respond to Him as *followers!*

Reflection Points

- Consider familiar stories in the Scriptures, and reflect on who is actually doing the initiating. Who initiated building the ark, walking around the wall of Jericho, or Paul going to Macedonia?

- In what areas of your life have you initiated instead of allowing Jesus to? Consider the energy put out and the cost to sustain it in:
  - » *Your personal life*
  - » *Your family life*
  - » *Your friendships*
  - » *Your calling/vocation*

- Think about a time where you sensed God initiated something in your life. Did you follow His lead all they way through? Why or why not?

- If you've initiated something that is now not going well, repent and surrender it to Jesus by asking Him what steps He would like you to take to get realigned to Him. Don't be surprised if He asks you to lay it all down. Also, don't be surprised if He creates a redemptive plan once you place it under His Lordship.

- As a result of this discussion, are you wondering whether you really know how to hear from God and follow His lead? If so, meditate on the Scriptures which show how He led and guided His people. How do these things apply to you?

- (Who) do you know that might be able to help you grow in this area?

- In light of those God has given you to influence and disciple, are you modeling "doing what the Father is doing" in your life? Or are you reproducing people that only rely on what they can initiate and sustain?

The Means of Jesus: *The Ways of God*

The Scriptures reveal that there is a difference between God's thoughts and man's thoughts and a distinction between His ways and ours. Isaiah 55:8–9 states, "For my thoughts are not your thoughts, neither are your ways my ways, declares the LORD. For as the heavens are higher than the Earth, so are my ways higher than your ways and my thoughts than your thoughts."

This truth is greatly evident in the story of Jesus' birth. If He is God, why in the world was He born in an obscure cave in the little town of Bethlehem and laid in a manger stained with the saliva of animals? Not only that, but why was He was born to commoners, given a very common name of the times (Yehoshua, or Joshua), and most likely pointed out by his peers as the one whose mom became pregnant before she was married? Not exactly the way you or I might script the coming of the Son of God to the planet! Yet He came in a way that would allow us to identify with Him as Immanuel, "God with us."

Sometimes Jesus did things that cause us to go "huh?" The story of Lazarus recorded in John 11 is one example. Why didn't Jesus rush to the aid of His dear friend when He learned that Lazarus was ill? Our typical response when informed of such news would be both swift and deliberate—swift to get to our friend's side at their home or the hospital, and deliberate to arrive with a card, food, or gift in hand. Not Jesus. He waited around until Lazarus died, and then He went! What's with that?

As much as Jesus was always deeply moved by people's needs, *ultimately He was obedient to God!* If we tie together this truth with what we learned from our last one, we understand that Jesus went to Lazarus when He did because that's when the Father led Him to go. Jesus was not being super-spiritual here, or out of touch with reality, but he was walking in the "ways of God." And after looking at the end of this story and the fruit in the lives of its key players, Mary, Martha and Lazarus, who could argue with His actions?

What are the ways of God revealed here? *We are not to be driven by needs, but rather we are to be led in obedience.* In reality, if each one of us were obedient to what Jesus asked us to do, every need would be met! Because He is the wisest, He knows what each one of us should do and why, as well as when and how it should be done. In the end, this gives Him the most glory!

Another "huh?" moment, also recorded in John, was when Jesus began to wash the feet of His disciples. It was common in the culture for hospitable hosts to greet their guests—who all wore sandals—by offering water for them to wash their own feet, or by offering to have their servants do it. Yet, in our story, Jesus, the Master, does it. Jesus' actions were nearly incomprehensible to Peter, who first refused before allowing Jesus to wash his feet. What's the deal here?

Jesus used this act to teach His disciples about the role of leaders in His Kingdom. He said, "Do you understand what I have done to you? You call me Teacher and Lord, and you are right, for so I am. If I then, your Lord and Teacher, have washed your feet, you also ought to wash one another's feet. For I have given you an example, that you also should do

CHAPTER FOUR : What Are You Reproducing?

just as I have done to you" (John 13:12–15). Our viewpoint as leaders can tend to be, "You're on my team to serve me." In His Kingdom, the ways of God are for leaders to serve those who follow them. Imagine the transformation that could occur in the lives of people, organizations, and domains of society if we modeled and multiplied this attitude!

As we've already defined it, God's ways represent *His path on a matter.* His ways are depicted throughout the Scriptures and are there for our discovery and application. God's ways were desired by Moses (Exodus 33:13–14) and by David (Psalm 25:4–5). Psalm 103:7 tells us, "He [God] made known His ways to Moses, His acts to the people of Israel…" and Micah 4:2 states, "Many nations will come and say, Come, let us go up to the mountain of the LORD, to the house of the God of Jacob. He will teach us his ways, so that we may walk in his paths. After allotting the land to the tribes of Israel, Joshua 22:5 says, "But be very careful to keep the commandment and the law that Moses the servant of the Lord gave you: to love the Lord your God, to walk in all his ways, to obey his commands, to hold fast to him and to serve him with all your heart and all your soul."

The ways of God reveal the "hows" of God: how He sees things; how He approaches things; how He acts and responds to things. Again, it's *His path on a matter.*

Here's a few examples to reinforce the ways of God in Scripture:

- God's path to receiving grace is to exercise humility (James 4:6).
- God's path on relating well to one another is to honor (Romans 12:10).
- God's path on living as a godly husband is to lay your life down for your wife (Ephesians 5:25).

- God's path on really living life is to lose it (John 12:24-26).

- God's path to inner freedom is through repentance and forgiveness (1 John 1:9).

- God's path on gaining wisdom is to walk in the Fear of the Lord (Proverbs 9:10).

- God's path on making wise decisions is to wait on God (Lamentations 3:25).

- God's path to reconciling relationships is to have an attitude of repentance and restitution as reflected in the Prodigal Son, and forgiveness expressed by the Father (Luke 15:11-32).

A chronic habit among sincere followers of Jesus is doing God's work *our* way. Francis Schaeffer said, "We must do the Lord's work in the Lord's way."[2] We often get the direction from the Lord, but then somehow we take it in our own hands to implement. In other words, we get the "where I am to go and what I am to do" part from God, but then we don't follow through on the "how do you want me to go about doing it?" part. To be clear, God has given us good minds and wonderful experiences to draw upon. However, even those can be flawed! Ask me (or better yet, ask my wife!) how I know.

Our God not only gave Adam a garden to tend, but He also shared with him *how* to go about doing it. He asked Noah to build an ark and cared enough to tell him *how* to construct it! He spoke to Moses to raise a Tabernacle for Him and provided the details of *how* He wanted it erected. The same is true with the Levites and priests when it came to worship; Joshua and the taking of the land; David's building of the Temple; the plan to reconcile man to God; the reproducing of disciples, etc. God's ways are revealed throughout the Scriptures. They show us how to do

Reflection Points

- What other examples from Scripture illustrate the ways of God?

- What comes to mind in your life when you think of the phrase "doing God's work my way"?

- In taking an honest heart evaluation, what percentage of time do you seek the ways of God when implementing what you believe the Lord Jesus wants you to do—both in your personal life and in your calling/vocation?

  - 0–10% — I rarely, if ever, seek God's ways.

  - 10–25% — Only when I'm really, really desperate.

  - 25–50% — When things aren't working, I sometimes do.

  - 50–75% — I'm seeking them more often than not.

  - 75–100% — It has been, or is becoming, my common practice.

- What is something you are currently walking through and how are you looking for the ways of God in the midst of it? Or not?

- What are some of the ways of God that He has taught you that have become norms in your life? What is the Scriptural foundation?

- Along with the Scriptures, who in your life represents your greatest source of learning the ways of God?

- In light of those God has given you to influence and disciple, are you modeling the ways of God for them through your life? Are you actively and deliberately reproducing those ways in them?

The Message of Jesus: *The Kingdom of God*

A read through the Gospels reveals that the core message of Jesus is the kingdom of God. We see kingdom references appear numerous times throughout the entire New Testament, with the most in Matthew. We find a kingdom reference in Jesus' first words following His baptism and testing by Satan: "Repent, for the kingdom of heaven is at hand" (Matthew 4:17). We then find him going "throughout all Galilee, teaching in their synagogues and proclaiming the gospel of the kingdom and healing every disease and every affliction among the people" (Matthew 4:23). Two truths about the kingdom emerge in Matthew 6 that help us grasp its message and its practical application. They are like a pair of lenses—one for each eye. When we look through both of them, we are enabled to view all of life with a "heavenly orientation."

The first lens is in the middle of Jesus' teaching on prayer (Matthew 6:10): "Your kingdom come, your will be done, on Earth as it is in heaven." What does it mean for God's will to be done "on Earth as it is in heaven"? What's going on in heaven? It's where His character is on full display, while He is worshipped and adored by every resident. It is where He rules supremely with absolute benevolence, justice, and wisdom. It is where His voice is heard, His ways delightfully demonstrated, and His will irresistibly exercised. It is the dwelling place of the "Lord God Almighty, who was, and is, and is to come," and of those who've arrived there ahead of us!

The chief cornerstone and sole attraction of the kingdom is the King Himself! Jesus intends to be revealed for who He really is on Earth through us—Earth's residents—just as He is in heaven. He wants His ways and will established on Earth, just as they are in heaven. He desires for people to encounter His Presence, to experience His character, and to worship Him, just as they do in heaven. Jesus demonstrated what the kingdom looks like when it comes in human form, and His intention is for His followers to reflect the same. He calls us to live with a "heavenly orientation" that puts His kingdom on display for all to see. As in heaven, so on Earth!

The second of our pair of lenses is found in Matthew 6:33, where Jesus said, "Seek first the kingdom of God and His righteousness, and all these things will be added to you." Jesus did everything with an eye on the kingdom: living it, teaching it, demonstrating it, building it, advancing it, and multiplying it.

Seeking first the kingdom of God means that we align all that we do through the "heavenly orientation" to God's will, as He desires for it to be expressed on Earth. It means the exact opposite of being locked into in our own little worlds. Instead we allow Jesus to increase our vision by showing us what He is up to in the Earth and then getting in on it. As Dr. Henry Blackaby states in his great resource, *Experiencing God,* "Look where God is working and join Him in it."[3] When we join God where He is working, we are free to cheer one another on sincerely, regardless of denomination or domain, because God's will is being accomplished!

Let's say, for example, that God is doing a great work in your city among young adults who are working together effectively to meet an urgent community need. A kingdom response means you don't fight it, devalue it with your words, or become insecure and threatened by it because it wasn't your idea. Instead, you embrace it and seek how you can serve them. In the end, if it is God's work, then there are "points on the kingdom scoreboard." When you have a kingdom perspective and attitude it doesn't matter what person/group/church puts points on the scoreboard—after all, we're on the same kingdom team!

Some of the greatest hurdles to being "kingdom players" are our own pride, insecurities, and the need to be noticed. Jesus said that to really live, we must first die to self and follow Him! Allowing Jesus to build His kingdom within our own hearts is the first step in overcoming these hurdles.

Jesus began a very special rebuilding project in us from the moment we responded to His amazing grace. He removes the debris of "our empires" and replaces it with His kingdom. His work in us exposes what's really in our hearts so we can repent and forgive, paving the way for Him to establish even more of His rule in our lives. Over time, we are shaped deep within through the work of the Holy Spirit, through obeying the Scriptures, and through our relationships. When yielded, we gradually display more and more of His kingdom in our lives as we demonstrate His character, ways and mission.

We have the opportunity as disciples of Jesus of living with a "heavenly orientation." We are privileged to be "carriers of His kingdom" where He's appointed us to serve. This opportunity and privilege is expressed through the lyrics of a wonderful song penned by my friend and Messenger Fellowship comrade Steve Fry, called *As in Heaven So on Earth*.[4]

> *Imagine a place where a holy race*
> *Delights to please the Father*
> *As in heaven, so on earth*
> *Where everyone lives to spend himself*
> *On the needs of every other*
> *As in heaven, so on earth*
>
> *Consider the day that men will say,*
> *"Please lead us to your Jesus,"*
> *As in heaven, so on earth*

Chorus:
As in heaven, so on earth, show your kingdom through your
church
A light that a world may behold
May we be a body yielded to the head who is Christ Jesus
Until all men see the glory of the Lord

Imagine believers flowing
As one river to their city
As in heaven, so on earth
Binding the strong man, tending the weak
And learning to be His Body
As in heaven, so on earth

Imagine the time when men shall rush
To behold His love through each of us
As in heaven, so on earth

Chorus:
As in heaven, so on earth, show your kingdom through your
church
A light that a world may behold
May we be a body yielded to the head who is Christ Jesus
Until all men see the glory of the Lord

Reflection Points

- What other Scripture portions comes to your mind about the kingdom?

- When considering your personal and family life, how much do you seek the kingdom?

- Are you building your "own empire" or are you building His kingdom where He's placed you?

 What currently hinders you the most from engaging as a true "kingdom player": pride, insecurities, a need to be noticed? Anything else?

- When you think about God building His kingdom within you, where do you see Him currently at work?

- When you look around in your family, vocation, church, and community, where do you see God currently working? How might you join Him in it?

- In light of those God has given you to influence and disciple, are you modeling for them what it looks like to be a "carrier of the kingdom"?

The Aim of Jesus: *His Father Glorified*

9/26/14

The solitary aim of Jesus is to bring glory to His Father. From the angels' songs of praise at His entrance to the world, "Glory to God in the highest" (Luke 2:14), to His acts that caused those present to glorify God (Matthew 15:31), to His conversational prayer found in John 17:4, "I glorified you on earth, having accomplished the work that you gave me to do", everything Jesus does is for His Father's glory. While walking this earth, Jesus carried within Him a deep concern about the reputation for the name that He represented. And He still cares about that today!

To catch the weight of what it means to glorify God, some background might help. In Jesus' time, people's reputations and the authority they carried were directly connected to their names. Their characters, actions, words, people skills, business dealings, and other attributes either significantly enhanced, or severely damaged, their reputations in the eyes of others. A person's name and his reputation were inseparable.

You would think that God's reputation wouldn't be of much concern to Him—after all, He's God! The Scriptures, however, tell us a very different story. They reveal an ever-expanding reach of His reputation throughout the Earth, via His name, as the major storyline from beginning to end! The Scriptures teach us that how His name is handled is of enormous importance to God.

The fourth of the Ten Commandments says, "You shall not take the name of the Lord your God in vain, for the Lord will not hold him guiltless who takes his name in vain" (Exodus 20:7). Somehow this command is often reduced to only mean we should not use God's name as a swear word. There is eternally more meaning to it than that. In Hebrew, vain is the word *shav,* meaning "emptiness, vanity, falsehood." When we make God's name worthless, we misrepresent Him. When we live in a way that distorts who God really is and what He's really like, it results in giving God and His name a bad reputation!

Leviticus 19:12 reads, "You shall not swear by my name falsely, and so profane the name of your God...." In Hebrew, the word for profane is *chalaland,* which means "to defile, pollute, desecrate, to make common, to violate the honor of." Another Hebrew translation of *chalal* is "wounded." It is found in Isaiah 53:5, where it talks about Jesus being "wounded for our transgressions." The people of God need to be careful not to profane or wound God's name and reputation, not only because it maligns and misrepresents Him, but also because it hinders His name from being spread throughout the Earth!

Jesus understood the ramifications of keeping God's name and reputation "on our radar" at all times. He realized that misappropriating God's name would be catastrophic. When people of different ethnicities or faiths have been killed over the centuries "in the name of Jesus," God's image is disfigured and His name profaned. When followers of Jesus say one thing but live the exact opposite, it wounds the reputation of God,

THE JESUS BLUEPRINT : PART ONE

hindering the momentum of the kingdom. When godly leaders who've inspired trust betray the name they carry through how they live and lead, the fallout often results in irreparable damage to God's sheep.

Weighty stuff, huh? When convicted on this front, repentance and crying out to God for His mercy and grace seems like the only right response to me. Following that, there may be some things that need to be made right with those who've been affected by our sin. Restitution must be exercised to begin the process of repair in people's hearts. As we walk this out, a door is opened for God to do His redemptive work of restoring His name and reputation in the hearts and minds of those we've sinned against.

How do we elevate God's name and reputation in our world today? I like Leith Anderson's practical way of expressing it: "Living to the glory of God means living in such a way that we enhance the reputation of God in the eyes of others."[5] Imagine if we approached every word, decision, activity, relationship, and task through the single grid of, "Am I enhancing God's reputation in the eyes of others?" We glorify God when we live our lives so that people see and are drawn to the beauty and wonder of who He really is!

Consider for a moment how different the following areas of your life look when viewed through the kaleidoscope of this understanding of glorifying God:

- *Your walk with God.* Your objective becomes being more like Him so you can more accurately reflect Him.

- *Your value.* He loves you so much that He's died for you and has made you an expression of His glory (John 17:22–26). What could possibly make you more valuable?

- *Your mission.* As an "ambassador of Christ" (2 Corinthians 5:17–21), you carry His name to the people He sends you to (Acts 9:15).

- *Your prayer life.* By praying as the Holy Spirit leads, in the name of Jesus, it allows Him to receive all the glory when prayers are answered (John 16:23–24).

- *Your relationships.* Because God's glory is at stake you are motivated to love, encourage, and serve people well, even lovingly correcting them when needed.

- *Unity.* A shared passion for giving God glory is what will produce unity in His Church (John 17:20–23).

- *Evangelism.* Evangelism is no longer primarily about saving sinners from hell, but about recognizing how much more glory someone will bring to God when living in an obedient relationship with Him.

- *Living life.* Our aim becomes very simple—glorifying Jesus each day in all things (1 Corinthians 10:31).

Has glorifying God so become a part of you that you're reproducing in those you disciple the desire to see "the name of Jesus famed and fol-

Jesus began a very special rebuilding project in us from the moment we responded to His amazing grace. He removes the debris of "our empires" and replaces it with His kingdom. His work in us exposes what's really in our hearts so we can repent and forgive, paving the way for Him to establish even more of His rule in our lives.

THE JESUS BLUEPRINT : PART ONE

lowed"? Have you purposely shaped them to understand that in all they think, say, and do, God's name and reputation is at stake?

Reflection Points

- What other verses from the Scriptures came to your heart and mind as we considered this topic?
- How has this discussion changed your perception of "living for the glory of God"?
- What was going on inside you as we looked at what it means to take the Lord's name in vain and to profane it?
- Did the Holy Spirit convict you as you read this passage? If so, in what way?
- How are you currently glorifying God in your life?
- In what areas of your life do you need to apply this truth more deliberately? Who might you know who can help you do this?
- In light of those God has given you to disciple, are you modeling for them what it looks like to "live for the glory of God," and has it become their primary aim?

In Summary

The Priority of Jesus: *Cultivating Relationship With the Father*

The Focus of Jesus: *Doing What the Father Is Doing*

The Means of Jesus: *The Ways of God*

The Message of Jesus: *The Kingdom of God*

The Aim of Jesus: *His Father Glorified*

If you're like me, the life of Jesus as follower reveals what's really in your heart. These truths continue to shape me and serve as a constant companion as I consider what I'm reproducing in the disciple-makers that Jesus has given me to lead.

So, what are you reproducing?

PART TWO

Windows for Making Disciple-Makers

Chapter Five

Disciple-Making and the Dozen Domains

Imagine for a moment with me the impact it would have on the world if *every follower of Jesus* was deliberately discipled to reflect His *character, ways, and mission* and reproduced the same in others. *Imagine if every follower of Jesus* aligned their lives to the *priority, focus, means, message, and aim* of Jesus. Imagine if that was the norm. How might that change the way we live our lives?

How might that change the way we do church? How might churches look and function if the only ones appointed to any kind of leadership role were first proven disciple-makers?

Imagine how it would change the way a parent parents, a government leader governs, and the way a business leader does business! How might the world be changed if the godly educator, artist/musician, athlete, news anchor, medical professional, techie, farmer, and cause-driven activist reflected and referenced the character, ways, and mission of

Jesus? What if this way of living is what Jesus intended from the moment He said to those first disciples and to us via the Scriptures, "Go, therefore and make disciples…"?

Now, consider the domain of society where Jesus has placed you. What if those leading you were shaped into the character of Jesus and led based on His ways? What if they were to finish tasks better than ever, and with great integrity, because they knew whom they ultimately serve? What if you saw them actually expressing a level of genuine interest and care for the people they work with? And, what if their bottom line was no longer the "almighty buck," but to make sure that customers/members/clients are treated with value and served in ways that meet their needs through whatever you have to offer? Life would be a little different, wouldn't it?

Imagine the ramifications if we determined to deliberately disciple people and leaders in the domains of society based on the character, ways, and mission of Jesus. Disciple-making is the blueprint of Jesus, and He knows the transforming power it holds for people and societies! Should we really be that surprised that the forces of hell work so hard to keep us from making disciple-makers?

A New Vantage Point

In March of 1976, while in my junior year of high school, I made my first trip to Kona, on the Big Island of Hawaii. My dad and a dear friend of his had accepted an invitation to participate in a month-long YWAM leadership seminar. In the midst of their seminar, my mom, brother, and I, along with dad's friend's family, made the trip to the beautiful Aloha State.

While enjoying the hospitality of the Polynesian people, the scenic beaches, the tropical scents, and the tastes of the "local kine grindz," we took in a session or two with dad. Following one of them, I was challenged by one of the leaders to come to the Discipleship Training School (DTS) after I graduated the following year. At that point in time, I was planning to attend the University of Minnesota's School of Journalism, aiming for a career in television broadcasting. How little did I realize that Jesus had another plan for my life on His heart.

Halfway through my senior year, I applied to the U of M and to the DTS in Kona. I was accepted at both! Through prayer, and the counsel of my parents and others, I decided to go where I felt the Lord was leading—back to Kona!

I remember well my last Sunday at North Heights Lutheran Church in September of 1977. Following the service, I knelt at the railing where my parents and Pastor Bob Burmeister laid hands on me and commissioned me for this new adventure. At the time, I believed I was just going to be gone for the five-month DTS and then return to Minnesota to pursue my journalism degree. I didn't really have a heart for the nations, but I recall my parents saying to me at that railing, "Just be open and see where Jesus leads."

As I began my DTS, we were asked to choose groups based around societal spheres. These were small groups focused around the family, the church, government, education, media, arts/entertainment, or business. With where I believed I was headed, I chose the media group.

We met twice a week in our media group to intercede for leaders in that area of society, learn more about it, and prayerfully consider strategies the Lord might share with us to serve people within that field. As an eighteen year-old, I was gaining a new vantage point. It began to shape how I viewed the Jesus blueprint and the world around me. Whether I would became a television broadcaster, missionary, or something else in the years following, I realized I could actively participate in making disciple-makers to live and lead in the ways of God within society.

What I didn't realize at the time was how this thinking around spheres came about. In the summer of 1975, the Cunninghams, YWAM's founders, were taking a little time away in Colorado. While there, the Lord impressed on Loren a new thought he'd never considered before—that nations can be reached through impacting their various spheres of influence.

During this same time, Loren and Darlene received an invitation to visit with Bill and Vonnette Bright, founders of Campus Crusade for Christ, who were also visiting Colorado. As they began comparing what the Lord had been sharing with them, they were amazed to find that Jesus had been putting in their hearts essentially the same list of the seven spheres of influence! As additional confirmation to where the Lord was leading, Darlene heard Dr. Francis Schaffer articulating a similar set of society shapers shortly after the Cunninghams and Brights had met. They knew God was up to something!

Two years later, this understanding of the spheres of influence was making an impact on me as I participated in my DTS in Kona. It provided me with a strategic way to pray for our nation and the world. It allowed me to see the value of each person's unique calling and role within society. I saw how people could be treated honorably and effectively served though each sphere, thus glorifying God. It also offered what would become a lifelong framework for me to view vocations through the lens of disciple-making.

The Dozen Domains

Following my YWAM years, I spent significant time pastoring within the local church. In doing so, I've had the privilege and opportunity of walking alongside people that serve within various vocations for many years. I've heard their heartaches and celebrated their wins. I've realized God's heart is for each one to be discipled and to become reproducible disciple-makers where they've been appointed by Him to serve—whether they are multi-ethnic students in Kona, faithful farmers in Minnesota, imaginative techies in San Jose, or talented artists in Nashville.

In the nearly four decades since Loren and Dr. Bright's divine insight about the spheres, I've noticed several other areas of society flexing their muscles. *Science and technology* has exploded in growth since the mid-seventies and has surged to become a leading influence on society and a growing vocation. *Health, medicine, and wholeness* has expanded as we've continued to learn more about the body, how to treat diseases, foster prevention, maintain wellness, and promote healing in all areas of body, soul, and spirit. With an increase of worldwide catastrophic events affecting land, sea, weather, plants, and animals, the importance of stewarding the Earth has brought *environment, agriculture, and zoology* to the forefront. Some of these same events, local and global, have given rise to many *non-profit and service organizations,* galvanizing volunteers to express God's heart of justice, mercy, and hope in the midst of desperate need.

Along with these four, another focus for many is on serving specific *"peoples"* or people groups, whose lives and communities revolve around shared affinities, geography, and/or a common culture. Let me illustrate this for you.

In the early-to-mid 1990s, I traveled to Russia eleven times. With several of my friends, I had the privilege on one of our trips of meeting and interacting with the Adyghe community near Krasnodar. The Adyghe are a Circassian people that emerged as a nation in the Caucasus in the 10th Century.[1] They warmly welcomed us and embraced the message of Jesus, whom they had only heard about from a showing of *The Jesus Film*.[2] As we spent time getting to know them, we laughed together, participated in their traditional dances (prompting even more laughter!), learned from them, and enjoyed the delicious food they shared with us. They had a distinct culture and well-established identity shaped around such things as similar physical attributes, language, dress, food, shared experiences, well-established traditions, and a communal history.

There are many people groups, based on ethnicity, gender, age, location, or numerous other criteria, who have become the focus of another's service. These "peoples" also need to be discipled in the character, ways, and mission of Jesus.

Building on the foundation and vantage point that I received during my YWAM years, I have found myself re-imagining the spheres in light of where I have been living, leading, and discipling over the last three-plus decades. In doing so, I have observed a "Dozen Domains" of society, all of which represent broad umbrellas of calling and service:

Family
& Social
Services

 Church
& Missions

 Government,
Law & Nation
Security

 Education
& Students

 Electronic,
Print &
Digital Media

 Arts,
Entertainment
& Sports

 Business
& Commerce

 Science &
Technology

 Health,
Medicine &
Wholeness

 Environment,
Agriculture
& Zoology

 Non-Profits
& Service
Organizations

 Peoples
(affinity/
cultural kinship)

Is this list the be-all and end-all list of societal spheres? No, not at all. Whether there are seven spheres, a dozen domains, fifteen fields, or eighteen arenas, the way we break these down is not nearly as important as intentionally identifying various domains and making disciples who will bring Jesus' character and ways to bear within them. These dozen happen to be ones that some of my friends and I in leadership identify with. We rally around them, with the goal of reproducing millions of disciple-makers as catalysts to serve and transform domains locally and globally.

In upcoming chapters, we'll take a little time to explore each of these Dozen Domains in snapshot form. For the moment, however, I want to share with you some aspects regarding these domains of society to provide you with more understanding regarding their value and function.

Defining Domain

The word "domain" is commonly used today within various sectors of society. For example:

- Related to government, it is a specific territory headed by a certain ruler.

- In Earth and Physical Sciences, it may represent a region containing specific types of plants or animals.

- In Law, it is the absolute ownership and right to dispose of land, known as eminent domain.

- In Mathematics, the domain of a function is the set of all possible input values (usually x), which allows the function formula to work.

- If intellectual property rights have expired or been forfeited, the ownership of a particular work is known as Public Domain.

- In the field of Philosophy, it is the range of significance known as the domain of quantification.

- In Electronics and Computer Science, it is a group of computers that have the same suffix—or in the popular vernacular, a domain name.[3]

For our context, a domain is a field of service or function. It's where one's knowledge, skill, expertise, interest, and/or concern is exercised. It's a broad umbrella representing an area of God-given callings and vocations, where things are created, cared for, changed, accomplished, or expressed. It's where we spend much of our time and energy, forty to sixty hours each week, stewarding what Jesus has given us to do.

Each Domain Is Rooted in the Character of God

As I began to consider and pray for leaders and people serving within these Dozen Domains, I've observed certain things about them. These various expressions of calling and service are not just good ideas or nice things to be able to do for a living. Eternally, they have significantly more value than that, as they are actually rooted in God Himself! That's right, these domains are expressions of the character of the God we love, worship, and serve. This understanding provides us with a whole different way of looking at and approaching what it is each of us is called to do.

Let me illustrate here what I mean. Today, I can get off a plane and turn on the device in my hand to receive, instantaneously, every message conceivable, from voicemail to email to text to social media. I am completely baffled as to how all this information is available at my fingertips. But, as I experience it, I am given the tiniest glimpse of the power of God's processing ability. I am reminded that He knows the past, present, and future and is alert to what's going on in the entire physical and spiritual realm at any given time. I am amazed that He is attentive to every single molecule and aware of the location of every person on the planet; conscious of the positioning of the sixty-four moons of Jupiter and knowledgeable of the deepest secrets of every heart—all at the same time! When I look at Jesus as the one behind technology, I stand in wonder and awe, worshipping Him in a way I had not previously considered.

What about Jesus, the Author of creation? The human body contains some 60,000 miles of blood vessels. If laid out in a single row they would wrap around the Earth 2½ times! What about the sun? Did you know that approximately 109 planet Earths would fit on the surface of the sun

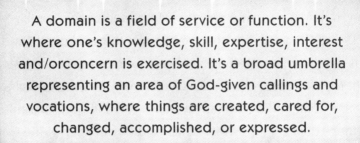

A domain is a field of service or function. It's where one's knowledge, skill, expertise, interest and/orconcern is exercised. It's a broad umbrella representing an area of God-given callings and vocations, where things are created, cared for, changed, accomplished, or expressed.

and more than one million planet Earths inside of it? Mind boggling! He also created the Earth just the right distance from the sun. If it were further away, we'd freeze. If it were closer, we'd all burn up! What about this thing we call water that makes up approximately 70% of our physical beings and around 75% of the Earth's surface? No living thing on the planet can survive without it! What amazing stuff—and what an amazing God!

Early morning sunrises on the beaches of Hawaii reveal the canvas of God. It begins with flashes of first light turning darkness into dawn with the morning clouds momentarily reflecting daybreak colors. Then, the sun begins its slow, majestic rise to reign daily over the vibrant blue Pacific waters. Welcome to the canvas of God the Artist! Think about the many other works that have originated from His heavenly hands—the perfect spots on the back of a ladybug, the flawless form of a rose, the grandeur of the Giant Sequoia, the bright and bold expressions of the sunflower and the uniqueness of each snowflake.

Have you considered God the Master Builder? When Noah was asked to build the ark, God provided him with detailed dimensions. It was to be made of gopher wood, and it was to be 300 cubits long, 50 cubits high and 30 cubits wide. Depending on whether the cubits of measurement were the typical 17.5 inches or the Egyptian royal cubit of 20.5 inches, it means the ark was 437 or 512 feet in length! With these measurements, there would have been over 100,000 square feet of floor space[4]—just what would have been needed for Noah's family and his thousands of paired creatures! The same kind of instruction and detail goes into the building of the Tabernacle and everything contained within it, including the Ark of the Covenant. Builders, your calling is rooted in God Himself!

As we watch governments collapse before our very eyes, I am grateful that we belong to an everlasting kingdom! The King of this kingdom governs with abundant mercy, consistent justice, and benevolence born of His own sacrifice. His subjects are never His slaves but rather His friends. His vision is such that the wealthy want to give generously and the poor are provided with opportunities to grow so both can give their lives in service for others. "God as Governor" is a much needed reference point in an age of "get what I can while I'm at the top."

I think you get my point. The domains aren't just places where we work and get paid. They are meant to reflect and display various aspects of God's character through our lives as we do what we do. It's a very practical way for each of us to bring glory to God!

Each Domain Has Its Own Strands of DNA

I've also noticed that each domain seems to have its own distinct "strands of DNA," which reveal unique components of the character of God and His ways. I've identified five strands common to the domains. Defining these for each domain helps determine their unique value and function, and results in improved goods or services produced, which betters the lives of others. These strands are part of the thumbprint of God. Not only is He glorified through them, but people can also be honored (treated with value) and well served (real needs met) through them.

First, each domain contains a *God-given capacity* that can be used to serve others. Of course, abilities, skills, and gifts overlap the domains. Yet, each domain has a certain contribution through which it can specifically serve others.

Second, each domain develops and/or makes available *distinct products and/or specific services* to meet the needs of others. Each domain shares with its community or the rest of the world their work for the betterment of society.

Third, each domain has a *unique sphere of influence* that it shapes and leads. With some domains, the influence is broad and expansive. With others, it may be narrow and focused.

Fourth, each domain contains *relationships that we can team together with and enjoy.* The like-heartedness that comes from working together allows for lifelong friendships to be built. It also allows people to get to know each other so well that they intuitively join together to accomplish tasks.

Fifth, and finally, each domain has a *specialized mission(s) to be accomplished* on behalf of others. The aims of each domain may be different yet each one is used to meet the real needs of people. Like everything else in the kingdom of God, as each one serves the other, every need is met.

Measures of Capacity and Influence

God apportions measures of *capacity* and *influence* to His servants. He gives us a measure of *capacity,* which are God-given abilities, skills, and gifts that He puts in our lives to serve and bless others. He also gives each of us a measure of *influence*, which relates to who and how many the Lord graces us to shape, oversee, impact, and help.

God is the source of both capacity and influence, and according to the Scriptures, He is the author of how they flow through our lives. As He combines our measures of capacity and influence with our various heritages, upbringings, personalities, and experiences, He makes us into effective servants in our domain(s).

Let me quickly illustrate from Scripture this concept of *measures of capacity and influence,* so that you can get a little better handle on what I mean.

- Abraham had a God-given capacity for stewarding property and wealth, and God continued to add both to him. His measure of influence: be a blessing to all families of the earth (Genesis 12:1–3).
- Moses had the capacity to be a deliverer and Joshua had a capacity to conquer. The primary measure of influence for both was the children of Israel (although Moses also significantly influenced Egypt, and Joshua the people he drove out of the land).
- David had been given the capacity by God to be king. His first measure of influence was over his sheep in preparation for leading people.
- Jonah had a capacity to bring the Word of the Lord. His place of influence was the people of Nineveh.

- Mary had the capacity by the Holy Spirit to be the mother of the Son of God. Her measure of influence was Jesus and her other children.

- Paul had an apostolic capacity and his measure of influence was Gentiles, kings, and the children of Israel (Acts 9:15).

Note that each one had a specific measure of capacity—abilities, skills, and gifts given by God. Each also had a measure of influence, decided by God. Once you understand the measures of capacity and influence assigned to you, it helps you work within the context of what Jesus wants to do through you. It also keeps you from drifting outside the areas where God has graced you to serve.

Joshua didn't go looking for another people in bondage to deliver, like Moses. Rather, he functioned within his God-ordained capacities and influence and helped Israel secure the Promised Land. Paul, tired from his many mission trips, didn't just decide to stay in Ephesus and pastor. Instead, he fulfilled his apostolic capacity and influence by furthering the message of Jesus among those who had not yet heard it. The New Testament letters that he wrote, Romans through Philemon, continue to influence generations of Jesus followers. That, too, is part of Paul's extended God-given capacity and influence!

There is a Greek word that appears thirteen times in eleven verses in the New Testament that can be a help to us here. It's the word *metron*. Among other places, it shows up in Romans 12 and Ephesians 4, where Paul is addressing the gifts and callings of Jesus followers. It means "a measuring rod" and is the root of such common words today as meter and speedometer. It speaks of a "determined extent, allotted measure, specific portion, limited degree."

In Romans 12:3 we find *metron* translated as "measure." The word is located right after the exhortation to be "transformed by the renewal of your mind" and right before the listing of various spiritual gifts. It says, "...by the grace given to me I say to everyone among you not to think of himself more highly than he ought to think, but to think with sober judgment, each according to the *measure* of faith that God has assigned." The word "assigned" in this verse is *merizo* in Greek and means "to apportion, divide, impart, bestow, distribute a thing among a people."

The following verse in Romans 12:4 states that although we are one body, "the members do not all have the same function." Verse 6 goes on to state, "Having gifts that differ according to the grace given us, let us use them."

What is Paul saying in these passages? God is the one who "assigns, bestows and distributes" various "specific portions and alloted measures." Our gifts differ according to God's choosing and grace, and how we function within our gifts varies based on God's design.

Each of us has been given various measures related to both capacity and influence. For example, I have two pastor friends, each functioning well in their gifts. One is a gifted teacher and the other is an effective organizational leader—these represent their measures of capacity. God has assigned one to serve a large flock and the other a smaller congregation with far-reaching missions influence—these represent their measures of influence. Both are God-given.

I see these measures expressed within my family and friendships. My son is currently a middle school teacher while a friend is a college professor. My daughter works in the domain of health with skin care, while my daughter-in-law works at a hospital in trauma care. My wife uses coffee to beautifully paint her water colors, while friends of hers excel at more traditional forms of art. Each one has a unique God-given capacity and sphere of influence that is incomparable and invaluable to others. Peter, one of the original Twelve who followed Jesus, passed this on to those he was discipling: "As each has received a gift, use it to serve one another, as good stewards of God's varied grace...in order that in everything God may be glorified through Jesus Christ." (1 Peter 4:10-11).

What's important is that we steward well what we've been given right where we are at, allowing God to determine the fruit, whether it be 30, 60 or 100-fold its original size (Matthew 13:1–23). The parable of the talents in Matthew 25:14–30 also reminds us that if we are faithful with what He's given us, He'll give us more! Ultimately we are judged on faithfully stewarding what God has assigned to us in both capacity and influence.

By the way, in case you tend to get caught up with a "bigger is always better" mentality, the life of Jesus reminds us that much can be done with few. His deliberate discipling of twelve men rocked the first century and continues to impact the nations of the Earth today, centuries later. Now, that's serious impact!

A Word of Caution: What God-Given Measures Are Not

From God's perspective in Scripture, measures of capacity and influence are always given for the building up of those around us (2 Corinthians 10:8). They are never to reflect the attitude of "I'm in charge, so do what I say. Honor me, serve me." Nor do they communicate a "We're the head, not the tail" mentality. In Matthew 20:20–28, Jesus takes the opportunity to address issues of power and control after the mother of the sons of Zebeddee vies for position for her two boys (James and John). He says, "You know that the rulers of the Gentiles lord it over them, and their great ones exercise authority over them. *It shall not be so among you.* But whoever would be great among you must be your servant, and whoever would be first among you must be your slave, even as the Son of Man came not to be served but to serve, and to give his life as a ransom for many."

Since the very beginning in the Garden of Eden, grasping and posturing for power and control has played a major role in human history. It is rampant today, and Jesus-followers can be caught in the middle of it as well! This desire for power and control exists within the sin-ridden heart of every man and woman. It is nurtured by a deep need to have things

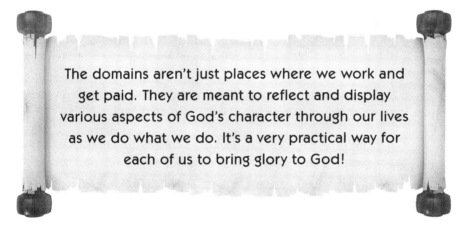

The domains aren't just places where we work and get paid. They are meant to reflect and display various aspects of God's character through our lives as we do what we do. It's a very practical way for each of us to bring glory to God!

"our way" and to be "one up" on others. But, Jesus told His followers, *"It shall not be so among you."* Regardless of our measures of capacity and influence, following Jesus means serving, giving, and laying down our lives for those around us, just as He did.

I've encountered countless stories of pain and disappointment from wonderful people who have been trumped, beaten down, and run over by leaders who may be sincere but are very misguided in their understanding of authority. Authority is never to be used to assert one's position or push one's agenda. It is for furthering God's kingdom and functioning in God's ways. Yes, authority is God-given, but always with His purposes and the highest good of others in mind. Over the years, I've seen how insecurity asserts authority. Often, someone who is needy or wants to "be somebody" jumps on the authority train. That person eventually crashes, often derailing his own walk with Jesus and the faith of those around them.

Nowhere does Scripture endorse manipulation, control, or power grabs. As a matter of fact, Scripture tells us that when Lucifer attempted a power grab God tossed him out of heaven (Isaiah 14:12–17; Luke 10:18). God certainly wasn't threatened; it just doesn't reflect His character and ways. God endorses and blesses humility, serving and honoring others, and fearing and obeying Him above all else—never control! To get a reality check of how God sees those who use authority to benefit themselves, consider Ezekiel:

> The word of the Lord came to me: "Son of man, prophesy against the shepherds of Israel; prophesy, and say to them, even to the shepherds, Thus says the Lord God: Ah, shepherds of Israel who have been feeding yourselves! Should not shepherds feed the sheep? You eat the fat, you clothe yourselves with the wool, you slaughter the fat ones, but you do not feed the sheep. The weak you have not strengthened, the sick you have not healed, the injured you have not bound up, the strayed you have not brought back, the lost you have not sought, and with force and harshness you have ruled them. So they were scattered, because there was no shepherd, and they became food for all the wild beasts. My sheep were scattered; they wandered over all

the mountains and on every high hill. My sheep were scat-
tered over all the face of the earth, with none to search or
seek for them.

"Therefore, you shepherds, hear the word of the Lord: As I
live, declares the Lord God, surely because my sheep have
become a prey, and my sheep have become food for all the
wild beasts, since there was no shepherd, and because my
shepherds have not searched for my sheep, but the shep-
herds have fed themselves, and have not fed my sheep,
therefore, you shepherds, hear the word of the Lord: Thus
says the Lord God, Behold, I am against the shepherds, and
I will require my sheep at their hand and put a stop to
their feeding the sheep. No longer shall the shepherds feed
themselves. I will rescue my sheep from their mouths, that
they may not be food for them."

— EZEKIEL 34:1–10

Trumpeting authority and keeping people around only as long as they are useful to one's purposes are ungodly expressions of a deceived human heart. Moving this sort of deceived leader toward godliness requires their repentance and the beginning a process of sincere restitution towards those who got caught in their web of ungodly leadership. Walking for a season with a gracious and truth-filled leader who can help realign someone to the ways of God is also a step of wisdom in the right direction.

A Look With Luther at Vocations

A long as I can remember, there seems to have been a gulf between those called into ministry full-time and those who work in so-called "secular jobs." Those who chose ministry appeared to be more sacrificial and spiritual, while the others were perceived to be less than holy and "caught up in the things of the world." Does Jesus really see it this way? Does He really intend for this gulf to exist or does He have something greater in mind?

Consider these words from German priest, professor, and reformer Martin Luther: "The idea that the service to God should have only to do with a church altar, singing, reading, sacrifice, and the like is without doubt but the worst trick of the devil. How could the devil have led us more effectively astray than by the narrow conception that service to God takes place only in a church and by the works done therein…The whole world could abound with the services to the Lord…not only in churches but also in the home, kitchen, workshop, field."[5]

As a Jesus-follower, I learned in Scripture that there really is no such thing as "the sacred" and "the secular." Psalm 24:1 reminds us, "The Earth is the Lord's and the fullness thereof, the world and those who dwell therein." John 1:3 affirms the same, "All things were made through Him, and without Him was not any thing made that was made." I really like what Pastor Jack Hayford says about this dynamic in the DVD series, *Fathers of the Faith: Wisdom for Difficult Times:* "The division in the mind of God is not between the sacred arena and a secular arena. But the division is between the light and the dark, and there's a darkened world in the secular and in the sacred. There's darkness across the face of the Earth, and the Lord wants to seed it all with the sons and daughters of light."[6]

Walking as disciples of Jesus means every area of our lives has been yielded to His Lordship, including what we do during a certain forty to sixty hours each week. Many view what they do during those hours as a way to put bread on the table so they can do what they *really* feel called to do. There may be some truth to that, but I think there is a broader way to look at it.

At the root of the English word "vocation" is the Latin word *vocatio* which means "calling." Luther believed that having a vocation is more than simply an occupation; rather, it encompasses the whole life of the follower of Jesus and is not limited to job, career, trade, or profession. He believed vocation was a calling for followers of Jesus to contribute to the world around them by serving others. Luther said, "A cobbler, a smith, a farmer, each has the work and office of his trade, and yet they are all alike consecrated priests and bishops, and every one by means of his own work or office must benefit and serve every other, that in this way many kinds of work may be done for the bodily and spiritual welfare of the community, even as all the members of the body serve one another..."[7]

The term "vocation" had long been used to describe "sacred" ministry and the religious orders. Luther was the first to use "vocation" to refer also to "secular" offices and occupations. Today, the term has become common, another synonym for a profession or job, as in "vocational training." But behind the term is the notion that every legitimate kind of work or social function is a distinct "calling" from God, requiring unique God-given gifts, skills, and talents. Moreover, the Reformation doctrine of vocation teaches that God himself is active in everyday human labor, family responsibilities, and social interactions.[8]

God created each of us to play a unique and meaningful role in society. He intended that we be linked by love, serving one another out of friendship while always benefiting the community at large. As each one serves through his God-given measures of capacity and influence, people are taken care of and real needs are met. William Perkins, the only Puritan author to describe callings in a systematic way, emphasized calling as "a certain kind of life ordained and imposed on man by God for the common good."[9]

One of Luther's examples, enhanced by Gene Edward Veith, helps us better understand the value and integration of our vocations: "We pray in the Lord's Prayer that God give us our daily bread, which He does. He does so, not directly as when he gave manna to the Israelites, but through the work of farmers and bakers—and we might add truck drivers and retailers. In effect, the whole economic system is the means by which God gives us our daily bread. Each part of the economic food chain is a vocation, through which God works to distribute his gifts. Similarly, God heals the sick. While He can and sometimes does do so directly, in the normal course of things He works through doctors, nurses, and other medical experts. God protects us from evil, with the vocation of the police officer. God teaches through teachers, orders society through governments, proclaims the Gospel through pastors. Luther pointed out that God could populate the Earth by creating each new generation of babies from the dust. Instead, He ordained that human beings should come together to bring up children in families. The offices of husband, wife, and parent are vocations through which God works to rear and care for children."[10]

Veith continues, "God is graciously at work, caring for the human race through the work of other human beings. Behind the care we have received from our parents, the education we received from our teachers, the benefits we receive from our spouse, our employers, and our government, stands God himself, bestowing His blessings."

"The picture is of a vast, complex society of human beings with different talents and abilities. Each serves the other; each is served by others. We Americans have an ideal of self-sufficiency and often dream of being able to grow our own food, build our own homes, and live independently of other people. But our proper human condition is dependence. Because of the centrality of love, we are to depend on other human beings and through them, and ultimately, we depend on God. Conversely, other people are to depend on us. In God's earthly kingdom, we are to receive His blessings from other people through their vocations."

"The purpose of one's vocation, whatever that vocation might be, is serving others. Though our justification through faith has nothing to do with good works, vocation does involve good works. And, those works have to do with fulfilling Christ's injunction to love one's neighbor. The Christian's relationship to God is based on sheer grace and forgiveness on God's part; the Christian's relationship to other people, however, is to be based on love. As Gustaf Wingren puts it, 'God does not need our good works, but our neighbor does.'"[11]

In framing vocations, Luther talks about them as the "masks of God," since God is actually the one at work behind what He's appointed us to do: "All our work in the field, in the garden, in the city, in the home, in struggle, in government—to what does it all amount before God except child's play, by means of which God is pleased to give His gifts in the field, at home, and everywhere? These are the masks of our Lord God, behind which He wants to be hidden and to do all things."[12] Luther's thinking leads to his characterization that "God Himself is milking the cows through the vocation of the milkmaid."[13]

Winkie Pratney has taken this idea a step further. In unison with the earlier thought that the Dozen Domains are rooted in the character of God Himself, Winkie has been on a journey through the Scriptures to identify what He calls the "vocations of God."[14] At last count, he had found almost forty vocations backed up with countless Scriptures where God Himself was operating in specific vocational expressions. Not only does Winkie's observations reveal something to us about God, it also divinely validates and endorses our calls and vocations.

Vocation Points to Ponder

For some, I am describing beliefs that fortify what you already understand about calling and vocation. For others, I may be introducing fresh thoughts that will invigorate you as you view life from this point forward. Along with the discussion we've had, I'd like to offer several thoughts for you to prayerfully ponder regarding calling and vocation as disciples and disciple-makers.

Work as Worship

While in YWAM, we would hold several all-hands-on-deck Saturday morning workdays each year. It was a time to deep clean, paint the facilities, and provide concentrated help on yard or maintenance projects.

> Our call and vocation is not ultimately to something but to someone—the Lord Jesus. We adopt His character, ways, and mission, as revealed in the Scriptures, as our sole standard and uncompromising point of reference. As His disciples, we want to do nothing that ever diminishes His character in someone's eyes, taints the goodness of His ways, or misrepresents His mission to a watching world.

During my time in Kona, we often had a guest from Indiana Wesleyan University speak at the base, Dr. Glenn Martin.[15] He was a tremendous teacher who shaped our thinking on living with a biblical worldview. One of the things that he taught us was "work is worship." Shortly thereafter, our Saturday workdays became known as "worship days"!

There are two things I want to highlight here. First, God is the one who initiated work. He works. He created the universe (Genesis 1 and 2) and He continues to advance His kingdom. God's work is an overflow of who He is and what He does. Some view work as a consequence of sin, believing that if it wasn't for Adam and Eve's choices, we'd still be relaxing in a beautiful garden eating fruit to our heart's content! Not so. God assigned Adam to work and tend the garden well before (Genesis 2:5–16) the "snake in the grass—sin in the hand—removal from the garden" scene ever happened.

Second, all of our work is to be done unto the Lord. Regardless of who is watching, we are ultimately working for His pleasure and glory. We should be offering our full effort to whatever we have in front of us to do: "Whatever you do, work heartily, as for the Lord and not for men, knowing that from the Lord you will receive the inheritance as your reward. You are serving the Lord Christ" (Colossians 3:23–24). Every expression of work we do—dishes after dinner, merging two companies, calling plays in the huddle on a football field, designing a new home or website, baking a pie for the widow next door, tending a contusion on a horse's hind quarters—can be done as worship "unto the Lord," and for His glory. "So, whether you eat or drink, or whatever you do, do all to the glory of God" (1 Corinthians 10:31).

Vocation as Ambassadorship

As disciples, we carry Jesus' presence wherever we go. We represent Him while interacting with every person we come in contact with and in everything we do. We are to reveal His character and ways, and we have been commissioned by Him to fulfill His mission!

Not long ago, I had the privilege of addressing ambassadors representing various nations around the world. These men and women were extremely gracious and diplomatic and weighed what they said and did very carefully. You could see that although they were being themselves, they also knew they were not there to represent themselves. Rather, they recognized that their every expression was a reflection and representation of the leader and nation that had sent them.

Every follower of Jesus is, in effect, a missionary.[16] You are His ambassador wherever you go and whomever you're with. It does not matter where He has put you. At all times and in all places, you represent His character, ways, and mission and are to steward what He's given you for the advancement of His kingdom and the flourishing of the people around you. Paul's words to the believers in Colossae underscore this concept: "Whatever you do, in word or deed, do everything in the name of the Lord Jesus" (Colossians 3:17).

Os Guinness writes, "Calling means that our lives are so lived as a summons of Christ that the expression of our personalities and the exercise of our spiritual gifts and natural talents are given direction and power precisely because they are not done for themselves, our families, our businesses or even humankind, but for the Lord, who will hold us accountable for them."[17]

You have been sent by Jesus to represent Him in your particular domain of society. Representing Him is your primary reason for being there! Now, you might not be in your God-given "destiny role" just yet, but He is using this time to shape and add to you, to teach you His

THE JESUS BLUEPRINT : PART TWO

ways, and to touch the lives of those around you. Who knows? Maybe as you're reading this, you are realizing that you are not really where you are supposed to be right now. That's okay. Jesus is always glad to reposition you where He wants you, as you humble yourself, seek Him in prayer, and glean from the godly counsel of those He has brought around you.

Consider Your Conscience

Tent-maker, disciple-maker, and writer of thirteen of our New Testament books, the Apostle Paul said, "So I always take pains to have a clear conscience toward both God and man" (Acts 24:16).

Our call and vocation is not ultimately to *something* but to *someone*— the Lord Jesus. We adopt His character, ways, and mission, as revealed in the Scriptures, as our sole standard and uncompromising point of reference. As His disciples, we want to do nothing that ever diminishes His character in someone's eyes, taints the goodness of His ways, or misrepresents His mission to a watching world. Like Paul, we must "take pains" to make sure we are walking cleanly in our conscience with God and the people around us.

Our conscience functions like an inner truth rudder. It is sharpened by the Word of God and calibrated by the Holy Spirit living within us. When we detach from what the Scriptures teach and become unresponsive to the nudges of the Holy Spirit, we find ourselves drifting into the waters of compromise. It happens subtly, one small turning from the truth at a time. Done often enough, we becomes disoriented and turn towards deception. If we continue this trajectory, we become acclimated to, and even defend, a virtual reality that is far from the course of where we once sailed with a clear conscience before God and man.

Luther's occupation was as a campus pastor, college professor, biblical scholar, and writer. He understood, however, his vocation to be true to the Word of God. When asked to recant his writings to the pope before Emperor Charles V at the Diet of Worms, Luther references the high calling of his vocation in order to defend himself. When asked, "Will you recant?" he simply replies, "I am bound by the Scriptures I have quoted and my conscience is captive to the Word of God. I cannot and will not retract anything, since it is neither safe nor right to go against conscience. I cannot do otherwise, here I stand, may God help me. Amen."[18]

Luther's vocation was regulated by his conscience. Bound by the truth of Scripture, it would not allow him to go against his calling to be faithful to God and his conscience—even if it meant losing his life.

How have you handled your conscience in light of your vocation as a disciple of Jesus? Has your conscience been clouded in the pursuit of status and position, the allure of sin, the buzz of celebrity, the chase of gain, and the sizzle of success? Have you ignored the conviction of God within? If so, you can restore your inner truth rudder by responding in repentance towards God and restitution towards man. Now would be a great time to move toward a clear conscience.

Call Ready

It is interesting to me how many people sincerely look to receive a call from God without referencing who God has already made them to be. You might say, "Moses, Paul, and others in the Scriptures received dramatic calls via a burning bush or an encounter on a road." Yes, very true. But I'm not speaking here of where or how God directs us, but rather that He's already wired us for what He has called us to do. Both

Moses and Paul were "call ready" when they received their directives from God. They had been prepared through life experiences, and in their abilities, skills, and giftings. If you examine their lives more closely, you will see that God's dramatic call on their lives matched what He's already placed within them.

Elizabeth O'Connor says, "We ask to know the will of God without guessing that His will is written into our very beings."[19] I believe finding our call and vocation begins by inspecting more closely what Jesus has already placed within us. What are your God-given natural abilities—things you've been able to do well since you were a child? What are acquired skills that Jesus has added to you sovereignly along the way? What spiritual gifts has the Holy Spirit deposited in you? Why does your mind work the way it does? Why do you lean to certain areas of interest? Why does something speak so deeply to your heart that it moves you to the point of deep emotion and action? Why has God brought certain people alongside you, and what might you have gleaned from them? Where do you see fruit in your life that advances the kingdom and glorifies Jesus?

Let me be clear. I am not talking here about self-actualization. I am simply saying that the God of the universe has intricately and wisely outfitted us to pursue and collaborate with His purposes. I know that how He has wired each of us must be considered through scriptural truths, such as dying to self, humility, relinquishing our rights, and being tested. I know we are called to obey the "who, when, where, and how" of the Lord Jesus! And God's calling happens within the framework of discipleship. As disciples, we serve at His command and for His pleasure.

We must do our very best to be prepared by stewarding well what He has given us. Our obedience to Jesus is often what sparks the marriage of preparation and purpose. Just like Moses and Paul, God may ask for

CHAPTER FIVE : Disciple-Making and the Dozen Domains

your obedience at any given moment. The question is, "Will you be call ready?" Doing the next thing He asks you to do on the journey will ultimately lead you to His destination for you.

I like this quote from Luther: "We should accustom ourselves to think of our position and work as sacred and well-pleasing to God, not on account of the position and work, but on account of the word and faith from which the obedience and the work flow."[20]

A Few Words to Move Us Forward

Although much more could be said here by many smarter than me, we've covered some good ground. I have introduced you to the Dozen Domains and their roots in the character of God. We examined their unique "strands of DNA" as well as measures of capacity and influence. We finished on vocation and some key areas to consider in light of our current roles within society as disciples of Jesus.

Recently, I heard Timothy Cardinal Dolan, the Catholic Archbishop of New York, make a very remarkable comment during a television interview: "Every great movement in American history has been driven by people of religious conviction. If we duct tape the churches…and morally-convinced people in the marketplace, that leads to a huge deficit and void. There are many people who want to fill it up, namely a new religion called secularism."[21]

If we obey Jesus and make reproducing disciple-makers our primary mission, godly people can then serve within the Dozen Domains with the aim of serving the common good and meeting the real needs of people. The result is lives transformed—personally, practically, and professionally—in our communities, cities, and countries for generations to come. It's all part of the Jesus blueprint.

As we venture into the next several chapters, I want to continue to make the connection for you between disciple-making and the Dozen Domains by taking a little look at all dozen, with the help of some of my friends.

Dozen Domain Snapshots 1

How can you impact a nation?
By influencing its domains of society.

How do you influence the domains of society?
By shaping godly leaders who serve within them around the character, ways, and mission of Jesus.

How do you shape godly leaders?
By cultivating disciple-making communities within domains of society where disciple-makers can be made.

Robert E. Coleman reminds us of the process of transforming a world when he says, "One cannot transform a world except as individuals in the world are transformed, and individuals cannot be changed except as they are molded in the hands of the Master."[1] As Jesus transorms individuals, they can then live in humility and service to their neighbors, teaming together within the domains of society to create a ripe environment for the flourishing of such kingdom qualities as beauty, justice, peace, provision, and joy.

Over these next three chapters we'll be looking at succinct snapshots of each one of the Dozen Domains. The aim of these chapters is simple. I want to help you envision disciple-making—and your incarnational role of expressing Jesus in and through it—within the context of your calling/vocation. You'll notice that each domain section contains three components:

- An introduction to the value of each domain and the necessity of making disciple-makers within it.

- In light of the fact that each domain is rooted in the character of God, each one will contain a sampling of some of the names, titles, and attributes of God from the Scriptures that are revealed and can demonstrated in and through that domain.

- Short essays by some friends—godly men and women—who have or are currently serving within that domain, regarding the role, influence, and need of disciple-making within it.

I fully recognize that you may find yourself involved in several of these domains—that's great! I also realize that these domains often overlap with other domains. For example, Agriculture might represent the source of food, while (Culinary) Arts highlights food's presentation. The domains containing Entertainment, Media and Technology often interface. Education & Students influences teenagers, as does the domain of Family and the Church—as well as the three we previously mentioned! You get the picture.

As we jump in, I'd encourage you to pay attention to both the big picture of disciple-making in the context of the Dozen Domains and the specific domain(s) where you are presently serving. As you focus on both, you will grasp both the concept of disciple-making within the domains, as well as its practical outworking in your life.

 ## Family & Social Services

After getting the Earth and the Garden of Eden ready, God's first expression of love was creating a family. Families are foundational to every culture on the planet and are the centerpiece of life. The potential of procreation resides within each family. God ordained it when He said to man and woman, "Be fruitful and multiply and fill the earth…" (Genesis 1:28).

The family unit provides us with meaningful relationships and nurturing as we grow and develop, a place for sharing life through love—and discipling into the character, ways, and mission of Jesus. In bringing Eve to Adam, joining husband and wife, God created the foundation for family life. Children were soon added to the first family which eventually grew into the extended family of aunts and uncles, cousins, nieces and nephews, and grandparents.

God's heart of love and concern for each and every person is expressed in the family. He intends that we experience family as a "safe place," where we feel we belong. God wants to surround each of us with unconditional love amidst the joys and challenges of real life. Within our families, we have a place to honor one another while pursuing truth. The home is a place where husbands and wives tend and serve one another. It's a place where children's lives can be formed around godly character through love, discipline, the joy of learning, and the discovery and development of their abilities and gifts.

In reality, many have not experienced this expression of God's heart in their family life. Their stories are those of rejection, abandonment, condi-

CHAPTER SIX : Dozen Domain Snapshots 1

tional love, and even abuse. In such cases, speaking of God as "Father" conjures up images that make the pursuit of knowing Him rather difficult. Some who've come from these backgrounds have been plucked from their difficult circumstances by God and placed in the embraces of loving families, where they've gained a taste of healthy family life. Others have been brought alongside godly men and women who have been used by Jesus to impart life to them and illustrate God's heart for them. When we become a part of God's family, He "re-parents" us, filling in the parenting gaps in our lives by aligning us to His character and ways through the Scriptures and through the relationships He brings in to our lives.

The Character of God and Family

- God started with a family in the Garden—a husband and wife who together bore children (Genesis 2–4).

- He chose a people to belong to Him who were called by His name (Deuteronomy 28:9–10; 2 Chronicles 7:14).

- He identified Himself with the children of Israel (Exodus 3:10; 1 Kings 6:12–13) in a generational, familial way as "the God of Abraham, Isaac and Jacob" (Exodus 3:5–7; Acts 3:12–13).

- One of His favorite names to be identified with in the Scriptures is Father (Psalm 89:26; Isaiah 9:6; Matthew 6:9–14), also expressed in the more informal term "Abba" (Mark 14:36; Romans 8:15; Galatians 4:6).

- The Church is affectionately known as His Bride (Ephesians 5:25–33; Revelation 19:7, 21:9).

- He is referred to as husband (Isaiah 54:5).

- He refers to us as His sons and daughters (2 Corinthians 6:16–18).

- He is the one who adopts us as His children (Romans 8:15; Galatians 4:5; Ephesians 1:5).

The Building Block of the Family

By Brian D. Molitor

The domain of family is the initial block upon which all the other domains are built. Here's why: God calls each person He creates to become an agent of positive transformation within one or more of the Dozen Domains. Whether called to impact the world of sports, music, business, or government, we all share one thing. We are all part of a family, in one form or another, before we move into any of the other domains. The degree to which each of us is lovingly and thoroughly discipled during our formative years has a direct impact on our ultimate success in our domains.

Obviously, children cannot disciple themselves, so those family members closest to them, ideally a father and a mother, must train them. So, the success of one generation depends not only upon the maturity, insight, and spiritual acumen of the previous one, but also on the elders' ability to transfer and transmit the truths learned from biblical study, sound teachings, and the life lessons that surface each day.

Those whose ultimate calling is to business must learn foundational lessons about work, rewards, consequences, and entrepreneurship early in life, or their rise to the top of any organization will be hindered. Those called to rule over cities or nations in the domain of government will do damage to themselves and countless others should their parents fail to teach them the values of fairness, self-sacrifice, and compassion before entering into the world of public service.

Since values and other positive practices are more "caught than taught", fathers and mothers must be more than just teachers of biblical truth. They must also be role models of those truths and living examples of how a healthy family looks, acts, sounds, serves, prays, and worships. The combination of the close personal connection between parents and children and a systematic process of biblical discipleship provides the greatest assurance that Christ-centered families will continue to be the foundation for great societies well into the future.

Brian Molitor is an international consultant, trainer, and executive coach. He also is an author of books on leadership, fatherhood, and ways to dis-

ciple the next generation. He has been married for thirty years and is the father of four children.

Website: www.briandmolitor.com

Spouse as Chief Disciple-Maker
By Dave & Cheryl Buehring

I won't forget that moment. We were still in our first year of marriage when Cheryl began pouring out her heart to me. I was listening—kind of—while at the same time crafting a brilliant solution for her in my mind. After all, she's the love of my life and I wanted to fix what was concerning her. If she would just finish, I could help her out! When she did, I blurted out my well-conceived answer thinking all would now be well.

It was at that very moment my life and marriage would change—and my disciple-ship towards becoming a godlier husband would enter new terrain. While kindly listening to me, she asked me to stop. The she uttered the life altering words, "Honey, I need you first to understand how I'm feeling—then I can hear what you want to say to me." I was stunned. I realized right then and there, growing up in a home with a brother and no sisters, that I needed a woman in my life to help me out! And although the solution I had concocted in my mind was a complete failure, the Lord gave me the wisdom to ask my wife to disciple me in "listening to understand."

It's important to recognize that along with love, companionship, and becoming teammates in life, Jesus brings to us a spouse that will aid us in His ultimate aim: for us to become more like Him! The friction of different backgrounds, personalities and gifts, the clash of different opinions, the little irritant of "not doing things my way" expose what's really in our hearts: pride, selfishness, fear, insecurities, etc. If in humility we are willing to see these differences as a gift of Jesus to us and respond to Him—instead of reacting to our spouse—He will use these moments to align us to His character and ways, forming us more into His image. This benefits our spouse, our children, and everyone else in our lives. It also glorifies Jesus as He is reflected in a greater way through us.

THE JESUS BLUEPRINT : PART TWO

A greater love, extreme gratefulness, and sharing deeper life together is awaiting those willing to receive their spouse as Jesus' "chief disciple-maker" in their
lives. Embrace them like never before and watch what Jesus will do!

....

**For an additional essay on discipling children within family life
by Paris Goodyear-Brown, visit www.thejesusblueprint.com.**

....

 # Church & Missions

Although every follower of Jesus is a part of His church, there are some
who are called to serve and to lead the church. We see numerous examples of those who lead God's people throughout the Old and New
Testaments. In the Book of Acts, we also see God's kingdom expanded
through the church, as it begins to send missionaries throughout the
world in obedience to Jesus' command to "make disciples of all nations"
(Matthew 28:18–20).

Moses, who was herding sheep when he received the call to lead
God's people, embraced that call (see Exodus 3–14) and led the children of Israel out of Egypt. Moses' call required significant faith and
obedience on many levels. First, Moses needed to come to grips with
going back to Egypt after being gone for 40 years, following his killing
of an Egyptian. Next, he faced the little matter of addressing the Pha-
raoh—who was overseeing Israel's 400 years of bondage in Egypt—to
bring him God's instruction to "let My people go." He also needed
to build some relationships with God's people, enable them to see
God's vision, and follow his lead. Once he actually leaves Egypt—with
millions in tow—he has to deal with tending to them in the desert!
Imagine the mind-boggling administrative and logistical challenges

accompanying that call! Welcome to the wonderful world of leading God's people!

Throughout the Book of Acts and the Epistles, we meet those encountering the thrills and trials of pioneering the church. On one hand, we see them enjoying oneness of heart (Acts 4:32) and on the other, some are being totally self-serving while celebrating the Lord's Supper (1 Corinthians 11:17–22). A complaint arises about certain ones being neglected, so new leadership is established and the kingdom advances. The number of disciples multiplies greatly (Acts 6:1–7). The missionary movement is off and running in an amazing way, but now the two "lead dogs" have a sharp disagreement. They each grab a new teammate and head off in different directions (Acts 15:37–40).

As with every other domain, we should engage in church leadership based upon God's leading in our life. It is not for the faint of heart! But, oh, the privilege of walking alongside God's people, whether pioneering new works or bringing the Word of the Lord to correct, equip, develop, or nurture them. How wonderful to prepare them to share Jesus with a lost and dying world! Thousands upon thousands of godly shepherds and leaders the world over have relinquished much to lay down their lives for the sheep. The church marches on today due, in part, to God's shepherds and leaders who've continued—in spite of many odds—to pray, worship, love well, and be faithful to Him and His Word.

While God calls some to lead the church locally, He calls others to take the disciple-making message of Jesus to the nations! God has laid on their hearts a burden to reach certain places or particular groupings of people. He might lead them to undertake a project or establish a beachhead for further outreach. He might call them to declare His message from house to house, display Jesus to people by meeting their practical needs, or stir communities as God moves in demonstrations of power. In the end, "ransomed people for God from every tribe, tongue, people and nation" (Revelation 5:8–10) will stand before the throne of God—and they will have missionaries, who were willing to sacrifice everything to get the Gospel to them, to thank!

The Character of God and Church & Missions

One term used often in Scripture to communicate God's heart for and relationship with His people is Shepherd—watching, tending, feeding, protecting, guiding.

- Jesus is called our Great Shepherd (Hebrews 13:20–21), the Chief Shepherd (1 Peter 5:4) and the Shepherd and Overseer of our souls (1 Peter 2:24–25).
- He is our Great High Priest (Hebrews 4:14–15).
- Our Apostle (Hebrews 3:1–3).
- Redeemer (Job 19:25; Psalm 19:14).
- He's also our Salvation (Exodus 15:1–3; Psalm 18:1–3)
- The Mighty God (Psalm 50:1–3; Isaiah 9:6).
- Our Teacher (John 13:12–14, 20:15–17).
- He is also the Light of the World (John 8:11–13, 9:4–6).
- The Desired of Nations (Habakkuk 2:7 NKJV).
- Immanuel, which means God with us (Matthew 1:22–23).
- The Lord of the Harvest (Luke 10:1–2).
- He is the Head of the Church (Ephesians 1:22–23, 4:15–16, 5:23).

The Command of Jesus: "Make Disciples"

By Henry Blackaby

The final command that Jesus gave His disciples as he returned to the Father was, and remains, crucial to the salvation of the world: "...make disciples of all the nations, baptizing them...and teaching them to observe (practice) all things I've commanded you; and lo, I am with you always, even to the end of the age" (Matthew 28:19–20 NASB). It is important that we recognize in this passage that this word was not merely a suggestion—it was His command! He expressed it to them, not only with great urgency, but with great clarity and simplicity as well. Without question, disciple-making to Jesus is an extremely vital process in God's eternal plan to redeem a lost world back to Himself.

Corporately, every local church is a "living body of Christ" and therefore vital to God's eternal purpose. God purposed that His churches take His good news to the world and make disciples. And it is through disciple-making that God equips believers to be on mission with Him. His desire is always to fashion each and every church according to His specific purposes. So, it is imperative in these critical days that local churches make discipleship a major focus in how they function. And, it should be a major focus among seminaries where the future leaders of our churches are being prepared to serve.

We should also recognize that since Christ promised He is with us always, He remains with us all the time, 24/7. Our lives, our homes, our churches, and our workplaces are all "holy ground" where He can draw people to Himself. Everyone touching our lives should be encountering Christ, too! With Christ living in us, we are accountable to make disciples wherever He leads us out in the marketplace. We can make disciples one-on-one with family members, neighbors, or co-workers. We can lead small group studies in our homes, at work, or on campus. Anywhere, anytime, we should avail ourselves to God for disciple-making.

We have been commanded to "go...and make disciples...and teach them." My prayer is that we will all answer His call, regardless of where He places us each day, and simply obey Him.

Dr. Henry Blackaby has served as a leader within the Baptist church for many years and is broadly known for his work, "Experiencing God," which has now been translated into multiple languages. He currently is discipling several hundred CEOs throughout America in the ways of God.

Website: www.blackaby.net

There is No "Plan B"
By Heather Zempel

Jesus' last command to his disciples was simple and direct: "go make disciples of all nations." He ascended into heaven and left the rest of redemptive history in the hands of a few dozen followers. That was the strategy, the entire game plan: "Go make disciples." There was no Plan B. To this group of unlikely revolutionaries, Jesus handed the keys to the kingdom—relationships. He gave them the plan for the deliberate and strategic passing of the faith from one person to the next. And it worked!

If there is one thing the church must do and do well, it is to make disciples. In our contemporary church culture, we have invested tremendous resources in improving our programming and constructing buildings, and we have devoted tireless energy to debating worship styles and mission strategies. Though valuable, these activities and conversations will not bring change to a generation. Nor are they at the core of our calling. We must make disciples.

I think it's worth noting that Jesus instructed us to "make" disciples and not simply to "find" them. We church leaders often take the easy route and expect disciples to materialize because we have dedicated a budget category and a sermon series to the idea. We insert the word "discipleship" into a mission statement that hangs on the wall and assume that we will crank out disciples as a result. Then we get frustrated when we don't find people transforming into Christ-likeness and growing in their gifts. Somehow, we miss the part of Jesus' command that instructs us to "make" disciples and forget that making disciples is hard work.

CHAPTER SIX : Dozen Domain Snapshots 1

We must return to the story of Jesus with fresh eyes and discover some ancient truths—that discipleship is more about the journey than the destination and more about the process than the product. Discipleship is more about relationship than program. It's more about completing spiritual workouts than completing spiritual workbooks. Making disciples focuses more on engaging in transformational conversations than on enlisting followers of rules and traditions. It requires time and relationship. And now, as then, there is no Plan B.

Heather Zempel is the discipleship pastor at National Community Church in Washington, DC, and the author of "Sacred Roads: Exploring the Historic Paths of Discipleship."

Website: www.heatherzempel.com

A Great Commission Context
By Randy Young

"We must be global Christians with a global vision because our God is a global God." *(John Stott)*

In both the design and strategy of our Lord Jesus, true discipleship is simply incomplete without a Great Commission context and passion. At the end of the day, no follower of Jesus is the "end-user" of his or her discipleship. But without a global life orientation, discipleship practices can subconsciously become religious avenues primarily pursued for greater self-understanding and quality of life. With Jesus, the disciple-making of the original twelve, from calling to commission, was all about others. When He first called them to follow, He promised they would be "fishers of men." And when He was ready to leave them, He charged them to "go into all the world." True discipleship, therefore, cannot be divorced from the Great Commission. It is not just "learn from Me," but it's also "follow Me…" into all the world.

Yet the Great Commission could be characterized as the Great Omission in many discipleship models today. Our challenge is to raise up a generation of global Christians—everyday disciples passionate to leverage time, talent, and treasure to see Jesus glorified among all peoples around the globe. This re-

THE JESUS BLUEPRINT : PART TWO

quires the recovery of two missing jewels of discipleship: worldview and world vision. Worldview is all about seeing life through the lens of Holy Scripture and aligning beliefs and behaviors accordingly. World vision is seeing our lost world as Jesus does, being moved to compassion and action as He was.

To raise up a new generation of global Christians, we must root them not only in the Word and ways of God, but also in His worldview and world vision. As one student said through her tears during her summer missions debrief: "This cross-cultural mission has helped me overcome my greatest obstacle...myself." True disciple-making is all about "others."

Randy Young has served many years as a senior pastor and missions mobilizer. He is the founder and director of The Agora Group, training next generation leaders to impact global cultures.

Website: www.theagoragroup.org

....

For additional disciple-making essays from R.T. Kendall, Bill Hull,
Dave Wells, Eddie Broussard, Jon Davis, Woodie Stevens,
Bill Miller, Grant Edwards, John Tolson, and Larry and Devi Titus
– all spiritual leaders representing various ministries and denominations –
visit www.thejesusblueprint.com.

....

 # Government, Law & Nation Security

According to Romans 13:1–7, God ordains civil government, and its leaders have been given by God "for your good." This passage reminds us that all authority belongs to God. It also helps us understand that God does not choose all rulers, but He delegates and divinely ordains all authority. Since we live in a sin-filled, self-centered world, most people will not be ruled by love—choosing another's highest good—and therefore they must be ruled by law.[2] "The design of civil government is to promote the security and well-being of its citizens and there would be no security of life and property if there were no human governments."[3]

Is society always ruled justly because a delegated-by-God government is in place? We know better than that by experience, don't we? Regardless, we need to live biblically: walking under authority (Romans 13:1–7), not speaking evil (Titus 3:1–2), and praying regularly for our leaders (1 Timothy 2:1–4). Jesus modeled this way by paying His taxes (Matthew 17:24–27) and providing wisdom on how to walk this road: "Therefore render to Caesar the things that are Caesar's, and to God the things that are God's" (Matthew 22:15–22). We owe to "Caesar" what is civil and we owe to God what is moral and righteous. Disciples of Jesus follow what Jesus did and taught—and disciple others to do the same.

Daniel, as a government leader-in-training, committed in his heart that he would not allow himself to be defined by culture, affecting the way he lived his life or the way in which he would lead (Daniel 1:8). He demonstrates for us what it looks like to walk rightly under authority and how to bring about change in a godly manner when needed and necessary (Daniel 1:3-16). Like Daniel, if we're ordered to do things that are in direct disobedience to the Lord in Scripture, then we must "obey God rather than man" (Acts 4:13–21, 5:25-29) and trust ourselves into His benevolent hands.

God has provided us with laws, such as the Ten Commandments, that reflect His character and ways and have everybody's best interest at heart. These laws, of course, apply to civil servants as well. Zacchaeus, a tax collector, repented when he became a Jesus-follower and made a four-fold restitution to all he had cheated (Luke 19:1–9). When civil laws are broken in society, it is the government's responsibility to punish the "wrongdoer" (Romans 13:3–4). It's interesting to note the principles behind the punishment meted out to the wrongdoer in the Old Testament: justice without partiality (Deuteronomy 13:6–10), without pity (Deuteronomy 19:13–21), and without delay (Deuteronomy 25:1–3).

When it comes to national security, police officers, firefighters, and soldiers, they are extensions of those in authority to secure and defend life, property, and the peace. Biblically, those serving in these roles are not to exercise unnecessary force, nor are they to extort those they are defending or conquering for selfish gain (Luke 3:14).

The Character of God and Government, Law & Nation Security

As we consider God's character and this domain, He is described as:

- The King of Kings and the Lord of Lords (Revelation 17:14, 19:16).

- He is the Prince of Peace (Isaiah 9:6).

- Majestic (Psalm 29:3–5, 93:1–3, 96:5–7).

- One who leads with Justice (Psalm 103:6–8; Isaiah 61:8; Revelation 15:1–4).

- He is the Lawgiver (Isaiah 33:21–23; James 4:11–13).

- Our Advocate (1 John 2:1).

- The Righteous Judge (Psalm 58:11, 96:11–13; 2 Corinthians 5:8–10).

- He's the Commander of the Lord's Army (Joshua 5:13–15).

- Our Fortress and Deliverer (2 Samuel 22:1–3; Psalm 18:1–3).

- Our Refuge (Psalm 46:1–3, 61:2–4, 118:7–10).

- Our Stronghold in trouble (Psalm 9:8–10; Jeremiah 16:18–20; Nahum 1:6–8).

- Our Shield (Deuteronomy 33:28–29; 2 Samuel 22:30–32; Psalm 3:2–4).

- Protector (Psalm 68:4–6).

Governing in God's Ways
By Darren Bearson

In a recent Gallup poll, members of Congress are ranked among the least respected professionals in America, with roughly half of people saying that the morals and ethics of these two groups are low or very low. It is no wonder this is the case when we are constantly hearing about elected officials on trial for taking bribes or that they have been caught having affairs. Scandals involving them don't shock us anymore. They have become clichés.

Government leaders who lack morals are not unique to modern times. The Bible is full of the stories of flawed and sinful kings, judges, and prophets. But the Bible is equally clear about the need for godly men and women to serve in politics and government. Proverbs 28:2 states, "When there is moral rot within a nation, its government topples easily. But wise and knowledgeable leaders bring stability"(NLT).

How do we raise up wise and knowledgeable leaders in government? We start by building a culture of discipleship within the domain of government, mentoring within the ranks of governmental leaders and requiring that these leaders live their lives in a way that glorifies God first. Imagine a whole network of politicians and government leaders who fell to their knees before God with every vote or decision they had to make. Imagine if they were willing to make unpopular decisions based on biblical principles, even if it meant electoral consequences.

Daniel was bold in following the principles of God over those of man, and his principled actions resulted in growing influence. He never worried about the consequences of his decisions because he knew they were a result of follow-

THE JESUS BLUEPRINT : PART TWO

ing God's guidance. He was willing to be put into a den of lions, literally, rather than compromise his beliefs!

We must deliberately disciple governmental leaders in God's ways. The result: a restored respect and public trust, and a more stable society.

Darren Bearson has served in government in Washington DC and across the country for many years, including four years in the White House. He also runs his own consulting company, Compass Point Strategies, LLC.

A Nation's Security
By Greg Campbell

In Old Testament times, the military and national security were important aspects of individuals, tribes, and cultures. For example, Joshua defeated the Amalekites (Exodus 17), Moses sent out leaders from each tribe to spy out the land of Canaan (Numbers 13), Gideon freed Israel from the Midianites (Judges 6–8), and David bravely confronted the Philistine champion Goliath (1 Samuel 17). Just as in Old Testament times, we need to have men and women of God involved in military and nation security. It is essential to our protection while we build God's kingdom.

Current literature suggests that the 9/11 attacks ignited a change in policing from a Community Oriented Policing era to a Homeland Security era, with a focus on terrorism and counterterrorism. According to the Defense Manpower Data Center,[4] between October 7, 2001 and July 3, 2010, 44,200 soldiers have been killed or wounded in action during Operation Iraqi Freedom and Operation Enduring Freedom. According to the National Law Enforcement Memorial Fund,[5] one law enforcement officer is killed in the line of duty somewhere in the United States every 53 hours on average and since 1792, nearly 19,000 U.S. law enforcement officers have died in the line of duty.

Men and women employed within the domain of military and nation security are entrusted to protect this country with their physical abilities, but it is even more important that they protect our homeland spiritually. In order to be living examples in an occupational environment that oftentimes prohibits spiritual socialization, prayer is essential! Prayer is the foundational component of strength, courage, perseverance, and protection for those who serve the public through this domain. The primary way of expanding discipleship in this domain will take place through an "each one reach one" concept, which encourages each military and national security disciple to engage in assertive efforts to identify and support at least one other believer within the organizational confines of this domain.

Greg Campbell currently serves as a federal law enforcement executive in Washington DC.

 # Education & Students

To raise up a generation of disciple-makers—children, youth, or adults—godly educators must disciple them. They must teach them to meet the needs of those around them, aid them in developing their full potential, help them cultivate healthy relationships, and encourage them to fulfill God's unique purposes for their lives. As they pass along knowledge and understanding, godly educators shape students using godly character and wisdom that comes from "the Fear of the Lord" (Proverbs 9:10).

A godly education begins in the home. God assigns parents the responsibility of training a child in His ways (Deuteronomy 6:6–8). Parents, then, involve others beyond the home, who foster a child's natural abilities and spiritual gifts, and add academic, physical, and spiritual skill sets. Together, this "team of guides"—drawn from local home schooling networks, private or public schools—leads a child over the years to discovering their God-given calling/vocation.

Educators come in different shapes and sizes, and serve in various capacities and roles. Some focus on pre-school children, and others work with

THE JESUS BLUEPRINT : PART TWO

elementary students or middle-schoolers. There are those who teach high school, junior college, and university or graduate level students. Some are skilled to equip others in assorted trades. Administrators, principals, university professors, and presidents help make the educational process efficient and effective. Each one, doing what he does best, prepares students to engage the world around them. By preparing his students to live in a godly way, a teacher can further God's kingdom.

Beyond the educational process and setting, the other focus of this domain is the students, themselves. Students who embrace their gifts and find where they've been appointed to serve within the Dozen Domains are effective instruments in God's hands. As they learn to love their neighbors—whether across the street or overseas—they can participate in outreach programs, both locally and globally. They learn to aid those younger and those in need through church youth group programs, campus ministries, and missions organizations. As students begin to combine all they have learned—academic knowledge and practical skills, with godly character and a sincere love for people—they change their world!

The Character of God and Education & Students

- According to the English Standard Version (ESV) Bible, the words *teach*, *teaching* and *teacher* are mentioned in 266 verses in Scripture.

- All knowledge and wisdom are rooted in God (Colossians 2:3).

- Jesus was referred to throughout the Gospels as "Teacher" (Matthew 8:19, 22:16). God's role as Teacher is one of the most significant and repeated roles we see throughout Scripture.

- We are to teach our children His ways (Deuteronomy 6:4–9).

- Ezra taught God's people His ways (Ezra 7:10). He recognized that teaching with authority was not just grounded in what he studied, but also in living it out first in his own life.

- We are to teach the next generation (Psalm 78:1–8; 70–72).

- He is the Historian, making sure the events of Scripture were recorded for generations.

- Part of Jesus' disciple-making commission was "teaching them to obey what I commanded you" (Matthew 28:18–20).

Transformational Education

By Bob Sladek

Did you know that students in grades K–12 spend, on average, 1080 hours per year within a school setting? In a child's most impressionable years, that number of hours represents an enormous amount of foundation laying; of worldview shaping. Parents have the God-given responsibility to train up their children, but as an extension of that authority, schools exist to support parents in the training process. When a child is old, he will not generally depart from that early foundation, be it oriented toward God, or away from Him. So, children rely on their authorities, primarily parents and teachers, to teach them about what is right, true, and real. The task of educating the next generation in the ways of God, therefore, remains paramount in an increasingly hostile world.

While some would suggest that education today is values neutral, we know that someone's values are being taught to our children every day. Education is not merely informational in nature, but transformational, in that it shapes the minds and hearts of children and how they view themselves and the world around them. In other words, the teaching process is a discipleship process, and the destinies of young people are always at stake. Is it any wonder that there is a consistent attack on the Judeo-Christian values taught to children in order to cut off future generations from the things of God?

Imagine what would happen if we could capture the hearts of young people for Christ now. The Church's task of discipleship must be as focused upon children as it is upon adults. We must move beyond Sunday school to Monday through Friday schooling, as well.

Knowing how seriously Jesus treated children, we must quicken our efforts to raise the next generation of spiritual champions.

Bob Sladek is head of school at Mariner's Christian School in Costa Mesa, CA. He has served as pastor to children, youth, and young adults in order to impact next generations.

Website: www.mcs-school.org

Discipling Students
By Mark Miller

Based on his extensive research, Dr. Tim Elmore, founder and president of Growing Leaders and an expert on the culture of emerging generations, wrote the following about Generation Y,[6] the generation born after 1990:

- *They are 40% less empathetic than earlier students.*
- *They are twice as likely to not finish high school.*
- *They are less altruistic and more self-absorbed.*
- *They are postponing adulthood—with 26 being the new 18.*

These generational qualities make the task of discipling young people in the ways of God much more difficult. Another obstacle is that the environment is hostile towards educators who desire to pass on timeless principles of Scripture (sacrifice, humility, obedience, discipline). But all is not lost. This generation is also highly relational, very spiritual, desires authenticity, craves mentors, and is extremely pragmatic. When a trusting relationship is established, this generation will dive headfirst into learning.

What works today, and is more necessary than ever, is similar to what worked in biblical times. We need:

- educators who listen and not just talk;
- students who humbly submit themselves to their teachers;
- educators who embody what they are teaching;
- students who embrace transformation, not just information.

The greatest example of this sort of relationship is the relationship Jesus had with his disciples. Jesus provides a beautiful template for the teacher: always in the moment, using metaphors and stories, asking powerful questions, and caring enough to patiently listen to the real need being expressed. In my experience as a discipler of young people, I have found that simply being available, listening well, being transparent, and following Jesus' example offers me a great opportunity to speak into the lives of young people. In turn, they challenge and inspire me!

Mark Miller serves as senior vice president at Andrew Coaching and as a speaker and author, including the book "Experiential Storytelling." He has coached and mentored people from various backgrounds, from students to corporate executives, with the primary goal of helping them live a better story.

Website: www.andrewcoaching.com

Chapter Seven

Dozen Domain Snapshots 2

 ## Media

Today's media shapes values, molds minds, and sways principles of people around the globe. It is powerful and persuasive. Its various vehicles offer tremendous services by affording us vital information, knowledge for decision-making, and awareness of what's happening. At its best, the media enables us to keep our lives well informed and our families safe. It also provides a necessary societal equilibrium, adding "checks and balances" to the potential abuses of power that can happen in government or in any other expression of leadership within the domains of society. When good character, a sincere desire to really help others, and excellence of skill in production and communication are combined within the media, they make an incredible impact.

In today's world, however, sizeable media groups championing particular agendas feed the consumerism of our times and pad pockets for personal or political gain. Too often, "truth telling" is lost in the hours of endless analysis and personal opinions. Sometimes, the media lacks wisdom when being "the first" on a news story, reporting information falsely or incompletely, and compromising the truth. As a result, lives and reputations are left in ruins while the chase for the next story begins.

Disciples of Jesus need to participate in media of all kinds—electronic, print, digital, and social—for the sake His kingdom. They need to disseminate information, communicate truth, and share fascinating stories to encourage others. Men and women who live their lives in great humility and the Fear of the Lord and are willing to counter the pride, self-exaltation and the fear of man that often dominates this domain can be uniquely positioned to use their God-given skills to serve many.

Social media, in particular, will continue to expand and offers abundant opportunities for disciples of Jesus. Even as I am giving you these statistics, I recognize they will be outdated momentarily; however, it makes my social media expansion point, so I'll give them to you anyway!

- Facebook now has over 900 million monthly active users; about 80% of people who own a Facebook page live outside of the USA.[1] If Facebook were a nation, it'd be the third largest in the world!

- Social media has passed pornography for the first time ever as the number one activity online.[2]

- Twitter allows people to get instant updates and send out information to large numbers of people instantly. Through Twitter, people no longer have to go searching for the news because the news now finds them.[3]

- More video is uploaded to YouTube in one month than the 3 major US networks (ABC, CBS, NBC) created in 60 years. In 2011, YouTube had more than 1 trillion views, or almost 140 views for every person on Earth. Sixty hours of video are uploaded every minute, or one hour of video is uploaded to YouTube every second.[4]

What might Jesus have in mind with these tools in our hands? Who will disciple a generation to use them for His purposes?

The Character of God and Media

- Jesus is referred to in the Scriptures as the Word of God (John 1:1; Revelation 19:11–16).

- He is the author of the Scriptures (2 Timothy 3:16–17).

- He is our banner (Exodus 17:14–16; Song of Solomon 2:3–5).

- He's the faithful witness (Revelation 1:4–6, 3:13–15).

- All truth is rooted in Him (John 8:30–32, 14:6).

- Jesus was a storyteller (see His parables in Matthew, Mark, Luke, and John).

- His character and word is fully trustworthy (Psalm 20:6–8; Proverbs 3:5–6).

- He is our source (Hebrews 2:10–12, 5:8–10).

Godly Journalists
By Sonya Crawford Bearson

The power of the written and spoken word is evident everywhere. We are inundated with information—on our computers, our phones, our televisions, our radios, and even through low-tech newspapers and magazines. Despite the increase in our access to information, we seem to be less trusting of the media we consume.

The media always ranks near the bottom in public opinion surveys of whom Americans trust. Political polarization, the proliferation of unconfirmed information, and the democratization of the Internet have only aggravated that mistrust. Journalists are under assault; not only from skeptical consumers, but also from an economic system that values quick profits over substance.

People who choose journalism as a profession consider it a calling. They seek to expose and solve problems, give voice to the voiceless. They are suspicious by nature, having seen the worst in humanity. They believe only what they can see and prove. This suspicion carries over to religion, especially Christianity, which claims there is such a thing as absolute truth and that there is only one way to reconcile with God.

Godly journalists must disciple and mentor other godly journalists because working in this field is like living in Babylon during Daniel's time. Godly journalists are in the minority and have to constantly battle against the dominant worldview, which holds that every opinion has equal weight, everyone must be tolerant, and that truth is relative. They must be salt and light. They must also be wise as serpents and gentle as doves, as they try to report the news fairly, answer colleagues' questions about "crazy Christians" in the news, and live the lives of Christ followers.

Sonya Crawford Bearson is a former correspondent for ABC News and KNBC Los Angeles.

Trustworthy Storytellers
By Tom Buehring

As it turns out, storytime never grows old. Closing the book to finish a child's day opens a lifelong appetite for more. Tales are timeless. And so is our craving to hear one, see one, and live one. Society is starved for packaged episodes with heroes and villains, rising tension, hurdles to jump and rewarded outcomes. Programming, newscasts, online media, and newspapers are filled with them. While fiction is viewed from a convenient distance, participant media (Twitter, blogs, reality TV) closes the margin, now thrusting anyone to become the story. The stage grows crowded. So the race to reach the largest audience relies more on hype than journalism, style than substance.

A story told is only as credible as the storyteller. But a polished image can be misleading. As a profession, broadcast TV is an alluring siren that draws the insecure. Those rare on-air positions can be perceived as a sure thing for recognition, worth, and control. More often than not, it nurtures a short cut for vanity, superficiality, and disillusionment. Disciples of Jesus who walk with integrity can bring a very sharp contrast to the industry. The professionalism demonstrated through character should be striking! Compassion, humility, authenticity, and excellence can embed a journalist favorably with both the viewing community and newsmakers they cover.

And who can best side-step the trappings of a media storyteller? One who walks with the author and finisher of our faith, capable of a principled perspective and mission when assignment coverage turns hideous and despairing! The larger than life residue from sensationalized reporting and media hype needs a poised sentinel whose spiritual self-esteem long surpasses a shallow, glossed identity.

Thousands of years ago, Daniel (12:4 NLT) saw today's eruption of information, prophesying "seal up the book until the end of the time when many will rush here and there and knowledge will increase." As information explodes exponentially, global media coverage will thrive meeting the demand for immediacy. Like the Old Testament prophet and lion den survivor, our 21st century society begs for trustworthy messengers, called and trained as professional storytellers, to steward both their positioning and window of influence with excellence.

Tom Buehring has spent more than two decades as an interviewer, anchor, and reporter in Seattle, Tampa, and Nashville. He also founded and developed an award-winning, accredited training program at the University of North Dakota.

Discipling Digital Natives

By Toni Birdsong

As Christ followers living in a digital era, we've been called to use the tools of our time to communicate the Gospel in relevant ways. Social networks such as Twitter, Facebook, and YouTube now lead as robust channels in the cultural conversation. The growth of social media has single-handedly surpassed the reach of television, publishing, and radio in a fraction of the time.

No doubt, the power and influence of social media in our daily communication tradition is here to stay. The call upon the Christ follower isn't cultural, however, it's biblical. And, it's twofold: to disciple inside the Church and to connect via evangelism outside of the Church.

Inside the Church, Digital Immigrants (those born before the 1970s) are called to disciple the next generation of Digital Natives (those born with iPods in their hands). Digital Natives process and interact with information far differently than their parents and require a modified approach to discipleship. Technology use without relevant biblical discipleship is a sure threat to the future of the Church and a forfeit of kingdom influence here on earth.

Yet, for generations, the Church has prayed for insight, access, and opportunities to engage in conversations with the lost. We must recognize that today's digital access is an answer to those prayers and that we must act on that blessing. Today, millions are pulling back a curtain on their lives and inviting us in through technology. For the first time in history, we can literally reach "the ends of the earth" with a click. Should we treat this opportunity with prayerful, digital savvy, we may find these to be fruitful days of reaching and then discipling people.

To seize such a (wired) time as this, the Body of Christ must work in the digital space together and leverage our collective influence as leaders in society. Only then can we effectively communicate the hope and love of Jesus Christ, both inside the Church and to a world that desperately needs it.

Toni Birdsong is the co-author of "@stickyJesus: how to live out your faith online," a field guide that equips and inspires Christians to make a kingdom impact in their social networks.

Website: www.stickyJesus.com

 ## Arts, Entertainment & Sports

A beautiful image emerges from nothing on a canvas. An actor with sword in hand fights with hundreds in the battle of his life on film. A dancer moves purposely with eye-pleasing ease and grace on a stage. A bat hits a ball with a cracking sound and soars through the night lights over a fence 400 feet away at a ballpark. A sumptuous meal prepared with such imagination and artistry that it is only surpassed by its pallet-pleasing deliciousness on a plate. A captivating chorus that sings words our souls identify with invites us to join in at a concert (or through earbuds!).

Arts, entertainment, and sports provide us with ways to see, taste, hear, smell, and touch life! They greatly impact us and "light us up" deep within, creating lifetime loves and loyalties to our favorite expressions. Without them, life would be much more monotonous—causing us to miss out on the richness of colors and sounds, the wealth of true stories that need to be told, and the encountering kinds of experiences that add to the joy of sharing life with one another.

We can take a peek at God's pouring out of His Spirit on those in this domain in Exodus 35:31–34 where it states, "...and he has filled him with the Spirit of God, with skill, with intelligence, with knowledge, and with all craftsmanship, to devise artistic designs, to work in gold and silver and bronze, in cutting stones for setting, and in carving wood, for work in every skilled craft. And he has inspired him to teach..." Notice at the end how the artist is to reproduce what they've been given in others—there's the disciple-making component!

Often, the various expressions in this domain reveal something of the beauty of the Lord. For some that beauty is conveyed through the hands of the sculptor as they fashion their clay creation. For others, it's expressed through a painter as they bring to life something they've only seen before in their minds. For sports fans, it's demonstrated through a well planned and executed play that combines exceptional teamwork and seasoned skill leading to a score on the gridiron, pitch, court, or ice. I like seeing this beauty on display every couple of years during the "parade of nations" at the opening ceremonies of the summer and winter Olympic Games—it gives me a little taste of what heaven will be like when the kings parade the glory of their nations before the King of Kings (Revelation 21:23–25)!

Like each of these domains, the devil would like to "steal, kill and destroy" those called to it—moving these artisans and players into places of isolation, perversion, vanity, and pride. He knows that if he can influence their lives, that he then owns the gateway that can alter their God-given craft. The Scriptures teach that our lives bring forth the fruit of what's really inside of us: "For no good tree bears bad fruit, nor again does a bad tree bear good fruit, for each tree is known by its own fruit. For figs are not gathered from thorn bushes, nor are grapes picked from a bramble bush. The good person out of the good treasure of his heart produces good, and the evil person out of his evil treasure produces evil, for out of the abundance of the heart his mouth speaks" (Luke 6:43–45). Therefore, the need for those in this domain to be shaped in the character, ways, and mission of Jesus is absolutely essential!

THE JESUS BLUEPRINT : PART TWO

- As mentioned already, this domain often reveals the beauty of the Lord (Exodus 28:1–3, 39–41; Psalm 27:4; Isaiah 62:2–4).

- Craftsmanship (Exodus 35:31–34).

- He was the designer of the first garments (Genesis 3:21).

- God was the one behind the building of the Ark of the Covenant—and besides being functional it was also beautiful (Exodus 25:10–22).

- He is also the Creator the New Jerusalem and all its splendor (Revelation 21:9–22:5).

- The greatness of God is often revealed causing us to worship (1 Chronicles 29:10-13; Psalm 145).

- The hospitality and culinary expressions of entertaining are rooted in God. He was the first to provide a place to stay and is our source of food (Genesis 1–3; Matthew 6:28–33).

- The Scripture reveals God's emotion of joy (Zephaniah 3:17), something we experience through this domain.

- He is ultimately an athlete's source of strength (Isaiah 40:29–31; Philippians 4:13).

- His discipline is like that of a coach training athletes for the prize (1 Corinthians 9:25–27; Hebrews 12:11–13) and playing by the rules (2 Timothy 2:5–7).

- He provides physical benefits for training (1 Timothy 4:7–8).

- The performance of the artist, entertainer, and athlete is to reflect the glory of God to the world (1 Corinthians 10:31).

Light Bearers

By Loren Johnson

"We become what we behold." *(Marshall McLuhan)*

According to the A.C. Nielsen Co., the average American watches more than 4 hours of TV each day (or 28 hours/week, or 2 months of nonstop TV-watching per year). In a 65-year life, that person will have spent 9 years watching film and television.[5]

A very successful advertising executive explained that he could tell who was discipling the teenager, within minutes of stepping into that child's room. It was apparent from the posters on the walls, the shoes in the closet, and the entertainment he watched or listened to.

One of the most powerful aspects of entertainment is that it allows the artist or creative team to communicate a message, philosophy, or ideal to a very large audience. Film, television, and music have been influential in taking the views of a small minority and imprinting our society as a whole by presenting those views in entertaining and compelling ways.

So, how do we disciple those involved in one of the most influential and powerful systems on the earth so that those disciples can, in turn, influence nations? We must first ask: Who are we, as Jesus followers, and who is it that we follow? The answer to this question allows artists and those in the entertainment industry to discover true love, acceptance, freedom, and understanding of the unlimited creativity that comes from a relationship with the Creator of the universe. The answer is a person, Jesus. The person is the King.

We are light bearers called to shine as lights in the world (Philippians 2:12–18). We serve for the pleasure of the King and we do so at His gracious invitation. We become free to express our gifts before a King and trust that He will use those gifts for His good pleasure and purposes, allowing Him to raise us up in His time (Psalm 75:4–7). We walk in humility (James 3:14–18). We draw near to God and know him intimately (James 4:7–8). We operate out of relationship, are intentional in our preparation, and are always being available to act according to God's Word and ways.

We were designed to capture the heart of every generation through creative expression. We can lead in innovation, insight, and creativity. We were designed to display and communicate the glory of God and to make disciples of every nation. For the pleasure of our King, we will.

Loren Johnson is an award-winning singer-songwriter, producer, and music entrepreneur. He's earned credits on over 50 national releases for various artists and Grammy award-winning producers and is a voting member of the National Academy of Recording Arts and Sciences. He's also recorded and released five of his own CDs.

Website: www.lorenjohnson.com

Influence by Imitation
By John Blue

As an athlete, your whole life consists of learning the fundamentals of your sport: strength, speed, agility, hand-eye coordination, shooting, passing. As a hockey player, I found myself doing the same things playing in the NHL that I was taught growing up as a kid first learning the sport. The consistency with which the athlete executes these foundational practices differentiates between the average, the good, and the great.

Paul says to Timothy in I Corinthians 11:1 (NKJV), "Imitate me just as I also imitate Christ." This principle is a familiar one to professional athletes, as we have spent our lives imitating fellow athletes. In athletics, discipleship takes place through teaching the next generation how to play the game. Those who have gone before us show us what to do and what not to do. They identify pitfalls. They help us become stronger, physically and mentally. They teach us how to finish the race.

To an athlete, finishing strong is everything. Winning is everything. We would never play the game just to be in the game, yet that is what we have done as Christians. Jesus gives us this great game plan in Matthew 28 to go and make disciples, but somehow we have managed to take this ever-so-important principle out of the Christian walk. Instead, we have taught people that just being on the team is enough. It's time we get back to imitating by making disciples.

Having spent three years of his life with twelve men, Jesus changed the world forever. One pastor spent countless hours praying, teaching me how to pray; reading the Scriptures, teaching me how to read the Scriptures; loving people, teaching me how to love people. The influence of athletes is matched only by celebrities and politicians. Just as Paul was sent to the Gentiles and Peter to the Jews, there are men and women that God desires to send into the world of the athlete to disciple them in God's ways and show them how to imitate His life for His glory!

John Blue played hockey at the University of Minnesota, on the USA Olympic hockey team, and in the National Hockey League. Today he serves as the lead pastor at Pacific Pointe Church in Irvine, CA.

Website: www.pacificpointechurch.com

....

**For an additional essay on discipling artists
by Byron Spradlin, visit www.thejesusblueprint.com.**

....

 # Business & Commerce

When considering the role of business in a given locale or within a nation as a whole, it is truly significant. Whether large sprawling corporations, regional franchises, small local businesses, or "mom and pop operations," every community is made up of these purveyors of products and services. Without them, we don't eat lunch, we won't get to our meetings, your kids don't get what they need for their latest school project, and you can't get the clothes you need cleaned for your upcoming trip. Maybe you haven't realized before just how important these businesses are that surround us—whether down the street or online.

The effects of business are felt broadly. Consider how many people businesses interact with on a regular basis, from customers and clients to vendors to other business leaders and community influencers. It's often the business leaders that rise up to address community concerns while also wielding influence in establishing public policy—locally, nationally, or globally. Of course, they also play a major role in society in generating and distributing wealth.

Although we sometimes like to think so, we really are not the "owners" of our businesses, but, rather, the stewards. After all, God is the one who owns it all and we're just passing through for a season of time. As disciples of Jesus we are to steward well what He places in our hands: abilities, skills and gifts, relationships and contacts, platforms of influence, products developed and services created. When put to use under God's oversight and in obedience to Him, there is no limit to what He can do through business leaders. And when these leaders are willing to team together, they can bring the kind of positive change to their communities that makes a real difference in the lives of people.

Over time, people who have served in the business world pick up a lot along the way that can be passed on to others. In church life, for example, they're not only the ones you can count on to contribute generously to various kingdom causes, but some also have leadership abilities to rally, organize, and mobilize people into some of those very same causes. Others have certain skill sets that can help meet real needs. Listen to their counsel. It is often sound and practical wisdom that might just help you through a tough spot!

One of the things I love about business leaders is that when they capture a vision, they're all over it—like bees on honey—to make it happen! They are not only good leaders, but good teammates—you can usually count on them. And, when they interlock with others, they are great disciplers and mentors. If you are called to this domain, you are greatly needed to disciple the next generation of godly business leaders, helping them to understand success in the marketplace through the grid of Jesus' character, ways, and mission.

The Character of God and Business & Commerce

- God owns it all (Deuteronomy 10:14; 1 Chronicles 29:11; Psalm 50:10–12; Haggai 2:8).
- God flexed his entrepreneurial muscle in creation (Genesis 1–3).
- God's "business model" is rooted in fruitfulness and multiplication (Genesis 1–3).
- He is the Landowner (Matthew 21:33–46); the Wise Builder (Matthew 7:24–27); the Vinedresser (John 15).
- He expects a return on His investment (Matthew 25:14–30).
- He's the first creator of goods and services that would meet people's real needs (Genesis 1).
- He positions people to use their gifts and talents both creatively and effectively (i.e. story of Joseph in Genesis 37–50; Book of Nehemiah).
- His central focus is the kingdom not money (Matthew 6:24, 33).
- He cares about those who work for Him (Ephesians 6:5–9).

Passing on the Heart of God

By Michael Q. Pink

When an emerging business leader wants to grow himself or his business, he turns to proven leaders who have track records of success and are willing to share their secrets. The "hungry for success" emerging business leader frequently submits himself to be discipled, mentored, or, at the very least, instructed by those who may hold the golden chalice of business success, but often deny or ignore the claims of Christ on this world and their lives.

Emerging leaders need strong discipling and mentoring relationships that pass on the heart of God for this world and not just the secrets of material success. Where are those godly, successful business mentors who will help the up-and-coming attain success in their chosen fields of endeavor, and also show them how to mesh their lives with the overriding purpose of God?

Jesus' method works! Elijah mentored Elisha, Stalin mentored Khrushchev, and Fidel Castro mentored Hugo Chavez, but those leaders, like all leaders, can only pass on the inheritance of their hearts. Where are the business leaders who carry the heart of God into the marketplace? Where are those who have a heart for providing leadership for, mentoring and, dare I say, discipling, the emerging business leader to help him step into the hope of His calling and the riches of the glory of His inheritance in the saints (Ephesians 1:18)?

Godly business leaders need to shift from a focus on personal accomplishment—and even great success in the realm of business done in the name of Jesus—to a more corporate view of accomplishment and success that folds into the master plan of making disciples of all nations (Matthew 28:19). That plan is the heart of God, the Great Commission and the blueprint for the ages We in the business community are invited to participate in this grand vision. Are we up for it? Let's disciple!

Michael Pink is a best-selling author, consultant, business trainer, and coach. He currently heads up the Rainforest Business Institute bringing transformation to cultures through innovative business training.

Website: www.michaelpink.com

The Marketplace Mission

By Mary Tomlinson

Webster defines a missionary as "a person who is sent out on a mission." For some of us, our mission field is the corporate business world.

Because he worked as an independent businessman in the carpentry business, I picture Jesus relating to the everyday work struggles of too much or too little work, dealing with challenging clients, and building a successful business.

In His adult ministry, He spent most of His time around business people—fisherman, tax collectors and those of wealth. In love, Jesus always accepted them for who they were but challenged them to grasp eternal truths and pointed them to their God-given destinies.

In *Jesus CEO*, Laurie Beth Jones states: "If everyone treated their staff the way Jesus did his, you would see an increase in morale and productivity. He created a lean, clean marketing machine. These people were motivated."[6]

In the marketplace our disciplng may come in many forms, such as consulting, coaching, leadership development, or team building. But like Jesus, our work is to love and accept our clients where they are and challenge them to know Him and His ways. We must intentionally:

- *Pray diligently for those He calls us to serve*
- *Honor each person as God does*
- *Discern needs and water with seeds of faith*
- *Live holy lives as we lead our businesses*
- *Be prepared to share the good news*

Billy Graham has said that one of the next big moves of God will be through believers in the marketplace.[7] To accept this call, we must know that the business world can be a holy place of work—one that is ripe for harvest and the making of disciples.

Mary Tomlinson has over 30 years of corporate/consulting experience, including 18 years at Disney. As president of On-Purpose Partners, she works with businesses, non-profits, and government organizations.

Website: www.marytomlinson.com

....

For an additional essay on the business of making disciples by Howard Partridge, visit www.thejesusblueprint.com.

....

 # Science & Technology

Not only is God just and kind in all His ways, the Savior of the world, and the Lord of our lives, He's also the most intelligent and wise person in the entire universe! Since God is the author of both the Scriptures and science there is complete harmony between them. As Galileo (1564–1642), wrote, "The world is the work and the Scriptures the word of the same God."[8] Johannes Kepler (1571–1630), a German mathematician and astronomer, and a contemporary of Galileo's, expressed it this way, "The tongue of God and the finger of God cannot clash."[9]

Kepler, whose discovery of the three laws of planetary motion laid the foundation for Sir Isaac Newton's theory of gravity, was a devout follower of Jesus. He regarded his study of the physical universe as "thinking God's thoughts after Him." His endeavors demonstrated for us Psalm 111:2, "Great are the works of the Lord, studied by all who delight in them." Kepler saw himself as "a high priest in the book of nature, religiously bound to alter not one jot or tittle of what it had pleased God to write down in it."[10] In light of this view, when revealing the motivation behind his work he wrote, "Since we astronomers are

CHAPTER SEVEN : Dozen Domain Snapshots 2

priests of the highest God in regard to the book of nature, it befits us to be thoughtful, not of the glory of our minds, but rather, above else, the glory of God."[11]

Over the last century-plus, the gap between God and science has widened, in part due to science's share in the increased secularization of Western culture. There is a tremendous need for godly men and women who call science their vocation/calling to step into the "disciple-making gap" and shape hearts and minds with the wonder of God's Word and works.

I want to switch gears and focus for a moment on technology—which likely represents the most remarkable advancement in our lifetime. When I realize that I hold significantly more power and memory in my iPhone than the astronauts had on board Apollo 11 when it went to the moon—it is staggering![12] Nevertheless, this fact represents the supersonic speed of the world of technology.

I remember sitting in front of the first edition of Mac computers in the 1980s, learning the basics, while being told "one day you'll sit at your computer and have access to more information at your fingertips than you could ever imagine." The sheer wonder today is not only how it all works, but in the reality that within three minutes I can see the top news story of the day, catch part of a football game live, be messaged on Facebook by someone I haven't heard from since high school, get a text from my daughter, and order my wife's birthday present at the same time! Those capabilities are not only remarkable, but they have been our norm for quite some time.

How does Jesus intend for us to use technology for His kingdom purposes? How will we disciple future generations who work with these technologies in the ways of God? How do we make sure that technology is there to serve us and that we don't become enslaved to it? These are the kinds of questions disciples called to this vocation will continually need to wrestle through with the latest gadget in one hand and the Scriptures in the other. Or, as they are referencing the Scriptures on their latest gadgets!

The Character of God and Science & Technology

- He's the author of life (Acts 3:15).

- He's the source of creation (Genesis 1–2).

- It's for Him, by Him, and through Him that all things exist (Romans 11:36; Hebrews 2:10).

- He is the beginning and end (Revelation 21:6, 22:13).

- He was and is and is to come (Revelation 4:8).

- He's unsearchable (Psalm 145:3; Isaiah 40:28).

- He's our source of wonder (Exodus 15:11; Job 5:8–9; Psalm 77:14).

The Great Engineer & Maker

By Winkie Pratney

"He has made everything beautiful in its time. Also He has put eternity in their hearts, except that no one can find out the work that God does from the beginning to the end" *(Ecclesiastes 3:11 NKJV)*.

There are three topics you may give yourself to that essentially cover everything: language, science, and theology. Language because we need the ability to describe what we know and see; science because we love to find things we might know and see; and theology because no one but the Maker has the ability to know, see, and speak not only everything, but all that may be behind it or beyond it.

Science and technology is one of God's great gifts to mankind: the knowing of worlds, dreaming of possibilities, and discovery of connections that can mark genuine greatness.

God is Himself the great Engineer and Maker. To deliberately divorce ourselves from His insight, wisdom. and direction in any quest we aim at is an invitation to arrogance. History is filled with records of what happened when those with such a gift did not have the sense to use this wonder wisely to bless the world. Babel was only the beginning; we can build another Hindenburg or Titanic for ourselves, but it will not be remembered on that day for how well it stood or flew or sailed.

When Jesus rose from the dead and came back to see His followers, He told Thomas, the born skeptic with the heart of a scientist, to reach for, see, and touch Him and not to be faithless, but believing; Thomas said: "My Lord and my God."

History holds the records of multitudes that used this gift for good; and time cannot tell all that was accomplished in their stand and by their hand. We must give ourselves to the discipling of those gifted and called to the sciences and technology—teaching them the ways of God so they might reveal to the world the Who behind the wonders!

Winkie Pratney has enjoyed both a research and experimental background in a number of sciences. He is a historian, apologist, teacher, author, and general editor of "The Revival Study Bible".

Website: www.winkiepratney.com

Technology With a Purpose

By Mike Gustafson

Technology and its advancement is the obsession of the modern era. It has created opportunity, wealth, health, and connections but also has brought with it pain, isolation, abuse, and death.

Our lives are embedded with technology. It is so pervasive we often do not realize the breadth and depth of our reliance on technology. It shapes how you think, how you communicate, and how you live your life.

God has not given us technology to use without a purpose. He wants us to use it in pursuit of redeeming this world. Technology is not the end in itself but a great enabler to accomplishing God's purposes in every other domain. Modern technology provides us with tools and abilities to live out this calling in ways unimagined to those even fifty years ago.

The world of technology is one of constant evolution. Those involved in this world feel and enjoy the exhilaration of the new, but are often overwhelmed by the speed and volume. There is a great and deep need for those who find themselves placed in this world to know the stability of our unchanging God. It is also critical that those who are shaping all other domains through the creation and use of technology learn and understand the ways of God. It is the responsibility of godly men and women in all areas of technology to undertake with great intentionality and earnest the mentoring, coaching, and discipling of those in our sphere of influence.

We must remember that our calling is not just to pursue our work with excellence and to glorify God with it, but to disciple those who are called to this world to encourage and embed within them the character and ways of God. Our legacy is not going to be the technology we create or put to great use but those that we disciple to put their gifts and talents to God's plan of redemption.

Mike Gustafson has been involved in the discipling and developing of leaders in various roles for the last 20 years. He is a partner at Rosetta, an interactive marketing agency, where he is responsible for leading and developing multiple technology teams.

Chapter Eight

Dozen Domain Snapshots 3

 ## Health, Medicine & Wholeness

In the Scriptures we encounter a man who's half-dead on the side of the road. Two who were "spiritual" saw him yet passed by him on the other side of the road. Along came a third man, not quite as "spiritual," who saw him and had compassion. He bound up his wounds, poured on oil and wine, and transported him to a place where he would be well cared for, covering all of the costs involved. Jesus then asks, "Which of these three, do you think, proved to be a neighbor?" They answer, "The one who showed him mercy," to which Jesus says, "You go, and do likewise."

The point? Our neighbor is not necessarily someone we like or the person who lives next door, but is the one in need that God places in our path. This parable reveals our heart motives and priorities in how we relate to people. Those called to this vocation have the regular opportunity of coming alongside people in their greatest moments of crisis and need—not only with their expertise and skill, but also by tending and treating patients as people created in God's image with great value and for great purpose.

This story underscores that Jesus cares about people holistically— body, soul, and spirit (1 Thessalonians 5:23; 3 John 1:2). Healthcare is an extension of God's heart for people—through wellness coaching and prevention, through medical and hospital care, or through whole- ness of body, soul and spirit. Those serving in this domain recognize the interconnectedness of our beings and how one area may affect the others.

The Scriptures teach that the body is His temple (1 Corinthians 6:18–20). God has called and equipped some to help us "tend our temples." They aid us in healthy eating, regularly exercising, and getting right amounts of sleep and rest—adding great value to our entire lives. Others help us walk in relational wholeness by helping us assess who "adds" to our lives and who "takes" from us. Of course, we are to receive friendship, strength, and encouragement from some and give our lives in sacrifice and service to help others, so the issue is not either/or—the issue is bal- ance. It's the same with our time. Do you intentionally take a Sabbath and time to recharge? Have you built an adequate margin into your life for "down time," or are you constantly "running on empty?"

God has called doctors, nurses, dentists, and medical professionals of all kinds to serve people. They help us with our hearts, eyes, teeth, skin, feet, allergies, knees, backs, and everything else that can possibly act up in our bodies. They have a God-given ability to take the knowledge they've received and combine it with the skills they've been trained in to help physically heal and at times rescue lives. They, too, are an extension of God's heart and hands of healing. Many become specialists, providing us with the understanding and unique care we need to be made well.

Some called by Jesus to this domain focus on wholeness of soul and spirit, and others on physical wellness. Counselors aim to aid people in

THE JESUS BLUEPRINT : PART TWO

getting on the inside—emotionally or spiritually—by combining their understanding of our souls with prayer. They wisely guide people out of the "stuck places" of their lives and into ones marked by joy, peace, courage, and hope—and health!

The Character of God and Health, Medicine & Wholeness

- Our Designer (Psalm 139:14–16).
- Our Maker (Psalm 95:6–7).
- Our Source of Care (Psalm 27:10; 1 Peter 5:6–7).
- The Giver of Life (Job 33:4).
- The Physician (Luke 8:43–48).
- The Healer (Exodus 15:26).
- Our Counselor (Isaiah 9:6).
- Our Consoler and Comforter (Psalm 23:4, 94:19; 2 Corinthians 1:3–4).
- Our Physical Trainer (Psalm 18:35; 1 Corinthians 9:24–25; 1 Timothy 4:8).

Matters of the Heart

By John McB. Hodgson, M.D.

As a cardiac physician, I have used my stethoscope to diagnose many illnesses and then performed many heart surgeries. Most of my patients get better and go home to their families, but very few are ever healed. As I work with their physical ailments, I also use my stethoscope as a disciple of Jesus to listen with my spiritual ears to their spiritual hearts. I have treated many patients with broken physical hearts, and they have taught me a great deal about our spiritual hearts as well. A story will best illustrate what I mean.

A retired soldier was admitted with a heart attack. We treated his blocked coronary artery and he did so well that he was ready to go home by the third day. Unfortunately, he returned two days later with a serious complication: he had developed a hole in his heart muscle. After 12 hours of emergency surgery he was brought back to his room with warnings that he was "unlikely to survive." I joined the family in prayer that morning and miraculously he improved and eventually went home. The man who left was not the same one who had presented to the emergency room six weeks earlier. He shared with me that he felt "different" about everything; the sun was brighter, his family dearer, his pet dog and his house that much more a comfort. I loved seeing him and his family; we had a special bond that only prayer can bring. He was always positive, even from his wheelchair, and he always had an encouraging word for the other patients. After he died, I was asked to give the eulogy at his funeral and remember using the analogy of the physical hole in his heart that we had repaired and the spiritual hole in his heart that had been miraculously healed at the same time. My patient had a sudden, divine, and miraculous experience.

Stories like these have taught me that all patients—whether they've never known Jesus, grew up with Him, or have been hiding from Him—are candidates for tune-ups of their spiritual hearts! Even in the sterile, scientific, fast-paced world of medicine, we need to disciple people to reflect God's character and ways, so that along with physical care, people's inner needs can be recognized and cared for.

John McB. Hodgson, M.D. is past chairman of cardiology for Geisinger Health System in northeastern PA. He is active in local and international missions work and serves as chairman of the board for Hope Educational Foundation, focuses on addressing systemic threats to children through education.

Website: www.hope-ed.net

Wonderful Counselor

By Phyllis Oswald Rogers, MA, LMHC

After returning to college in my forties, I finished my degree and became a licensed family therapist. Five years earlier, my husband had been in a serious accident that left him in a vegetative state and us without financial security. Through those difficult years I learned to depend on God for even the smallest decision. It was during this time that He taught me what later became an essential skill in my profession as a therapist—how to hear His still, small voice.

Three years into private practice, I could see that the theories and approaches I had learned in school were helping my clients, but the deep wounds in their hearts were not getting healed. In answer to my prayers, I read Proverbs 2:1–3 (NLT), "My child, listen to what I say, and treasure my commands. Turn your ear to wisdom, and concentrate on understanding. Cry out for insight and ask for understanding."

With the client's permission, I began to ask God to reveal to them the origins of their emotional wounds, while I listened for His direction on how to proceed. He would reveal where the pain originated and pinpoint where there were lies about who they were in their belief systems. I began to apply God's truth like salve to their wounds. Miracles began to unfold—most of which I had little to do with other than getting out of the way. My clients who preferred a more standard therapeutic approach benefited because I was relying upon God's wisdom rather than my own. Many of them had been seeking just such help, but had not found it.

As a disciple of Jesus I still value and use my educational tools, now under God's direction. Each morning as I prepare for clients, I invite Him, the Wonderful Counselor, to sit with me in my therapist's chair, and I ask Him to make my office a place of healing, restoration, and refreshment. As I strive to incorporate the ways of God into my own practice, I pray and look for opportunities to disciple and mentor godly therapists to walk in the ways of God in our professional calling. The goal is worthy and the rewards are great.

Phyllis Oswald Rogers, MA, LMHC, is the founder and director of the inLife Clinic in Bellevue, Washington. She also serves her community as a police and fire chaplain.

Website: www.inLifeClinic.com

....

**For additional essays on a lifestyle of health and wholeness
by Lynell LaMountian and being physically fit to serve by Tim Powers,
visit www.thejesusblueprint.com.**

....

 # Environment, Agriculture & Zoology

It all began in a garden created by God. He called it "good" (Genesis 2:8). He placed within it water, land, plants, trees, fish, birds, and animals of all kinds. When He created Adam and Eve He placed them in that garden to work it and keep it (Genesis 2:15) as His stewards of His creation. God cares about His creation and, as Jesus' disciples, we need to embrace our roles as representatives of His care for it.

Have you ever paused to consider that some of our current environmental issues may actually be rooted in sins such as selfishness and greed? Consider water pollution, for example. How hard is it to make sure we don't put something in the water, as a person or as a business, which causes the water to be contaminated? When we do contaminate water, others "down stream"—whether literally or generationally—can't enjoy the same blessings from it as we do. Our selfishness is focused on our own convenience—it's easier to leave our trash than throw it away—and our carelessness—not thinking how what we do might affect creation and others enjoying it. Greed can also blind us as we choose to destroy something because we only have our own gain in mind. As followers of Jesus, we need to humble ourselves and reference God's perspective as we deal with the growing list of environmental problems at hand.

My grandparents were farmers in northwest Minnesota, home to the rich, fertile soil of the Red River Valley. While pastoring there in my twenties, I had the privilege of gaining friends who are hardworking, godly farmers. Through their lives they taught me the value of the land. Agricultural themes run throughout the Scriptures. Agriculture is often used as a metaphor to provide us with greater insights into our walks with Jesus (i.e. the Sower in Matthew 13:1–9, 18–23; and the Vine and the Branches in John 15:1–9). We also find that God is concerned about fields, crops, and land and even how food we grow is shared with the hungry (Leviticus 25–26). Hunger and malnutrition are rampant throughout the world—as of this writing there are approximately 925 million people[1] around the world classified as "hungry." That is almost 1 out of 7 of us! Those who view this domain as their vocation/calling can play a very significant role in making an impact here on behalf of Jesus and His kingdom.

As we see in Genesis, God created animals. They are seen throughout Scripture from Genesis to Revelation and are also used as symbols or pictures in the Scriptures: Jesus is pictured as the "Lion of the Tribe of Judah," we are the "sheep of His pasture," and Satan first appears as a "serpent." Some of our favorite Bible stories as children include animals: Noah and the ark, Jonah and the whale, and Daniel in the lion's den. A reading of Psalm 104 reveals God's provision of food, water, and places to dwell for these special creatures of His making. Whether furry friends that live with us in our homes, animals on the farm, or those in the wild, it's important to reference God's truths of humility, justice, and kindness as we interact with them.

CHAPTER EIGHT : Dozen Domain Snapshots 3

All three of these areas—environment, agriculture, and zoology—affect all of us around the world in various ways. The question I have is, who is willing to disciple the next generation of godly leaders to represent His character, ways, and mission within this domain? Jesus-followers called to this domain: We need you to pour into others so that His perspective, based on Scripture, is understood, embraced, modeled, and forwarded.

The Character of God and Environment, Agriculture & Zoology

- He's the creator of the earth and everything in it (Psalm 104:25,30; John 1:3; Colossians 1:16–17).
  - » *The plants (Genesis 1:11–12).*
  - » *The fish and birds (Genesis 1:20–21).*
  - » *The animals (Genesis 1:24–25).*
- He relates to all of His creation.
  - » *The heavens, earth, the seas, fields, trees (Psalm 96:10–13).*
  - » *The wild animals (Isaiah 43:20–21).*
  - » *The clouds and lightening (Job 37:14–18).*
- His creation expresses worship to Him.
  - » *The heavens tell of the glory of God and the work of His hands (Psalm 19:1).*
  - » *The mountains and hills burst in to song and all the trees of the field clap their hands (Isaiah 55:12–13).*
  - » *Every creature in heaven and on earth, under the sea and on the sea, and all that is in them (Revelation 5:13).*
- He instructs through nature (Job 12:7–10; Proverbs 6:6–11; Romans 1:19–20).

- He protects and preserves animals (Genesis 6:19–21).

- He's made a covenant that includes plants and animals (Genesis 9:8–13).

Stewarding God's Creation
By Winkie Pratney

"In the beginning, God created the heavens and the earth…And God said, Let the waters under the heaven be gathered together to one place, and let the dry land appear: and it was so. And God called the dry land Earth; and the gathering together of the waters He called Seas. And God saw that it was good" (Genesis 1:1, 9).

The dominant metaphors of God's creative work in Scripture for our world are those of the environment, agriculture, and zoology. The very structure of life is upheld by His amazingly interlinked planetary design. In Genesis, our stated created origins are set in the context of the sheer beauty, size, and power of Earth's majestic supporting structures, where wonders are unveiled. In all creation, beneath what seems like apparent simplicity, lays mind-blowing sub-microscopic maintenance of previously unseen and unknown complexity.

The Scriptures clearly reveal that God has given man responsibility to steward His creation (Genesis 1:28). Not only is this to be done out of reverence for and obedience to God, but also so that generations might reap the fruit of sustenance and enjoyment that flows from His glorious creation. Because followers of Jesus realize this is a command and value of God's, they should be on the leading edge of care, wisdom, and service in regards to tending this domain.

Healthy soil conditions and crops, clean air and water, the wellbeing of the many organisms and species within the plant and animal kingdoms are all part of being responsible for things assigned to us by our Maker. Environmental, agricultural, and zoological researchers, scientists, and practitioners must continue to seek to wisely manage God's creation. At the same time, we must deliberately disciple leaders in this domain with God's heart and ways, ensuring a godly perspective and excellence in competence as it relates to stewarding the Earth.

Winkie Pratney has enjoyed both a research and experimental background in a number of sciences. He is an historian, apologist, teacher, author, and general editor of "The Revival Study Bible."

Website: www.winkiepratney.com

The Beauty of the Beasts

By Dr. Kit Flowers

We constantly fight the challenge to segment our lives into the secular and the sacred. We go to church on Sunday and take the rest of the week to work, play, or rest. We especially face this segmentation as we serve through our work. After spending many years pursuing education in order to serve others, we find ourselves well equipped to administer skills through our vocations. Yet, we often do not have any planned strategy of how those professional skills are to be integrated into His kingdom work. In His design, our service to others—to His creation and to His creatures—is intended to be part of His work of redemption.

"And God made the beasts of the earth after their kind, and the cattle after their kind, and every thing that creeps on the ground after its kind; and God saw that it was good" (Genesis 1:25). What an amazing and beautiful image—the creation of all living things—and God saw that it was good. In the midst of that creation, God charged Adam to engage in His purposes for the animals by asking him to name them. The Scripture is full of references to the role that animals play in this world and in His story.

"A righteous man has regard for the life of his beast. But even the compassion of the wicked is cruel" (Proverbs 12:10 NASB). Our heart toward God is reflected in our heart's attitude toward His creation. God's redemptive purposes include man's responsibility in the care of animals. "Know well the condition of your flocks, and pay attention to your herds" (Proverbs 27:23 NASB). The heart of a disciple demonstrates the Father's love for this beautiful part of His creation and actively looks for ways to replicate that heart—and the skills that go with it—in fellow disciples.

By living with the heart of a servant in the care of this part of creation, the disciple provides a witness of God's care for all living things. In living a life of service to people and their animals, others are challenged to know Him and become His disciples.

Dr. Kit Flowers serves as the president of Christian Veterinary Mission, serving to challenge, empower, and facilitate veterinary professionals to serve others by living out their faith.

Website: www.cvmusa.org

 # Nonprofits & Service Organizations

This domain may include activities of many kinds. Gathering boys and girls to participate in organized athletics. Distributing food and clothing to those in need. Taking care of families in the midst of health emergencies. Translating the Scriptures into a native tongue. Giving blood. Facilitating mentoring opportunities for those with limited adult leadership in their lives. Raising money for people with physical challenges. Providing resources for the arts. Protecting wildlife. Responding to those affected by natural disasters. Connecting needy children with sponsors. Developing societal leaders with character, wisdom, and perspective. Picking up roadside trash. Educating single moms to raise their children. Providing places for families to stay during a loved one's cancer treatment. Rescuing children and youth from the snares of human trafficking. Digging wells so entire villages have clean water to drink. The list goes on and on.

Where there is a need for such things as justice, hope, and mercy, you'll find nonprofits and service organizations ready to jump in to help. According to the National Center for Charitable Statistics (NCCS) there are over 1.57 million nonprofits, accounting for 9% of all wages and salaries paid and $1.4 trillion in total annual expenses. In 2010, individuals gave over $211 billion and foundations contributed $45 billion towards their causes.[2] From September of 2009 to September 2010, approximately 26% of Americans over the age of 16 volunteered for a nonprofit organization over a one-year span.[3] Obviously, the nonprofit sector plays an influential and dynamic role in our communities!

One of the things you'll notice about people who lead nonprofits and service organizations, and the many who volunteer with them, is their passion and commitment. They are cause-led and mission-dedicated. A need surfaces, an opportunity to make a real difference in people's lives emerges, a way to change the culture around them in a positive way arises—and not far behind is a man or woman with vision of a better future. They engage this newfound opportunity with great passion and tireless commitment, rallying others, raising funds, and running volunteers through training so they can multiply their impact.

Some of the greatest challenges for these groups when it comes to fulfilling their missions are:

- *Volunteers*—There is always a need for more committed volunteers who are willing to be trained and serve the mission.

- *Organizational Assistance*—Because the needs and tasks of nonprofits and service organizations are ongoing, there is a demand for those with skills in organization, communication, technology and support to lend a hand by giving freely of their time and expertise.

- *Funding*—Often, the greatest of the three challenges is to match monies with the mission. Meeting this need is where individual donors, tithing companies and foundations come in, as they look for relationships, a like-heartedness of purpose and biblical accountability that both satisfies their needs as givers and frees the organization to pursue its ends.

Leaders within nonprofits and service organizations need to also be making disciples—reproducing the character, ways, and mission of Jesus in those God brings around them so that He is honored in how they live and lead.

The Character of God and Nonprofits and Service Organizations

- He is merciful (Psalm 69:16;103:2–5,8; Ephesians 2:4–7).

- He is just (Deuteronomy 10:17–18; Psalm 103:6).

- He gives hope (Psalm 62:5;42:5).

- He is present for the poor and needy (Psalm 12:5; 34:6; Luke 4:18).

- He defends the widow and fathers the orphan (Psalm 68:5; 146:9).

- He is companion to the hungry, thirsty, stranger, naked, sick, and the prisoner (Matthew 25:31–46).

- God is the giver/donor (Luke 12:32; Acts 17:25; Romans 12:6–8).

- He is a very present help in trouble (Psalm 46:1–3).

- He is a stronghold and refuge in the day of trouble (Nahum 1:7).

Discipled for Compassion
By Jack & Cherie Minton

Tsunamis...Hurricanes...Floods...Fires...Earthquakes...Most of us have found ourselves watching the nightly news, moved by the heartbreaking calamities

---

195

around the world. In the midst of it, we ask: "What in the world is going on... and what can we do?"

Jesus commissioned His Church to lay their lives down in loving service to a broken world. We are to love through compassionate—and often times, spontaneous—acts of kindness, reflecting the very glory and nature of God to those whose image of Him may have been distorted through suffering and loss. Throughout the teachings of Jesus, it is simply impossible to miss the mandate that He has given to His followers: to show love for Him by serving others in need.

Before actively engaging his disciples in acts of service, however, Jesus purposefully invested himself into their lives—spiritually, relationally, and practically. This pattern of modeling and molding His team was evident throughout the time He walked with them on Earth. It was woven into the fabric of His relationship and the various tasks He assigned at any given moment. His first priority was to prepare them for the demands that would soon be placed upon them. Jesus knew that without this foundation, they could not follow His example by laying their lives down for others.

Discipleship just doesn't happen by itself. As followers of Jesus serving in compassion ministries in the nonprofit world, we must be intentional about investing into the lives of those bearing the burden of service. The rush to serve must be tempered by the example of Jesus; care for those entrusted to us first, so that they, in turn, can care for others. This care is not a one-time event, but rather an ongoing expression of loving God and loving one another. The careful and continual attention to the well-being of our team will result in far greater effectiveness, and bear transformational fruit in the lives of the served as well as the servant.

Jack & Cherie Minton are the founders of Hope Force International, a nonprofit organization created to provide a clear pathway to mobilize Christians into rapid disaster response scenarios around the world.

Website: www.hopeforce.org

Peoples (Affinity/Cultural Kinship)

Jesus loves people. He made them diverse and dispersed them around the globe. Groups of people naturally hub around what they have in common, forming an identity and creating culture. Cultures represent such things as shared heritage, family systems, language, food, clothing, mutual interests and needs, and similar aims. These traits bind a group of people together and are reinforced by the way they relate to each other over time. Some people have Jesus' heart for certain groupings of people and they are called by Him to lay down their lives in service for them. Some might be called to their "own people."

Each people grouping has been given a unique deposit from God that accentuates certain attributes of His character and conveys a distinctiveness of call. Have you ever considered that God has a call upon groups of people just like He does on individuals? Have you noticed that through various people groupings certain things are created, developed and distributed to serve and bless other peoples?

As a simple example, consider one of our favorite topics—food! Can you imagine life without tacos, guacamole, chips and salsa—we have to thank Mexico! What about lasagna? It originated among Greeks and Romans, and after being a lost dish for decades it resurfaced in its present form through the Italians! How about Chinese food?

On another front, have you ever noticed how the trains run like clockwork in the nations of the Germans and Swiss—where some of the best clocks and watches in the world are made? Every people grouping has God-deposited "redemptive gifts" that are part of their unique call and

CHAPTER EIGHT : Dozen Domain Snapshots 3

are intended to bless others. What are the redemptive gifts of the people you're a part of and called to?

We must remember that God desires for us to celebrate the uniqueness of His diverse cultures. In this context, we must also remember that God's ways always trump culture. In other words, if a particular aspect of culture doesn't align to God's ways as revealed in Scripture, it must be repented of and rightly aligned to His ways. Satan will do his very best to spoil and pervert the redemptive gifts of God within a culture. As a matter of fact, one of the greatest ways to discover the redemptive gifts of a culture is to locate where the enemy has worked hard to damage or destroy it. It may be within this very area that we'll find the truth of how God intends to use them to be a blessing to the world!

Are you called by God to give yourself in the service of a certain people grouping? If so, consider what attributes of His character He desires to put on full display through them. What is their calling as a people? What are their redemptive gifts and how has Satan tried to hinder them from fully expressing them? And in this context, are you making disciples among them in such a way that they are reproducing the character, ways, and mission of Jesus in others—both among their own people and beyond?

What a glorious day it will be when we experience together the scenario foreshadowed in Revelation 5:9, "And they sang a new song, saying,

> *"Worthy are you to take the scroll and to open its seals,*
> *for you were slain, and by your blood you ransomed people for God*
> *from every tribe and language and people and nation..."*

The Character of God and Peoples

- He's made us in His image (Genesis 1:26–27).

- He's made people from all nations (Psalm 86:9).

- He's the redeemer of nations (Revelation 5:9).

- He's the discipler of nations (Matthew 28:18–20).

- He's worshipped by kings/nations (Revelation 21:22–26).

- He's Messiah to the Jews (Luke 1:30–33).

Discipling the Young African-American Man
By Dr. John Perkins

We are all well aware of the drastic statistics related to young black men today and how these negative numbers increase when there is not a father in the home. We need to ask the question: What is being done to communicate what young black men need in order to succeed?

Discipleship is central here. God incarnated in Jesus Christ the perfect example of how to do this. Christ developed godly character in others. Developing godly character is our commission as well. We are called to be men who walk in the ways of God and exercise authority for the good of others. We are formed by what we believe and how we are anchored. We ought to be anchored in Christ, expressing the fruit of the Spirit (Galatians 5:22–23) in honesty, truth, and respect.

I grew up without a father, but God blessed me with a man of God who discipled me in my youth. I am ever so thankful for the time he spent casting dreams into my life that have come true today. I encourage older black men to take time and cast godly dreams into the lives of young black men. I know that these young black men can only arrive at their dreams as older black men care, love, and affirm the young ones in their personhood.

There are three core principles to build in the lives of young black men. First, each one should be encouraged to discover his special talents. God has created each man for a specific purpose and has equipped him with the tools and gifts he needs to accomplish that. Second, a strong vision must be cast to follow God's will. A desire and vision must come from within, centered on Jesus Christ. The third principle deals with bearing suffering. In our walks with Christ, there are many struggles and opportunities to "carry the cross" that we must be willing to embrace and endure to accomplish Jesus' mission through our lives.

We have a holy heritage to uphold. I invite you to join me in laying godly tracks for generations of young black men to follow and walk in.

Dr. Perkins is a leader, teacher, and author. As a reconciler and community transformer, he founded the Christian Community Development Association and leads the John M. Perkins Foundation for Reconciliation and Development.

Website: www.jmpf.org

Next Generation Disciple-Making

By Dan Sneed

Some time ago, I had the privilege of having lunch with an incredible group of youth pastors—sharp young leaders who were passionate about their relationships with Jesus and their love for people, especially for the young generation. To say I was impressed with them would be an understatement.

I was also impressed by their desire to find mentors—spiritual fathers and mothers who were willing to invest their lives in them. I was blown away by the fact that they wanted to "hang out" with an old guy like me. At their age, I would have never thought that anyone over the age of thirty had anything to contribute to my life. These guys were different. They sought me out, asked me to have lunch with them, and opened their hearts and lives to me.

As we were getting ready to leave, one of them thanked me for taking the time just to be with them. I'll never forget his words: "You have spent more time with us at lunch today than my pastor has in the almost two and a half years I have worked for him." At first, I was sure he was joking or at least exaggerating. How could that be? But, I quickly realized that he was not exaggerating. Several of the others spoke up, affirming his statement and acknowledging to varying degrees that their experiences were similar. Although the discussion that followed was brief, it has troubled me for years. Those exceptional young leaders all came to their positions not only with a specific job to do, but with a deep desire for someone to invest in them—their lives and their future.

As an older leader, "a father," I have taken the challenge to invest, not only what I have learned about ministry, but also my life—in an emerging group of leaders, who, I believe, can become much more than I could ever be. They are ready to listen if we are willing to invest. I'm also finding that my greatest days of ministry are now giving myself to develop spiritual sons and daughters who will touch their world in ways I have only dreamt about.

Dan Sneed currently travels the world as a Bible teacher and conference speaker, ministering to and advising leaders, while serving on numerous ministry boards. He is the author of "The Power of a New Identity."

Website: www.dansneed.com

....

For an additional essay on discipling the next generation by Brenda Bertrand, visit www.thejesusblueprint.com.

....

PART THREE

A Framework to Build Upon

Chapter Nine

Cultivating Disciple-Making Communities

Go back in your mind with me—way back to the original disciple-making community—Jesus and twelve. For three years he walked with twelve men from various domains. He allowed them to experience life with Him and view the world through the lens of His kingdom. Nothing more—nothing less. As we briefly viewed in Acts, the end result was a world impacted and a disciple-making model and mandate passed on for future generations to carry on.

I wonder what things would have looked like over the centuries, and today, if this first disciple-making community—based on the Jesus blueprint—remained the church's primary mission? How much further ahead would we be in displaying the wonder and wisdom of God's kingdom in the world around us? How many trappings of religiosity would we have avoided altogether? How much hotter would the spiritual passion of the church be today? How many lives and societies would be bettered and blessed around the world had Jesus blueprint disciple-making impacted the Dozen Domains throughout the centuries? My guess is, there'd also be no concerns about "the church in decline," numerically or in influence.

I've traveled around the globe enough to recognize that the Jesus blueprint can be implemented anywhere at anytime. Of course, I realize each culture will adapt it to make it unique to itself, but the Matthew pattern we viewed earlier with the ingredients of *teaching truth, community, obeying Jesus, and reproducing disciple-makers* remains the same, as does the paradigm of imitation.

Are you currently an active part of a disciple-making community? I'm not asking if you're a part of a church, in a neighborhood Bible study, or part of an on-the-job prayer group. Are you engaged in a disciple-making community where you and the others are being shaped by the scriptures and the leading of the Holy Spirit into the character, ways, and mission of Jesus? Are you where relationships are genuine and going deeper; where obeying what Jesus has been revealing to you is valued and applied in your life and through where you serve in the domains; and where you are expected to be reproducing the same in others?

Thinking Outside the Box

Whether you are currently involved in disciple-making or not, I want you to think outside of the box with me for a moment. Where, when, and with whom could you help create disciple-making communities?

Imagine the many innovative ways disciples could be made if we would simply think outside some of the boxes that we've previously built. I've actually been quite encouraged with what I've been experiencing and hearing about over the last several years. I'd like to share a sampling of them with you. I've noticed that some of these disciple-making communities are related directly to church life, but many are not. I've seen some fledgling, some flourishing, and others currently being experimented with. Prayerfully consider how these kinds of expressions, and others, may work in your world.

You'll note that I've purposely left names and organizations out, to highlight the concept and to provide those involved with the room they need to experiment and grow their disciple-making communities. As these groups emerge and begin making some noise in their communities down the road, you might bump into them along the way. Each example represents people that I'm either in relationship with or circumstances that I am acquainted with first-hand.

Within the Dozen Domains:

- *Family:* I'm finding couples and families that are moving well beyond the morning devotional to serious discipleship in their homes. Some use the day-by-day slow drip method, while others take an evening each week to deliberately build their marriages around key discipleship themes or build their sons and daughters into solid disciples of Jesus. Imagine combining families that already enjoy hanging with each other and translating that into regular disciple-making moments together!

- *Business:* Recently, a godly businessman said to me, "You know, business people are great at designing systems to make their businesses a success. However, I've just realized that even though I have every possible business system in place, I've left an important one completely out—making disciples." With that in mind, he has begun the process of bringing Jesus-followers around Him and forming them into His character, ways, and mission.

- *Environment, Agriculture & Zoology:* I've been having some conversations with a network of godly veterinarians who serve as short-term and long-term missionaries. They do a great service to people locally and globally by tending to the wellness of their animals. This group is taking seriously the need to disciple veterinarians who deliberately pass on God's ways to the next generation of Jesus-followers in their domain.

- *Education & Students:* Imagine university students catching a vision for creating a disciple-making community on campus that leaves a multi-decade disciple-making legacy in place when they graduate! It's fun to watch what happens when this age group catches the disciple-making fire!

- *Missions:* I've had the privilege of receiving reports from long-time friends who are actively engaged in establishing disciple-making among tribal people. They are accomplishing this task through discipling indigenous leaders who are, in turn, growing multipliable disciple-making communities.

- *Arts, Entertainment & Sports:* I'm seeing more and more people in arts and entertainment catching a disciple-making vision. I know of disciple-making communities being established on tour buses, among managers and artists/entertainers, and with entire bands. I have also seen disciple-making taking place among coaches, athletes, and entire ball teams.

- *Nonprofits & Service Organizations:* I have the privilege of regularly interacting with a wonderful nonprofit organization that makes the discipling of its disaster relief teams a priority. Because of these efforts, I see their reservists better equipped spiritually, mentally, and emotionally to serve those in desperate need.

- *Peoples:* Dr. John Perkins, a champion of reconciliation and justice, has said, "I really believe that we should live our life out in a shepherding relationship throughout our lives. Taking 2 Timothy 2:2 real serious, 'That what you've heard from me, that commit unto faithful people.'"[1] At his urging, many have committed to make a difference over the next decade through deliberately discipling the young African-American man. Satan has put up such a fight for them for so long! From where I sit, the Lord Jesus must have some pretty special plans for them to change the world!

In Cities and Counties

Based in a large city, a local Christian Chamber of Commerce has looked to bless and serve the five-county area where its members all live and serve. Not long ago, some of the key leaders approached me to brainstorm with them how they might use the Dozen Domain concept as a way to organize chamber members for the purpose of disciple-making and serving their community. I'm looking forward to seeing the impact resulting from its deliberate efforts, both in its members' lives and in the community.

In a county of several million people, a pastor is praying through plans to challenge and equip pastors in all thirty-some towns within the county to make disciple-makers. As he does so, he's considering the use of the Dozen Domains as a county-wide framework and rallying point for disciples to team together to serve and bless their county.

Online Disciple-Making Communities

Multiple disciple-making communities are being established online and they are thriving. These communities enable disciple-making to happen with relative ease, extending our reach past any one geographical · location. By seeing and communicating with each other online we can disciple others who live across the country or globe, while implementing all of the elements from our Matthew Pattern. No one with access to a computer is out of reach.

Lionshare, the organization that I have the privilege of leading, has been using this online method effectively for several years now. In doing so, we use material from *A Discipleship Journey (ADJ)*, containing both video and written content. Imagine a group of six people— one from Mississippi and one from Michigan, two from Ohio, another from Washington DC, and two more from Tennessee—all who commit to a discipling relationship over a period of one year. The glue here is the disciple-maker who knows each of the participants. Following an initial relationship-building retreat in Nashville, each one commits to watch a 12-15 minute video and dig into the Scriptures via their *ADJ* manuals for a total of about 90 minutes each week. Every other week, they gather together online where they see one another and discuss their takeaways and the obedience points highlighted by the Holy Spirit. Additionally, the disciple-maker spends time with each of them individually, applying the truths they are learning to their unique worlds.

Currently, we are using our *ADJ* online resource and mobile app to come alongside the disciple-making purposes of various groups in multiple denominations and domains that serve and impact others around the globe.

Pre-Discipleship

Although discipleship usually has more to do with followers of Jesus pouring into other followers, we often are presented with opportunities of "pre-discipleship." Born out of genuine friendship, Jesus followers can express and pass on His character, ways and mission in the midst of walking real life with their "not-yet-follower friends." I've experienced the impact of this personally as I walked with a friend who had a common interest in the Minnesota Vikings. Mostly through football seasons, we built a meaningful friendship. After several years, my friend would ask my advice about how to handle things with his life and career, allowing me to teach him some of Jesus' ways. He also joined my family for Thanksgiving and participated in some of our important family events. One day, after eight years, he asked me how to follow Jesus. My "pre-discipleship" provided groundwork for him as he entered the kingdom.

Obviously, these are just a sampling of the kinds of disciple-making communities currently being cultivated. Was the Holy Spirit prompting your heart and mind as you were reading? What kinds of ideas might work effectively in your setting?

The Church as Disciple-Making Hub

Consider what Bill Hull has to say about the centrality of disciple-making in the church: "Discipleship isn't a program or an event; it's a way of life. It's not for a limited time, but for our whole life. Discipleship isn't for beginners alone; it's for all believers for every day of their life. Discipleship isn't just one of the things the church does; it is what the church does. A commitment to be and make disciples must be the central act of every disciple and every church."[2]

For quite some time now I've had the joy of interacting with numerous pastors, churches, and denominational leaders about this matter of disciple-making. I find it remarkable how the Holy Spirit is leading and guiding across the body of Christ as many are discovering afresh this commission of Jesus and are aligning themselves—and those they lead—to it. I have participated in many conversations locally, regionally, nationally, and globally with those who are recognizing the sound of Jesus wooing His beloved church back to His disciple-making mandate.

The current interest in disciple-making does not appear to me to be the latest fad, but a blend of the Holy Spirit's conviction and the pursuit of godly leaders. They are acting on a sincere desire to repair rotting foundations, muscle-up spiritually thin churches, and return to obeying Jesus' command to reproduce. From my vantage point, this movement toward disciple-making is absolutely essential for the health, role, and existence of Jesus' Bride on Earth.

I believe the local church should serve as a "disciple-making hub" for the reproducing of disciples. We desperately need a disciple-making revival in the local church! Imagine the transformation if every Jesus follower in your church experiences being discipled and then reproduces several disciples every year who in turn become disciple-makers!

Consider the impact if you rally your church members around Dozen Domain Teams that could disciple others in their domains and strategically serve and bless their city! Your church could serve as a launching pad for disciple-making teams into society and throughout world. The possibilities are endless! They are left for you to discover as you and Jesus daydream together in times of fellowship and prayer!

Please don't mishear me. I am *not* talking about "discipling" people to be at a certain place on a certain day of the week. Nor do I mean to shape them around our pet doctrinal themes and preferred methodologies, or to encourage them to carry on programs that the Holy Spirit has been trying to shut down for quite some time. I am talking about a prayed through, thought out, leaders-in-unity game plan to deliberately reproduce the character, ways, and mission of Jesus in every person in your church, expecting them to multiply the same in others!

With that said, there are three questions I like to ask pastors and church members to help them gain a reality check about where their churches currently stand on the disciple-making front. How would your church family answer these simple "yes" or "no" questions?

- *Does your church currently have a deliberate game plan in place to obey the command of Jesus to make disciples?*

- *Are your current members actively engaged in making disciple-makers?*

- *Do you have a scripturally sound, proven, and practical resource to aid you in the disciple-making process?*

What did you just discover? If you're like the vast majority I talk with, then you're probably among the 80% or so that answered "no" to all three questions. As you well know, until you clearly understand where you are, you won't be able to get to where you want to go. The great news here is you don't have to remain where you currently are! You can fully embrace Jesus' disciple-making blueprint and move forward into a brand new day!

Impart—Implement—Invest

When I have the opportunity to speak to a new group of people about disciple-making, I will often ask the leader, pastor, or facilitator ahead of time to help me understand where they are in their disciple-making journeys. I want to know where they are currently so we can "move the disciple-making ball down the field" together. Once I find where the church or group of people stands, I know where to begin the three-fold process:

- *Imparting vision*
- *Implementing disciple-making*
- *Investing in the domains*

Let me briefly describe each of these to you. As I walk you through them, I would ask you to consider prayerfully where you are and where the church/community you're a part of is currently. I know that understanding this process can be very helpful as you and your group move toward embracing Jesus' disciple-making mandate.

I begin by *imparting vision* to those who don't yet see or grasp the Jesus blueprint. I share with them about the value and central role that Jesus intends for disciple-making to play in our lives and churches, according to the Scriptures. It still surprises me to see many people who've never even had this command of Jesus on their radars! Some may understand the concept of disciple-making but have not walked in obedience to it. Or they've never been discipled so they don't know how to go about it. When the majority of the people I'll be addressing lack vision, I'll do my best to build some relational bridges with them and then, with passion and compassion, trust Jesus to use me to help them see it for themselves. As I speak and pray with them, I'm looking in their eyes for the "I've got it!" moments, which often leads to repentance and a fresh alignment to obeying Jesus in this area of their lives.

If I know that I am speaking to a group that has already caught Jesus' vision of making disciples, then I can focus on *implementing disciple-making* so they can become disciple-makers who are effective and fruitful. While speaking, I do my best to make things very practical, reminding them all along that Jesus' blueprint is about reproducing disciple-makers, not just making a disciple. I help them understand what it means to reproduce the character, ways, and mission of Jesus in those God brings around them. We dive in to the disciple-making expressions

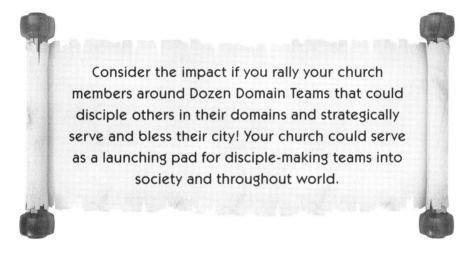

Consider the impact if you rally your church members around Dozen Domain Teams that could disciple others in their domains and strategically serve and bless their city! Your church could serve as a launching pad for disciple-making teams into society and throughout world.

of *foundational discipling* for newbies in Jesus (first 6–12 weeks) and how to implement and apply a *formational framework* for every Jesus follower. We also help them discern who Jesus might have them disciple, while answering many of the "what do I do" and "how do I do it" questions (more on these fronts in the next chapter).

Should vision already be imparted and implentation be in full swing, I focus on *investing in the domains*. I introduce them to domain discipleship, which is shaping disciples around key scriptural truths and principles that specifically relate to leading and serving in their domain. As we've already considered, each domain is rooted in the character of God, and He desires to reveal the wonder and workability of His ways within them. But it takes people who've been discipled to do so!

So, where are you personally? I hope, through this book, that you're becoming envisioned with the blueprint of Jesus. Maybe, you see your need to be discipled or to implement disciple-making in your context. Or, possibly, you've been making disciple-makers for awhile already, and investing more intentionally within your domain is your new place of growth!

What about your church, the community of Jesus followers that you're a part of? Do they carry Jesus' blueprint vision? Are they in need of practical help to implement disciple-making? Perhaps they've been reproducing disciple-makers for years and now's its time to explore how to invest in and impact the domains through making disciples?

As you can see, finding answers to questions about imparting, implementing, and investing gives you a way to assess a person or group and to know where to begin to lead in the discipleship process. You will find that any group of people usually has a mix of all three components in it. Find where the majority is and begin to move forward from there. You can always point to those that are further along as examples for others to follow.

A Brief Word for Church-Planters

Church-planters, you have the freedom to cultivate a disciple-making community from the ground floor like no one else, so take full advantage of it! Make it simple: love Jesus; love your neighbor; make disciples. That's it!

If you reproduce the character, ways, and mission of Jesus, you're connecting people directly to Him. This is where it gets wonderfully dangerous! Those you lead on this path will start looking like, acting like, and having attitudes like Jesus. They'll actually obey what He asks them to do and people's lives will be eternally touched—removing your anxiety of having to "think up" how to reach your city! What's also nice is everyone will know what to do with new people: love Jesus; love them as neighbors; make them disciples! Sow this principle in them from day one and watch what God will do. No excuses, church-planters. Don't ever make this about numbers; it's always about making disciple-makers! Healthy things naturally multiply—God made it that way. Sow the right things and the fruit will be harvested in due season!

Am I saying that it is easy? No! Whenever you set your heart and mind to make disciples you will have to contend every step of the way. It's Jesus' will, so Satan will attempt to undermine it, dissuade you, discourage you, and distract you. Even though he'll attempt to throw all kinds of obstacles at you, stand convinced and committed, trusting the weight of His authority ("All authority in heaven and earth has been given to me, therefore go and make disciples"—Matthew 28:18–19) and His presence ("I am with you always"—Matthew 28:20). God's grace and the Holy Spirit's power are well able to keep you right on target.

Transitioning to a Disciple-Making Church

As you've been reading you may have found yourself thinking, "How in the world is our church going to become a disciple-making community? Aren't we just better starting from scratch?" If so, this next section is for you!

I've had the privilege of being a part of a pastoral team in four wonderful flocks, serving in youth ministry, men's ministry, missions, equipping, and as the lead pastor. I want to share with you some principles I've learned from my journey in the local church that I believe can aid you in transitioning from where you currently are to reproducing disciple-making community. I discovered these principles through both success and failure.

Whether you're a pastor, church leader, or member, the same comments I just made to the church-planter apply to you as well. Transitioning into a disciple-making church will not be easy. If you obey Jesus, however, and follow His lead, He can do some pretty amazing things that look nearly impossible to you at this very moment!

> Watching churches attempt to transition into disciple-making communities over the years, I've come to this conclusion: If the lead pastor and leadership team don't "own" the vision of a disciple-making community, it's nearly impossible to pull off.

✳ The Primary Mission of the Leader(s)

The primary leader and leadership team of the local church must be absolutely convinced that disciple-making is the central task in the day-to-day life of the church. He must view his primary mission in the church—next to loving Jesus and his neighbor—as making disciple-makers in obedience to Jesus' command. The authority to lead a disciple-making community comes from living and modeling it in his own life first. He must fully understand that making disciple-makers is not something that simply can be delegated to the "discipleship pastor" to do. It must be the chief expression and overflow of his life and ministry.

Consider the comments from two spiritual fathers of our day on the role of the pastor in discipleship. Dr. Lloyd Ogilvie reflects, "I really think that we're all in the process of becoming what we dare to envision. And whatever the focus of that image of what we are to say, what we are to preach, and what we are to produce is very, very important. And I think the basic thrust of the ministry of the pastor and of the local church is to produce disciples. The pastor has to model it, reiterate it in every sermon with the application of how does it apply to the discipleship you're going to live out this next week?"[3]

Pastor Jack Hayford adds, "We've got to disciple pastors to disciple. That's the thing. And too many times our seminaries, our colleges, our training programs, whatever the name of the system is, doesn't do that. Pastors need to be discipled how to disciple a congregation."[4]

At this point, you may be thinking, "How did something of such importance slip through the cracks?" As a leader and/or participant in church life, you've been intentionally or unintentionally "discipled" to do things a certain way—so you've done them that way. You may have only known one way—until now. If that's you, I'd invite you to join me in repentance, receive Jesus' forgiveness, and then ask Him to do a mighty work in and through you in this area for His glory and the advancement of His kingdom.

Watching churches attempt to transition into disciple-making communities over the years, I've come to this conclusion: If the lead pastor and leadership team don't "own" the vision of a disciple-making community, it's nearly impossible to pull off. Certain segments of a church might function in disciple-making such as youth, young adults, men, or women, but disciple-making won't take hold among the whole flock.

Agreement among leaders is essential to birth a vision. God blesses unity—moving in one heart and one mind (Psalm 133). Agreement among leaders in regards to transitioning to a disciple-making community allows it to move forward successfully. I've experienced both agreement and disagreement in church leadership on this front. When leaders didn't agree the results were very limited. When they did agree the fruit tasted delicious!

If you're the primary leader, or a member of the leadership team (elder, deacon, or staff person, for example), how will you respond to what Jesus has been speaking to your heart? If you're a member of a flock where you deeply love your pastor and leaders, you can begin to praying for them to catch the vision of becoming a disciple-making hub. You can also model it within your delegated sphere of influence. You will find that once people begin to see good fruit, they want to know more!

The Role of the Holy Spirit

The Holy Spirit is absolutely essential in moving toward disciple-making. He knows your flock, so He best knows how to go about getting people's hearts on the same page. Without His empowering and enabling, your efforts won't amount to much.

As you know, you must spend a significant amount of time seeking Jesus in prayer to effect a transition that has as many ramifications as this one. As a leader or leadership team, give yourself to praying over the situation as a whole. Also, take time to seek the Lord about specifics: who, what, when, and how to do it. Follow His lead. Do what He asks you to do. I'd also encourage you to ask intercessors to pray. You might fast as you seek God, should the Holy Spirit lead you in that way.

Move forward with your first step only after you believe you've heard from the Lord together and you're in unity as a leadership team. Continue to reference this principle of prayer and agreement as you launch into different phases of transitioning to a disciple-making community. Praying, agreeing, and obeying will serve you well every step along the way!

Pioneer With a Prototype

Don't feel under any pressure to get "the whole body on board" from the start. Once all the leadership team is on board, begin the discipling process with them. At the same time, simply look for those who are most hungry to be discipled. Is it the men? The women? Could it be the youth or young adults? Small groups?

So often we focus on the percentage of people that aren't involved. Don't fall prey to that paradigm. Robert Coleman reminds us of Jesus' perspective on this: "His concern was not with programs to reach the multitudes, but with men whom the multitudes would follow."[5] Martin Luther King Jr. had this principle in mind as well when he said in one of his sermons, "An increase in quantity does not automatically bring an increase in quality. A larger membership does not necessarily represent a correspondingly increased commitment to Christ. Almost always the creative, dedicated minority has made the world better."[6]

I learned many years ago to secure the committed and build from there. I can't tell you how often that has helped me to stay faithful to what was in front of me and how it has guarded my heart from discouragement. When what you do bears good fruit, the uninvolved will come running! Don't get caught up in the numbers game. Focus on the committed few. Dawson Trotman, the founder of the Navigators, steers us right when he reminds us that, "More time with less people equals greater impact for the kingdom."[7]

Often, the most effective way to move towards a disciple-making community in church life is to pioneer a prototype—a model that you can tweak until it's most effective, fruitful, and ready to be replicated. I like the idea of a church leader selecting a dozen people or so—could be half a dozen couples—and inviting them to prayerfully consider walking together over the period of year. If they accept, tell them it is with the understanding that after nine months they'll be asked to pray about who they are to invite into a new group that they will launch when the first group finishes its yearlong journey. After the first year, the original group would multiply into six groups, with two leaders per group. After the second year, members of each of those six groups, having been discipled as leaders, would be expected to launch new groups the third year.

The pastor and church leaders either launch new groups as well or serve in a continued discipling role in the lives of those who are now leading the newly launched groups. After several rounds of multiplication, many in the church will be active either being discipled or making disciples. After three to five years of multiplying groups, you'll see a noticeable difference in reproducing disciple-makers and you'll be well on your way to becoming a true disciple-making community.

Please note that this phase is a great time to choose what disciple-making resource(s) you are going to use. You may think this isn't that important, but it really is. Whatever resource you disciple people with, in tandem with the Scriptures, is the resource they are going to feel most comfortable with in discipling others. John Tolson[8] told me that he believed that the number one reason people won't continue discipling others when they know they should is because they don't have a resource they are comfortable with. Please note this very practical wisdom that will serve you well when it comes to reproducing!

Another practical step, as you begin to multiply groups, is to seek the Lord about where they are to be launched. Are they to start a group where they are already serving within the church or within another area of ministry within the church? In their neighborhood? Or, might they launch a disciple-making group where they serve within the Dozen Domains? The sky is the limit, and obedience to Jesus is the key!

Foster a Disciple-Making Culture

I know that changing a church culture requires time and intentional action. Somewhere along the way I learned that if 15% of a group gets on board with a vision or project, that number could influence the group as a whole. I have seen that building relationships, not programs, leads to disciple-making, and once relationships are built, disciple-making activity can spread quickly.

Here are a few suggestions on how to "seed" a disciple-making vision among a flock.

- *Prototype*—We've looked at this one already.
- *Teach*—Take a couple of months and lay the foundations and framework from the Scriptures on disciple-making. Teach about Jesus and the twelve, and the disciples in Acts. Let people marinate in it, giving them time to think about it and

ask questions. Answer for them the "why" question as well as the "what" and "how." Help them envision the next practical steps of participation and be ready to engage their questions as they walk those out.

- *Small Groups*—Launch disciple-making within in the context of small groups. You can do it with a few or have every small group in your church community do it at the same time. I've seen it work both ways. Jesus will give you wisdom on which way to go.

- *Questions*—Questions open a door for answers to be given, and they also help you understand where people are coming from and what they really need to know. Make sure you're creating an environment where there's freedom to ask questions.

- *Credible People*—Ask credible people who are excited about the disciple-making vision to serve as mouthpieces for it.

- *Share Real Life Stories*—Provide time and opportunities for those whose lives have been deeply impacted and transformed to share their stories. These people inspire those who identify with them.

- *Honoring*—Another way to further disciple-making is to consider publicly honoring people along the way. Some people will value being honored and others will honor the value of disciple-making.

When moving a church toward a disciple-making culture, it's good to build various layers of discipling into the process from the beginning. I find these four layers to be helpful:

1. *Foundational*—Discipling the brand new Jesus-follower for the first 6–12 weeks of their new walk.

2. *Formational*—Deliberately building a scripturally sound spiritual framework within the lives of Jesus-followers that they can reference, add to, and reproduce in others throughout the rest of their lives.

3. *Needs/Interests/Gifts/Domains*—Once someone has been discipled in a foundational and formational framework and is now a reproducing disciple-maker, they will desire to be equipped further based on needs ("I'm a single dad with a teenage daughter—help!"), interests ("I really want to learn more about the book of Esther), gifts ("I have a gift of mercy, what do I do with it?"), and domains ("How do I reflect God's character, ways and mission where He's appointed me to serve in society?").

4. *Leadership*—There should be an intentional plan to disciple the up and coming leaders and to take current leaders to the next level. Each pastor, elder, and leader should pray for and invest in someone who can eventually take his place. Don't let insecurities based on position keep you from doing this kind of discipling. God will never "bench" anyone who constantly reproduces His character, ways, and mission in others!

> You cannot force people to participate in disciple-making. But you can make it so attractive by the transformed lives they see that they can't help but want to be a part of it!

Moving Forward While Aiming to Win Hearts

Identify and engage your key players (usually around 2–3% of your church) and your early adopters (12–13%). These become your first generation disciple-makers. Pay attention to your early majority (34%) and get them connected as they step up. If you reach the point where these three groups are on board, you are well on your way to becoming a disciple-making community. Late adapters (34%) may eventually join, after disciple-making has been "proven" while the remaining (16%) may or may not bring up the rear.[9]

Solicit your people to pray regularly and actively for God's activity in the church as you obey His commission to make disciples. Be aware when you make this transition that people will react out of fear, insecurity, self-interests, differing opinions, and loss of control. Continue to move forward graciously, doing your best to win hearts as you go.

Remain open to suggestions throughout the process. Remember, if you don't give people time to own this vision with their hearts, they'll become your greatest obstacles when it comes time to implementing it.

Make sure you build in the "reproducing DNA" right from the very beginning. It's essential that your first disciples and groups reproduce. Otherwise, you'll be fighting an uphill battle.

You cannot force people to participate in disciple-making. But you can make it so attractive by the transformed lives they see that they can't help but want to be a part of it!

Be prepared for bumps in the road. Persevere, and continue to respond to people with great grace and a desire to include them.

Find disciple-makers to disciple you in this area as you attempt to transition.

Finally, slow and steady wins the race. Remember, you are making a significant "generational turn," so it will take time.

Getting Started

As you begin to prayerfully consider cultivating disciple-making communities within your world, there's one other thing we need to look at together before we wrap-up: gaining some practical wisdom on the "what do I do's" and "how do I do it's" of making disciple-makers!

THE JESUS BLUEPRINT : PART THREE

Making Disciple-Makers

"Christianity without discipleship is always Christianity without Christ" *(Dietrich Bonheoffer).*[1]

Have you considered what the future could look like if followers of Jesus committed themselves to obey the command of Jesus to reproduce disciple-makers? Can you imagine how differently the church would look and function if next to loving Jesus and our neighbors we all made making disciple-makers a primary focus? Here are some things we stand to gain:

- We'd be obeying what Jesus actually asked us to do, giving the Great Commission the thrust He intended for it to have.

- There would likely be less self and more selflessness.

- More humility, less pride.

- Squabbles of insignificance giving way to everyone maintaining oneness of heart and mind.

- New expressions launched from obedience born out of prayer, versus brainstorming sessions that result in rallying people to something that Jesus never initiated.

- An unending supply of spiritually maturing and trustworthy people desiring to serve and lead.

- Every Jesus-follower discipled and making disciples as the new norm.

- God's presence tangibly experienced and transforming lives as His character, ways, and mission are fully embraced and engaged.

- Our ambitions becoming more about Jesus being satisfied and glorified instead of each one trying to find his own fulfillment.

- A watching world being drawn to the person of Jesus.

- The ongoing multiplication of generations of disciple-makers.

Imagine the impact if disciple-makers had the opportunity to serve in roles of leadership in society:

- Strong marriages and wise parenting resulting in greater health and wholeness for families.

- Leaders of nations skillfully are leading out of godly character and wisdom for the common good, ensuring an environment where their people have opportunities to flourish in every way.

- An educational system that honors teachers and equips students to serve the current and future needs of society.

- A media culture revolving around the communication of stories and truth rather than the slanting of information for political/personal gain.

- Artists, entertainers, and sports figures that inspire, instruct,

THE JESUS BLUEPRINT : PART THREE

and uplift, both in their performances and through their godly lives.

- Businesses that create goods and services that put people to work, cultivating a healthy economy while reproducing godly entrepreneurs and managers to benefit those they lead and influence.

- Scientific discoveries and technological tools that solve real problems and benefit people worldwide.

- Health services that provide quality patient care physically, mentally, and emotionally at a fair rate.

- God's creation stewarded for the benefit of those currently residing on the planet and preserved for future generations.

- Volunteer passions ignited, and people overjoyed to use their gifts and skills to extend mercy, hope, and justice both locally and globally.

- God's love for diversity reaffirmed (He created it!) and the lives of distinct groupings of people enhanced through acts of service and training.

Dave Buehring for President

The *end* of disciple-making is one who reproduces the character, ways, and mission of Jesus in others. The *effects* of a discipled life, however, should extend to blessing and bettering those in the world around us.

Words and Deeds

In light of a discipled life being a bearer of transformation, let's look for a moment at the *words* and *deeds* of Jesus. In Matthew 5:13–16 Jesus said to His disciples, "You are the salt of the earth, but if salt has lost its taste, how shall its saltiness be restored? It is no longer good for anything except to be thrown out and trampled under people's feet. You are the light of the world. A city set on a hill cannot be hidden. Nor do people light a lamp and put it under a basket, but on a stand, and it gives light to all in the house. In the same way, *let your light shine before others, so that they may see your good works and give glory to your Father who is in heaven.*"

Light provides guidance, helping people see what they may not have been able to see on their own. As light bearers, we are like beams from a lighthouse, pointing to safe passage. Salt, among other things, counteracts corruption. Where pride, selfishness, greed, control, and exploitation abound we are to be a neutralizing agent that seeks grace, truth, justice, and mercy while meeting the real needs of people, enhancing their lives.

People tend to view God differently when they witness disciples doing good works. Many people are stuck in the way they view God. Often, they carry an image of God that is vastly different from Who He really is! This image has often been distorted by the sin and difficulties of life and disfigured by the devil himself. It may have come through years of experiencing an angry father or one who abandoned them, a teacher or coach who spewed harsh words, or a "Christian" whose actions fell far short of reflecting God's character and ways. Before anybody with that kind of marred God-image is open to hearing about Him, he first needs to experience His love, kindness, and goodness towards him.

As it relates to Jesus' deeds, Acts 10:37–38 tells us: "...you yourselves know what happened throughout all Judea, beginning from Galilee after the baptism that John proclaimed: how God anointed Jesus of Nazareth with the Holy Spirit and with power. *He went about doing good* and healing all who were oppressed by the devil, for God was with him."

THE JESUS BLUEPRINT : PART THREE

Jesus went about doing good, and He told His disciples to do the same! Jesus equipped people and pointed them towards their God-given destinies. He fed the hungry. He offered freedom to those who found themselves stuck and oppressed by the devil. He restored a son to a widow by raising him from the dead. He intervened on a woman's behalf when she could have been stoned. On and on it goes. Through loving, teaching, forgiving, serving, healing, meeting human needs and setting free—Jesus went about doing good!

It doesn't stop with Jesus, it includes us as His followers. Ephesians 2:10 states, "For we are his workmanship, created in Christ Jesus for good works, which God prepared beforehand, that we should walk in them." As His disciples, we are to reveal our Father in heaven through our good deeds—which He has prepared in advance for us to do!

Based on our God-given measures of capacity and influence, each of us is strategically positioned to serve and bless others. I can't even begin to tell you how often I have been on the receiving end of such blessings. My very real needs have been met, and I have been blessed in ways I have never expected as people have shared their experience, wisdom, expertise, resources, and relationships. Even as I have been writing this book, several friends have opened up their homes and cabins to provide me with a quiet and reflective place to write. Their "doing good" in Jesus' name came at just the right time for me, and the result is what you are reading right now!

Over the last several years I have established some practical reference points to gauge our effect on the world around us. I've been asking: *"Is Jesus being glorified and are people being honored and served?"* By the way we are living and leading are we helping people to see what Jesus is really like? Is *His reputation* being enhanced or blemished by how we who carry His name are relating to those around us? Are the people in our lives being treated honorably because of their unique blood-of-Jesus-shed-for-them eternal value? And, are their real needs really being met? The fruit of a discipled life should be real transformation—first, in our lives and then in those around us.

Now, to accomplish this we must become effective disciple-makers. Because we tend to multiply what's been modeled to us, each of us has a little different perspective on what making disciple-makers looks like. You might already be an excellent disciple-maker so this may be old hat to you. However, for the rest, I trust this will get you practically thinking and moving towards obeying Jesus' disciple-making command.

Making Disciple-Makers Practical

Our aim in disciple-making must always be life transformation, not just the passing on of information. We want to allow Jesus' character, ways and mission to "rub off" on the lives of others, life-on-life. I like the way Greg Ogden describes this process: "The only way for Jesus to grow flawed and faithless common people into mature disciples and make sure that His kingdom would transcend His earthly ministry was to have a core who knew in depth His person and mission. His life and mission needed to be internalized in the lives of the disciples. The way to ensure that they internalized his mission was through 'purposeful proximity.'"[2]

Foundational & Formational Disciple-Making

As we dive into some of the practical content that needs to be applied in the lives of disciples, I want to begin by reminding us of our working definition of disciple-making: *reproducing the character, ways and*

234

mission of Jesus in those God brings around us, expecting them to multiply the same in others. This reflects His kingdom: revealing the character of its King; demonstrating the wisdom of His ways; and fulfilling His mission of reconciling the lost and discipling the nations.

Regardless of nationality, gender, or experience, *every follower of Jesus* needs to be grounded in truths that will enable him to walk closely with the Lord Jesus and relate well with the world around them. Imagine if every follower of Jesus in business was discipled around humility and servanthood, every artist and athlete walked in obedience to Jesus, and everyone serving within agriculture learned to hear God's voice! What if government leaders feared God above all else, educators reflected God's ways, and leaders of families revealed the character of God to their children by the way they lived their lives! If every Jesus follower were to walk in the truths attached to foundational and formational disciple-making, it would benefit him and others no matter where he served in society.

Core Discipleship: Foundational

I want you to think with me about two stages of core discipleship. The first expression occurs in the initial 6–12 weeks after someone commits to follow Jesus. I have found that we often leave new followers in a real place of vulnerability unless we help them get connected fairly quickly with other followers. Not only must they get connected, but they also need a follower who is further along that will help them lay foundations that they can build on for the rest of their lives.

My friend, Grant Edwards, a pastor and fruitful foundational disciple-maker, has found that new Jesus followers need to be immediately grounded in four foundational disciplines: *prayer, Bible study, fellowship, evangelism, and discipleship.* Along with learning these disciplines, he believes they need to learn to overcome temptation patterns that are familiar to most new Christians. He has developed a one-on-one discipleship model for new followers focusing on the first three months of one's new walk with Jesus. Grant and his team have seen good fruit in their own church from this methodical approach and have used it to help many other churches in the foundational disciple-making phase.[3]

LeRoy Eims reinforces this approach when he says, "Disciples cannot be mass produced. We cannot drop people into a program and see disciples emerge at the end of the production line. It takes time to make disciples. It takes individual personal attention."[4]

Looking back at my own life, I realize that having a season of laying a foundation in my early teens allowed me to better receive the spiritual input and investment that followed. I have noticed that a good foundation provides a solid base for building a spiritually mature disciple of Jesus. Without it, I have seen followers of Jesus struggle. When new followers are engaged in laying a healthy foundation early in their walk with Jesus, it fosters in them the godly expectation of a lifetime of learning as disciples. It is the kind of investment that will serve them well for the rest of their lives.

When we are not deliberate in helping to lay solid foundations for new followers we are irresponsible. And, there's even more at stake. It is not only that a new follower's lifetime discipleship journey could start off on the wrong foot. His entire walk with Jesus hangs in the balance. Coleman says, "Clearly the policy of Jesus at this point teaches us that whatever method of follow-up the church adopts, it must have as its basis a personal guardian concern for those entrusted to their care. *To do otherwise is essentially to abandon new believers to the devil.* This means that some system must be found whereby every convert is given a Christian friend to follow until such time as he or she can lead another."[5]

Where we have not embraced disciple-making as a primary focus in our churches, we have seen people quickly drifting away. Or, we have produced new converts, but not mature disciples. To see a preferable outcome we must immediately go to work to shore up this phase of disciple-making.

Core Discipleship: A Formational Framework

When building a home or any building, a foundation is essential. Without one, nothing lasting takes shape. No foundation exists, however, for the sake of leaving it as a slab of cement. It's meant to be built upon! A foundation works the same way in discipleship-making. Once the first 6–12 weeks foundation is laid, it's time for the next stage of core discipleship, which I'll refer to as a *formational framework*.

The Scriptures teach that God desires to conform us to the image of Jesus (Romans 8:29) that we might reflect His character, ways, and mission. This process, of course, requires a lifetime. Nevertheless, as with laying a good foundation, providing a *formational framework* that allows one to deliberately and effectively build on that foundation is equally necessary.

As we've already seen, the pattern of Jesus' discipling included: truth taught, demonstrated, and replicated; a context of relationships in community; real life application expressed in obedience to

---

237

Him; and an expectation that what's passed on will be reproduced in others.

In my reading of the Scriptures over the years, I've observed the disciple-making of Jesus throughout the Gospels, and His disciples in the Book of Acts. I've gleaned from the body of teaching in the Old Testament and from the letters of the New Testament. In doing so, I began to make some determinations about the formational body of truth I was to pass on to those God was bringing around me to disciple. I have come to believe there is a *formational framework* that needs to be at the core of every Jesus follower. Not only does this grow new followers, but it also provides a framework for their spiritual development for the rest of their lives! It equips them with what they need to become effective and fruitful disciple-makers!

I've used the following *formational framework* for three decades to aid people in their discipleship journeys and to equip them as disciple-makers. As I've learned over the years I've added and adjusted—and will do so for the rest of my life. *Scripture is the source; the character, ways, and mission of Jesus are the focal point; the Holy Spirit is the Guide and Transformer; and the application of truth through obedience to Jesus is the engine of transformation.*

Knowing God

> *"Thus says the Lord: 'Let not the wise man boast in his wisdom, let not the mighty man boast in his might, let not the rich man boast in his riches, but let him who boasts boast in this, that he understands and knows me, that I am the Lord who practices steadfast love, justice, and righteous-*

THE JESUS BLUEPRINT : PART THREE

ness in the earth. For in these things I delight, declares
the Lord.'"

— JEREMIAH 9:23–24

Who is God? He is not like the limited image that we conjure up in our minds or the contorted image the devil has tried to frame for us. What is He really like and how do we come to know Him? Throughout the Scriptures God unveils Himself to us through His names, titles, and attributes. Jesus revealed what He is really like to His disciples. He reveals who He is and what He's like through His ways, His works, and His words. His desire is that we know and experience Him in our daily lives.

By helping disciples explore God's nature and character, my aim is to provide the framework for ongoing encounters with God that leads to intimate friendship with Him. By sharing with them 52 attributes of His character—taking one a week over a period of an entire year—I teach them to renew their minds through scripture while allowing God to show them what He's really like. *We must constantly be renewing our minds.*

A Call to Discipleship

> *"And calling the crowd to him with his disciples, he said to them, 'If anyone would come after me, let him deny himself and take up his cross and follow me. For whoever would save his life will lose it, but whoever loses his life for my sake and the gospel's will save it. For what does it profit a man to gain the whole world and forfeit his soul'?"*

— MARK 8:34–36

A disciple of Jesus is not somebody who merely believes in Jesus, goes to church, or does good things. A disciple is someone who voluntarily places himself under the Lordship of Jesus Christ. By doing so, a disciple's character and ways begin to conform to those of Jesus, and he begins to understand and move toward His world-changing mission. A disciple allows other followers who are further along to walk alongside him, to challenge, equip, and encourage him in the things of God, and to be formed more effectively into His image.

My focus here is to reaffirm and establish disciples in their commitment to follow Jesus with their whole hearts and lives. I help them understand the conditions, cost, characteristics, and cause of the disciple, and encourage them to allow Jesus to mold them around seven life altering godly qualities: love, forgiveness, humility, brokenness (God's process of forming a yielded heart), obedience to Jesus, servanthood, and the Fear of the Lord.

The Grace of God

"For by grace you have been saved through faith. And this is not your own doing; it is the gift of God, not a result of works, so that no one may boast."
— EPHESIANS 2:8–9

The grace of God is evident throughout the Scriptures. It is displayed through God's everlasting love in the Old Testament and repeated in the writings of Paul in the New Testament. Jesus came "full of grace and truth," according to John 1:14–17. He modeled for us what a grace-filled life looks like, how it expresses itself to those we relate to, and how it empowers us to fulfill God's purposes.

Teaching about grace offers an opportunity for disciples to allow the Holy Spirit to remove any legalism, dislodge "stuck places" (strongholds) and uproot lies in how they see themselves and the world around them. As the Holy Spirit begins to reveal these places in disciples' lives, truth from the Scriptures pours in. They come to understand who they are "in Christ," and His heart for them as a heavenly Father. Grace is also revealed as His enabling power to change their hearts, helping them to live godly lives that fulfill His purposes.

The Cross, Sin & Repentance

> *"...We implore you on behalf of Christ, be reconciled to God. For our sake he made him to be sin who knew no sin, so that in him we might become the righteousness of God."*
>
> — 2 Corinthians 5:20–21

The cross has been the symbol of Jesus followers for centuries, but the full ramification of His death for our lives is often drastically unappreciated. Through His shed blood we have been completely reconciled to a holy God. Our sins have been forgiven and the power of Satan has been broken over our lives. Because of the cross, it is fully possible to reconcile relationships and walk in like-heartedness with others.

Walking alongside a disciple as he grasps the nature, progression, and real consequences of sin from a biblical perspective allows him to understand more clearly the depths and richness of the cross of Jesus and the meaning of the Atonement. As a godly heart response to the cross, I explain to him the biblical foundations of repentance and forgiveness, which are practical gateways to freedom.

Hearing the Voice of God

> *"...The sheep hear his voice, and he calls his own sheep by name and leads them out. When he has brought out all his*

CHAPTER TEN : Making Disciple-Makers

own, he goes before them, and the sheep follow him, for they know his voice."

✟ — John 10:3–4

In the Book of Acts we observe various ways God spoke to, led, and guided Paul. He had been trained in the Scriptures. He then encountered the audible voice of Jesus on the road to Damascus. Next he heard His words through a man named Ananias. Later, when in the place of worship and fasting with other leaders, Paul heard the Holy Spirit speak about his next step of obedience. While on one of his missionary journeys, he sensed the Holy Spirit leading him to avoid one place, and then, in a vision, He clearly led Paul to another place. On his way to Jerusalem, Paul received prophetic words, and later, on a ship, an angel appeared to him with a message from God.

Many ask me, "How do I hear from God?" As one who continues to grow in this area myself, I pass along what I'm learning in my own walk with Jesus. I share with disciples the purposes of hearing from God, His promises of guidance and how He led people throughout the Scriptures. I want them to understand that cultivating a hearing heart is important for them and to learn some of the ways God speaks: through Scripture; through the leading of the Holy Spirit; through an inner peace; through circumstances; through other people and leaders in our lives; by waiting on Him in prayer; and by supernatural means.

The Disciple's Disciplines

"Share in suffering as a good soldier of Christ Jesus. No soldier gets entangled in civilian pursuits, since his aim is to please the one who enlisted him. An athlete is not

crowned unless he competes according to the rules. It is the hard-working farmer who ought to have the first share of the crops. Think over what I say, for the Lord will give you understanding in everything."

— 2 Timothy 2:3–7

Olympic athletes compete against the world's best to prove they're champions. But no one is born competing on an Olympic level! These athletes develop their skills over many years, honing them through hours of hard work with the world's best coaches. Becoming masters of discipline, they forsake some of life's enjoyments in the short-term so that they might ultimately receive the prize they've set their sites on—a gold medal.

To walk as a disciple of Jesus is no less daunting. It, too, requires commitment, sacrifice, and endurance. To resist the onslaught of the flesh, the devil's lures, and the temptations presented by others—and to develop strength in our inner man—we must embrace and exercise godly disciplines. I encourage disciples to develop godly disciplines through regular times in the Scriptures (reading, reflecting, memorizing, studying), worship, prayer, waiting on God and the giving of our time, resources and gifts for the sake of the kingdom.

Relationships

"A new commandment I give to you, that you love one another: just as I have loved you, you also are to love one another. By this all people will know that you are my disciples, if you have love for one another."

— John 13:34–35

God pursues relationships with man. He is a relator—the ultimate relator! Even before creation God was relating within the Trinity. Relation-

CHAPTER TEN : Making Disciple-Makers

ship is an expression of the Godhead—it exists at the core of who He is and what He values most. In light of who God is, followers of Jesus should be the best relators on the planet—reflecting Him! We must relate well with others. Outside of relating with God, nothing is as important.

All of us come into the kingdom with relational baggage. When discipling in the area, I like to start with principles for godly and healthy relationships out of Romans 12, and teach how to maintain peace and oneness out of Ephesians 4. I think it is vital to impart truth about relationships within family life—the role of a husband and wife, parents and their children—from a biblical perspective. I also teach disciples how to walk under authority in a godly manner, and how to properly appeal to authority in a way that honors the Lord.

Spiritual Warfare

We must know our enemy to fight successfully

"Behold, I have given you authority to tread on serpents and scorpions, and over all the power of the enemy, and nothing shall hurt you."

— LUKE 10:19

When we give our lives to Jesus we are enlisted in an ongoing battle of spiritual warfare. We have an enemy—the very same enemy that opposes the God we love and serve. Satan exists as surely as you and I, and he preys upon those from whom he can "steal, kill and destroy" (John 10:10). He aims to distort, disfigure, and defame the character and ways of God. He attempts to derail God's purposes, destroy the precious lives of those Jesus died for, and rob Gof of glory.

Disciples of Jesus must understand the truth about spiritual warfare as a part of their *formational framework*! I ask them to undertake a search of the Scriptures to gain an understanding of Satan's origin and power, and to learn about his names and titles that serve as descriptors of his character (i.e. accuser, god of this world, murderer and liar). I want them to be aware of his schemes, and embrace their authority and weaponry as spiritual warriors, in order to defeat him.

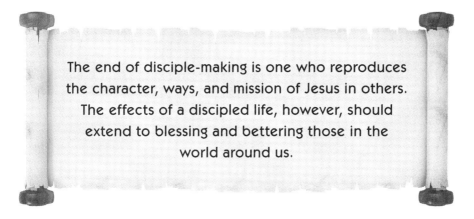

The end of disciple-making is one who reproduces the character, ways, and mission of Jesus in others. The effects of a discipled life, however, should extend to blessing and bettering those in the world around us.

The Church in Acts

"But you will receive power when the Holy Spirit has come upon you, and you will be my witnesses in Jerusalem and in all Judea and Samaria, and to the end of the earth."

— ACTS 1:8

The Book of Acts records what many would refer to as the birth of the Church. It tells of the whirlwind of 3,000 new believers being added to the 120 disciples, and details how the more seasoned followers did their best to do what Jesus taught them to do in discipling the new followers. They gathered the new recipients of God's grace together and committed themselves to relay all that Jesus had taught them. The Church, empowered by the Holy Spirit, became a hub of people where disciples were made and served as an outpost of outreach to the world around them—locally and globally.

For some, the Church is a whole new and delightful concept. For others, it's been soured by bad experiences. Either way, gaining a biblical perspective of the Church and the role of the Holy Spirit is key. The Church is people—not buildings, empty rituals or a meeting on a certain day of the week. I like the New Testament word portraits of the Church: the Body of Christ, the Building of God, the Bride of Christ, the Family of God, etc. I also like to consider the Church's mandate, messengers, message and mission. I share about the vital role of the Holy Spirit, who brings the presence, likeness and power of Jesus, into the life of the disciple, and into the Church.

Advancing the Kingdom

"And this gospel of the kingdom will be proclaimed throughout the whole world as a testimony to all nations, and then the end will come."

— MATTHEW 24:14

The kingdom of God is the central message of Jesus. He taught on it extensively until the time he ascended to heaven (Acts 1:1–3). It represents the arena where He is Lord and where His character is on full display, His ways are honored and followed, and His will is being done. Like a multifaceted gemstone, the truths of the kingdom are enormous and innumerable. The kingdom of God is to be displayed on Earth just as it is in heaven. To that end, Jesus commissioned His disciples to be carriers of His kingdom to every tribe, tongue, people, and nation.

When I disciple others in this area, I relay the huge role the message of the kingdom had in the life of Jesus. I like to bring some biblical definition to it, describe its scope and values, and reference the heartbeat of the kingdom—God being glorified. I help them translate this truth into practical ways that can help them advance His kingdom in their neighborhoods, within the Dozen Domains of society, and in the nations. I like to help disciples learn how to share the testimony of what Jesus has done in their lives and how to present the Gospel to someone. While on this topic, I also give them some tools to help them discern authentic messengers of the Gospel while exposing counterfeits.

Purpose, Passion, and Giftedness

"For you formed my inward parts; you knitted me together in my mother's womb. I praise you, for I am fearfully and wonderfully made. Wonderful are your works; My soul knows it very well."

— Psalm 139:13–14

When we were still in our mother's womb God determined our physical makeup—our gender, facial and body features, our intellect and aptitudes. He also chose our social heritage—our race, culture, language, and family. His hand was in the complete formation of our being, to the extent of redeeming the ugly effects of sin in our lives! His purpose for us is divine. He has equipped us with abilities, skills, and gifts that allow us to impact the world around us for His purposes and glory.

Disciples of Jesus need followers who are further along to walk alongside them in the discovery, development, and deployment of their unique kingdom contributions. They need to determine what they are passionate about, as it often assists them in embracing their purposes. Because God created them as whole persons, they awaken to an understanding of how Jesus may want to work through them to touch others as they identify natural abilities, acquired skills, and spiritual gifts.

Making Disciples

*"And Jesus came and said to them, 'All authority in heaven
and on earth has been given to me. Go therefore and make
disciples of all nations, baptizing them in the name of the
Father and of the Son and of the Holy Spirit, teaching them
to observe all that I have commanded you. And behold, I
am with you always, to the end of the age'."*

— MATTHEW 28:18–20

Obviously, we've already covered this terrain pretty well. We understand that each one of us has been commissioned to *reproduce the character, ways, and mission of Jesus in those God brings around us, expecting them to multiply the same in others.* As more experienced followers, we must demonstrate and model these principles, by building them into the hearts and minds of new disciples from the get-go. We must help them embrace the reality that disciple-making is the primary way of advancing, multiplying and expanding God's kingdom. It's what Jesus did. It's what He's asked us to do.

Is this *formational framework* a be-all and end-all? No, of course not. Yet, my experience tells me that approximately four out of five followers of Jesus have never been discipled with this kind of deliberate formational framework in mind! Imagine what would happen if we jumpstarted the spiritual growth process of every Jesus follower concerning these scriptural themes? I've seen the fruit of it over and over again and I've watched new disciples become primed to receive more as they continue to be formed into the image of Jesus. And, just as important, they are equipped to function as disciple-makers!

I've used this very *formational framework* to develop a resource to serve disciple-makers and their multipliable communities, called *A Dis-*

cipleship Journey. This tool facilitates a yearlong journey and is available for small groups, as an online resource, and as a mobile app. You can learn more about it by visiting www.lionshare.org.

Domain Discipleship

So, we've identified the two stages of core discipleship for every follower of Jesus: foundational and formational. There is another important facet to molding a follower of Jesus that we need to talk briefly about, something my friends and I refer to as *domain discipleship.*

Domain discipleship is specifically for those who serve within a particular domain. It is an added dimension of disciple-making in someone's life. Business people need different development than those who serve in the arts. Government leaders require input that is unique to what they do, as do those in science, the media and all the other domains of society.

Domain discipleship must be deliberate and can be done in tandem with foundational and formational discipleship. Journeying over the years with people who serve in these various domains of society, I've seen several areas where specific development can and must occur:

- *Character*
  Every domain has it's own challenges, enticements and pitfalls. As disciples of Jesus serve within a particular domain they should be aware of where they may be tested, and where they need to be strengthened in character. For example, counteracting an environment of greed will require a greater deposit of generosity. A disciple-maker functioning within an

entertainment culture where vanity, pride, and selfishness tend to flourish will need to cultivate a humble spirit.

- *Connecting*
As mentioned earlier, one of the greatest strengths of a disciple of Jesus should be the way he relates to the people around him: staff, employers, employees, partners, boards, clients, customers, vendors, members, and others. Learning to relate well builds good teams, creates cultures of mutual honor and respect, and benefits the communities, cities, countries, or continents that a domain influences.

- *Competencies*
The Scriptures clearly teach that we should offer our very best to those we serve and lead (Ephesians 6: 5–9). When doing things "unto the Lord," disciples of Jesus should take opportunities to be shaped and equipped so they can excel in serving others better at every level in their domains. This includes mastering theological and philosophical perspectives and paradigms, as well as godly principles and practices so they can lead well. As they serve where they are assigned, they honor Jesus, gain value within their organizations, and are greatly appreciated by those they work with and the world around them.

- *Commitment*
Functioning within each domain requires different layers and levels of commitment. Whether committing to a company, project, program, team or mission, a disciple's commitment will be tested. They will reap the rewards of godly character in their lives as they serve out their commitments. Disciples can benefit those they work with when the qualities of faithfulness, endurance, a stellar attitude, and a unifying spirit are evident. They can also finish well in everything they put their hands to.

So, the two stages of core discipleship represent key pieces of truth that *every disciple* needs to apply in his life. Domain discipleship equips a disciple in the principles of character, connecting, competencies, and commitment that are unique to their domain. Both kinds of deliberate discipling result in displaying greater Jesus-likeness in the life of a Jesus follower. And it provides them with what they need to reproduce the same in others.

Disciple-Maker Considerations

If you just add "making disciples" to your to-do list, or throw it in the mix with everything else you want to accomplish, you will not get it done. You must begin by taking a look at your own life. As you embrace the in-gredients Jesus used to make disciple-makers—teaching truth, community, obedience, and reproducing—you must make a deliberate choice to effectively engage in disciple-making. You might want to consider a process I've observed in walking with those who've made this choice.

Commit

Jesus taught the multitudes, but His primary thrust was investing in the twelve. He didn't allow the pull of the crowds, the opinions of the religious leaders, or the side-tracking attempts of Satan to draw Him away from making disciple-makers. What do you allow to draw you away?

One thing that I've learned after three-plus decades of disciple-making is this: Without a revelation from the Scriptures by the Holy Spirit to your heart of the centrality of Jesus' disciple-making mandate, you won't gain any real traction in your efforts to make disciple-makers! You must see it like Jesus sees it. You must comes to grips with the reality that Jesus

CHAPTER TEN : Making Disciple-Makers

did not intend for disciple-making to be optional but rather the responsibility of every follower of Jesus. You must be utterly, unreservedly, and wholeheartedly convinced.

One of the ways that you'll know that you've turned that corner is that the Holy Spirit will lead you toward both repentance and a conviction to make disciples. There will be a turning away from past ways and a turning toward Jesus out of love and a fresh desire to obey His disciple-making command.

While there, allow the Spirit of God to do a deep work in you. Like some of our Old Testament heroes, build an altar in your heart that establishes His Lordship over this area of your life. Commit yourself to obey His disciple-making mandate by applying it as a norm in your life.

To make sure we're clear, what I mean is a commitment to core discipleship and to domain discipleship in light of where God has you serving. Foundational and formational disciple-making become good soil that domain discipleship can be nurtured in.

Examine

Once you've seen it from Jesus' perspective and commit to walk the road of disciple-making obedience, the next leg of the journey is implementing this belief and conviction into your every day life.

As you know, our values are born out of our beliefs, and our priorities emerge from what we really value. So, as you embrace what you now believe about disciple-making, your new beliefs need to be applied to your value system. What you value you give your time, effort, and resources to, or, should I say, the best of your time, the best of your efforts, and the best of your resources!

Becoming one who makes disciple-makers requires changes in thinking and actions. How will this new commitment affect what you've currently been doing? How does it touch the way you view and relate to those around you? How does it affect your other commitments and your calendar? What might you need to adjust or take off your plate?

To make my point, let me offer an illustration. If you have a large glass jar, one big rock, a dozen small rocks, some sand and some water, and you're asked to get them all into the jar and then seal the lid, how do you do it? After experimenting, in the end you'll come to only one conclusion: you have to start with the big rock. If you attempt to do it any other way it just won't work. Once you get the big rock where it needs to be, everything else falls in to place just right.

When it comes to fleshing out our values and priorities, disciple-making can only really take hold in our lives if we make it the "big rock." As I've said previously, next to loving Jesus and our neighbor, disciple-making is to be our primary mission. It's what He's commissioned His followers to do, regardless of what domain He's appointed us to serve within. It means clearing the decks and prioritizing your life, calling, calendar, and relationships around it.

Identify

Once you've committed yourself to making disciple-makers, and establish it as a value and priority, it's time to start asking the "who" questions, as in, "who do I need to disciple me?" and "who should I disciple?"

CHAPTER TEN : Making Disciple-Makers

If you've never experienced foundational and/or formational disciple-making, begin to pray and look for someone who can disciple you in the truths we've looked at in this chapter. If finding someone in your church or sphere of relationships to do this task doesn't come easily, don't become discouraged. Because we've not given ourselves to deliberate generational disciple-making there is a huge void in this area. Many need discipling but there are not many disciple-makers. Keep praying and pursuing God until you find an appropriate person or disciple-making community.

A disciple-maker is somebody who is just a step or two ahead of you in an area that you need to grow in. Maybe he can't help you grow in every area but he can in a couple of them. Pray and then go to him, asking if he would be willing to help you grow. Look for ways to get with him at times that work in his schedule. It's important, once he commits to give you some of his time, that you make every effort to be where you need to be when you need to be there, honoring his time and effort.

Now, who are you to disciple? Begin by looking at your current God-given sphere of relationships: family, friends, neighbors, staff, team members, small group participants, and others. These are people Jesus has already brought in to your life. You might be thinking, "That's great, but how do I narrow this group down?" That's a good question!

Because I want to see every Jesus follower and godly domain leader shaped in the character, ways, and mission of Jesus, choosing becomes hard for me too! So, I have had to develop a bit of a grid to help me discern whom I am to invest in at any given time. I'd like to share that with you in case it may be of some help to you.

First, I like asking the question that my friend, David Shirk, once asked

THE JESUS BLUEPRINT : PART THREE

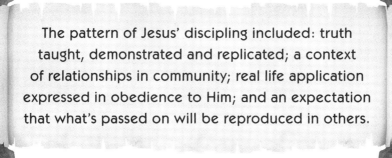

The pattern of Jesus' discipling included: truth taught, demonstrated and replicated; a context of relationships in community; real life application expressed in obedience to Him; and an expectation that what's passed on will be reproduced in others.

me: "In whose ears are your words big?" Have you noticed that with some people your words and wisdom carry the weight of a feather, while others weigh your words like gold? The latter actually listened, did what you suggested and came back for more! I've learned that when you find someone responding to your words, it's important to note that Jesus may be giving you a cue that this person is someone He desires for you to disciple and invest in. Expressions of unusual favor and receptivity help you identify God-ordained heart-links—connections of the heart that make it easy for you to give and for them to receive.

Next, I consider where a person is coming from through the qualities of faithfulness, availability, a servant's heart, and a teachable spirit. *Faithfulness* speaks of someone's character and commitment. If he says, "I'm in," I need to know that I can count on him. *Availability* tells me whether or not he is willing to carve out the time that it's going to take to be discipled. A servant's heart shows his desire to serve and invest in others, reproducing what he's being discipled in. *A teachable spirit* reveals itself in humility of heart and a willingness to obey Jesus and apply to his life what he is learning in the midst of the disciple-making process.

CHAPTER TEN : Making Disciple-Makers

The other thing I look for is whether they are willing to match my commitment. In other words, if I commit a certain amount of time and effort to invest in them are they equally committed to follow-through with what they've committed to do? If they can't, I'll still love them, pray for them, help them, and enjoy their company—but I won't disciple them. Jesus required His disciples to match His commitment so how can I do anything different?

This three-fold identification process provides me with a pool of people I can really pray about discipling. I then spend time seeking Jesus about who He is giving me the "green light" to pour into at the time. Because Jesus spent the whole night praying about who He was to disciple (Luke 6:12–16), I want to give myself to purposeful prayer about this as well. I want to spend my time where it will bear the most fruit for His kingdom purposes, and Jesus knows best who needs what He's poured into me. Sometimes my "obvious" choices are not His! Because I want to obey Him, I stay dependent on His leading and guiding in my life.

You might ask, "How many should I disciple at a time?" Everyone's experience is different. Some will tell you one-on-one is the way to go, others like groups of three, and some prefer small groups of 8–12. Jesus discipled twelve at a time. I've found that a lot depends on the disciple-maker's time and gifts, and what resources/tools are being used. In the end, it needs to be effective and fruitful in the one being discipled and done in such a way that it is easy for them to reproduce it in others.

The process I've just described is meant to facilitate formational discipleship and domain discipleship. Foundational discipleship (remember, the first 6–12 weeks) should be initiated immediately when someone has given his life to Jesus, by people trained to do so. It seems that discipling foundationally usually works better in one-on-one settings or in smaller groupings.

Multiply

Disciple-making math is not addition, it is multiplication! Because each one who is discipled also makes disciples, the increase happens in leaps and bounds. To ilustrate, consider this disciple-making multiplication table.

Imagine if you start with 50 disciple-makers each committed to disciple two people per year, who in turn, do the same. At the end of the first year you'd have 150 disciple-makers—the original 50 plus the 100 that had been discipled by them. With this in mind, look at the ramifications of disciple-making math over less than two decades:

End of Year Total Disciple-Makers

1	150	10	2,952,450
2	450	11	8,857,350
3	1,350	12	26,572,050
4	4,050	13	79,716,150
5	12,150	14	239,148,450
6	36,450	15	717,445,350
7	109,350	16	2,152,336,050
8	328,050	17	6,457,008,150
9	984,150	18	19,371,024,450

Nearly 3,000,000 disciple-makers after the first decade, beginning with only fifty committed to discipling two per year who each do the same!

CHAPTER TEN : Making Disciple-Makers

With the United Nations 2030 population estimate[6] being 8,308,895,000, we could impact the entire world through multiplying disciple-makers in under 18 years! Even after the passing of centuries, never has a man devised a better plan to impact the world than the blueprint of Jesus!

Teach—Demonstrate—Replicate

I want you to think for a moment of how often you were given something to do, yet you never fully understood it yourself. Or, how often you had to figure it out on your own because no one ever modeled if for you? Pause now for a moment and think how often you've done this same thing to others. Not only is it true that you simply pass on what you know—but you also pass along what you know in the manner you've received it!

If you recall, Jesus' game plan for passing things on and fanning the flames of disciple-maker multiplication is: *teach—demonstrate—replicate*. So, this process needs to become every disciple-maker's refrain: *teach—demonstrate—replicate*. It needs to serve as the disciple-maker's compass. If you want someone to really catch the character, ways and mission of Jesus you must *teach—demonstrate—replicate!*

Teach

Teaching is communicating a truth in such a way that the person you are discipling relates to it, understands its meaning and ramifications, and grasps how it can be applied to his life in obedience to Jesus.

Demonstrate

Demonstrate is the modeling of truth—or the the show-me-what-it-looks-like aspect of Jesus' blueprint. It's what gives the truth taught real credibility and authority—seeing it displayed before our eyes. It must be an overflow of who we are. Willard reminds us, "The people to whom we minister and speak will not recall 99 percent of what we say to them. But they will never forget the kind of persons we are."[7]

Replicate

Once disciples fully understand and see truth via teaching and demonstrating, it is their turn to replicate it in front of you. It's their opportunity to show you what they've really learned and received, and your opportunity to coach them by guiding and encouraging them.

I've been able to apply this portion of Jesus' plan as a dad, leader, pastor, disciple-maker and football coach. When coaching high school football this method became the primary one I used to help our guys grasp what it meant to be good tacklers. I had the opportunity to brush up on tackling technique by participating in an NFL/NFF Coaching Academy hosted for high school coaches by the coaching staff of our hometown Tennessee Titans.

After that experience, "hit, wrap, and drive," became a regular part of our afternoon practices. "Hit" meant placing one's facemask in the numbers of the ball carrier. "Wrap" represented the position of a tackler's arms around the ball carrier with one hand being locked around the other arm's wrist. "Drive" was used to describe the movement and momentum of the back leg thrusting forward to stop the runner in his tracks.

CHAPTER TEN : Making Disciple-Makers

When one of our defensive players was not tackling correctly I would apply the *teach—demonstrate—replicate* principle right then and there. First, I would pull him aside privately to remind and *teach* him the "hit, wrap, and drive" technique. Then, I would place a helmet on my head, instructing this big, padded, ball player not to touch me (or he'd run laps!), and I'd *demonstrate* for him how to position himself to make a tackle on the field of play. All the while, he stood and watched from the sidelines. I would then return him to his position where I would have him *replicate* what he had learned in front of me on the field of play, allowing me to guide, tweak and encourage him. It worked, and we soon became known league-wide as a tremendous tackling team. Our success in this area helped contribute to a league championship.

So, how do you pass things on? The refrain of a disciple-maker is *teach—demonstrate—replicate*. In light of this pattern, what adjustments do you need to make in the way you live, lead, and disciple?

Wrapping Up: Where Do We Go From Here?

We've covered a lot of ground together. What's most important, however, comes now. What are you going to do with what you've received from reading and reflecting through *The Jesus Blueprint*? Here are a few suggestions and encouragements to get you started.

1) Your Life

First, if you've never been deliberately discipled around the character, ways, and mission of Jesus, prayerfully consider who you might approach about discipling you. As you pray, watch for someone who is further along in his walk with the Lord that you naturally connect with and someone who is wiling to give of his time. I encourage people to seek out those whose *character* consistently reflects Jesus over time, whose manner of life is marked by *God's ways* and godly wisdom, and who references the *mission of Jesus* in all that they do.

When someone is willing to give of his time, do your very best to make time together work within his schedule. Whatever you commit to do together as a part of the discipleship process, be committed to it! Be faithful to apply what you're learning, obeying Jesus as He leads you. As you are growing be praying about who Jesus would have you disciple in the days ahead.

Now, if you're ready to make disciple-makers, review this chapter again. If you didn't do it the first time, make sure to personalize it the second time through. Pay close attention to the *Commit—Examine—Identify—Mulitply* portion. Also, as you begin to walk with others remember the disciple-maker's refrain we've just touched on, *Teach—Demonstrate—Replicate*.

Being a disciple-maker doesn't mean you've got a degree in biblical studies or that you live life perfectly. It simply means that you're willing to deliberately pass on what Jesus has taught you to those you're "one step ahead" of. By the way, make sure you stay open as Jesus often uses the ones we're discipling to pour things right back in to our lives!

2) Making Disciple-Makers Within Your Domain

Begin to pray about how you can reproduce disciples within the domain of society where Jesus has appointed you to serve. Think about it. If you don't do it, who will? Imagine the impact that can be made, over time, if you intentionally launch disciple-making communities within your domain!

The domain where you serve is part of your "metron" or measure (remember from chapter five?) assigned to you by the Lord Jesus. It's not "second best", nor can be compared to anything or anybody else. It's where Jesus desires to express Himself through you for His glory. Use that unique God-given grace for your domain to pray for and disciple Jesus followers, and to influence and bless others by walking in God's ways.

I don't know if you've noticed this before, but as Bobby Clinton has said, "like attracts like."[8] In other words, people of like gifting and calling are often drawn to one another. Ask Jesus to provide you with "disciple-making radar" that allows you to identify people you could disciple whose gifts and callings are similar to yours. Look for those who already are Jesus followers and start there. However, always keep an eye open for like-gifted people who don't yet know Jesus, and with whom He's given you favor. Begin to pour into them by serving their greatest needs and watch what Jesus will do! It may eventually lead to discipling them into His character, ways, and mission!

Just a quick word here about your disciple-making approach. Disciple-making is based on genuine relationships of love, truth, trust, and honor. Don't walk up to somebody and announce, "I am going to disciple you." Rather, gently come alongside, encouraging and serving as an expression of your relationship. Look for ways to meet real needs and be available to answer questions. Over time, if a greater desire emerges to spend more time together in deliberate discipleship then seek the Lord about what it should look like and commit to it. If this happens with several people around the same period of time, consider drawing them together as a group.

For those of you whose primary domain of service is the church, I'd like to point you back to the portion in chapter nine under "The Church as Disciple-Making Hub." There are practical things there for you to consider, whether transitioning a congregation or planting a new one.

3) A Resource for Making Disciple-Makers

As mentioned previously, it's important that you choose a resource to use in disciple-making that those you're discipling will be able to use as they disciple others. There are some very good resources available that I would highly recommend to you, many of them created by my friends.

The resource that my team and I use is *A Discipleship Journey*. It's a scripturally sound, proven, and practical resource to aid in the disciple-making process that I developed based around the twelve formation framework themes mentioned earlier in this chapter. It's been used effectively in its current form since 2004. It has been used in local churches, within the Dozen Domains of society, among men and women, with youth and young adults, and nationally and internationally. It's also a tool that is easy for those you're discipling to use to disciple others.

A Discipleship Journey is available in a one-year format, allowing disciples to digest and apply one major theme each month, and to renew their minds by reflecting on 52 aspects of God's character from Scripture. It is a flexible tool that can be applied in any kind of setting. It can be obtained as a Small Group Kit, Online Subscription or Mobile App at www.lionshare.org.

4) A Disciple-Making Network to Connect With: NetDMC

For many who have faithfully focused on the disciple-making mandate of Jesus for years, we've learned that no one person or group can do this by themselves. Those functioning as independent "silos," by not acting in concert with other like-hearted disciple-makers, significantly limit what could be the strategic combined impact on the church and the world around us.

> One thing that I've learned after three-plus decades of disciple-making is this: without a revelation from the Scriptures by the Holy Spirit to your heart of the centrality of Jesus' disciple-making mandate, you won't gain any real traction in your efforts to make disciple-makers! You must see it like Jesus sees it. You must come to grips with the reality that Jesus did not intend for disciple-making to be optional.

Originated in prayer in 2006 and launched in 2009 by Lionshare, NetDMC[9] is a relational-based mission-maximizing network made up of leaders throughout the Dozen Domains of society who are committed to making disciple-makers. Along with disciplers, some participants are active mentors and professional coaches. NetDMC "Teammates" build relationships and prayerfully strategize on domain teams, cross pollinate with other domains to glean from them and serve them, share disciple-making tools and resources, and rally together around a shared "2020 Vision."

The term NetDMC is not as much a name as it is a descriptor of our ever-expanding network of disciple-making communities within the Dozen Domains.

Our shared "2020 Vision" is:

Teaming to reproduce one million disciple-makers as catalysts in domain transformation locally and globally.

Note that this number refers not to disciples, but to *disciple-makers*—reproducers of the character, ways, and mission of Jesus who expect those they disciple to multiply the same in others.

One million disciple-makers by the end of the year 2020 spread through-out the Dozen Domains and the nations of the Earth! We are working toward this primarily with a "you and two" approach. While *"you"* continue to be discipled, you are actively discipling *"two"* others over the period of one year, who in turn, will do the same. Our concentration is on making sure those "two" you disciple receive foundational and/or formational disciple-making during that year (depending on where they're at spiritually), and, at the same time, begin to gain an understanding of domain discipleship.

If you remember our disciple-making math from a few pages back, you'll recall that if we start with 50, each one discipling two each year, we'll actually be pushing the 3 million threshold at the end of a decade. Is this 1 million aim doable? By God's grace, with His power, and by humbly teaming with one another—absolutely!

Consider some of the ramifications and possibilities of fulfilling this "2020 Vision":

- It begins in one's own backyard (relationships/domain) and can be replicated anywhere around the world.

- As churches become "disciple-making hubs" they could impact cities, counties, countries and entire continents via "disciple-making domain teams."

- We could be on the verge of an unprecedented mass mobilization of discipled Dozen Domain leaders like never before who can come alongside leaders of villages, cities, and nations to serve, disciple, and bless them and their people.

- It's possible that "domain transformation via disciple-making" could become one of the next great thrusts of world missions!

- Consider the impact on generations to come if making disciple-makers became the norm of every Jesus follower.

- The scope is broad: Making disciple-makers within the Dozen Domains in every country and among every people group on Earth.

There is no limit to what is possible when we team together to obey Jesus' disciple-making mandate! *Together* we can accomplish what none of us can do individually. *Together* we can see the local church become an effective and fruitful disciple-making hub. *Together* we can see society transformed as godly domain leaders disciple current and next generation leaders in the character, ways, and mission of Jesus. *Together* we can watch the overflow of disciple-making meet people's real needs. *Together* we can see Jesus glorified—enhancing His reputation in the eyes of the world around us. *Together.*

To learn more or to become a NetDMC Teammate, visit our NetDMC page at www.lionshare.org.

A Few Final Words

At our first NetDMC Summit, hosted in July of 2009 in Nashville, Henry Blackaby and Winkie Pratney participated with us as "spiritual fathers in residence." Listening to the Lord and hearing from them in that round-table experience proved to be a significant launch-pad for what we are now doing.

As I combed through my takeaways from those couple of days together, it was something the Lord Jesus dropped in my heart while I was listening to that wonderful multitude of counsel that resonated the loudest in my soul. It was a two-fold tactic that I was to take in my life and with those who team with me.

First, we are to cultivate disciple-makers among leaders within the Dozen Domains. They must catch the vision and be equipped as godly leaders to make disciple-makers within their spheres of influence—among those whom they lead and peers they're connected with.

Second, and with equal emphasis, we are to cultivate disciple-making communities among the next generation. Pouring the character, ways, and mission of Jesus into someone early on—as a child, teen, young adult—allows them to grow up discipled and with the understanding that making disciple-makers is the norm.

I commend these thoughts to you as you prayerfully move forward to cultivate disciple-making communities and reproduce disciple-makers where you live and lead.

Finally, let me end where I began in the introduction. We are living in a period of time where we must engage Jesus and rediscover His disciple-making blueprint. We desperately need a disciple-making revival in His

Church. Her health, effectiveness, and fruitfulness is dependent on our obedience to His last command. We must "own" His Great Commission in order to transform people and societies for His purposes and glory.

It all comes down to obeying Jesus.

The great pastor, preacher, and author A.W. Tozer said, "Have you noticed how much praying for revival has been going on of late—and how little revival has resulted? I believe the problem is that we have been trying to substitute praying for obeying, and it simply will not work. To pray for revival while ignoring the plain precept laid down in Scripture is to waste a lot of words and get nothing for our trouble. Prayer will become effective when we stop using it as a substitute for obedience."[10]

Will Jesus' last command be your least concern? Or will His mandate now become your mission, making disciple-makers where you live and lead?

> *"All authority in heaven and on earth has been given to me. Go therefore and make disciples of all nations, baptizing them in the name of the Father and of the Son and of the Holy Spirit, teaching them to observe all that I have commanded you. And behold, I am with you always, to the end of the age."*
>
> — JESUS

Endnotes

Chapter 1: The Acts of the Discipled

1. Dr. Tim Elmore, *Intentional Influence* (Nashville: LifeWay Press, 2003); www.growingleaders.com.
2. Randy Young, The Agora Group, www.theagoragroup.org.
3. An Interview with Cal Thomas. *Christianity Today*, April 25, 1994.
4. Dallas Willard, *The Great Omission* (New York: HarperOne, 2006).
5. Ibid.
6. Philip Schaff, *History Of The Christian Church*, Vol. II., *From Constantine The Great To Gregory The Great, A.D. 311-600* (New York: Charles Scribner & Co., 1867).
7. N'tan Lawrence, *Hebrew Thought Compared with Greek (Western) Thought.* http://www.hoshanarabbah.org/pdfs/heb_grk.pdf.
8. Michael Beer, "Greek or Hebrew?" http://www.wildolive.co.uk/Greek%20or%20Hebrew.htm.
9. Ibid.
10. http://www.barna.org/teens-next-gen-articles/545-top-trends-of-2011-millennials-rethink-christianity.

Chapter 2: The Fruitfulness Factor

1. www.ywam.org.
2. http://en.wikipedia.org/wiki/Washington_for_Jesus.

3. Rose McDermitt, "The Iranian Hostage Rescue Mission," *Avoiding Loses/Taking Risks,* http://www.press.umich.edu/pdf/0472108670-03.pdf.

4. www.bobbyclinton.com; jrclintoninstitute.com.

5. Bobby Clinton, "Three Articles on Finishing Well."http://www.bobbyclinton.com/articles/downloads/3FinishWellArticles.pdf.

6. Dr. J. Robert Clinton and Dr. Richard W. Clinton, *Getting Perspective Using Your Unique Timeline.(Barnabas Publishers, 1993).*

7. Dr. J. Robert Clinton and Dr. Richard W. Clinton, *The Life Cycle of a Leader. (Barnabas Publishers, 1995).*

8. http://iagenweb.org/boards/wright/obituaries/index.cgi?read=203266.

9. Dr. J. Robert Clinton and Dr. Richard W. Clinton, *The Life Cycle of a Leader. (Barnabas Publishers, 1995).*

10. www.messengerfellowship.com.

11. Dr. J. Robert Clinton and Dr. Richard W. Clinton, *The Life Cycle of a Leader. (Barnabas Publishers, 1995).*

12. Dr. J. Robert Clinton and Dr. Richard W. Clinton, *Boundary Processing. (Barnabas Publishers, 1992).*

13. Dr. J. Robert Clinton and Dr. Richard W. Clinton, *The Life Cycle of a Leader. (Barnabas Publishers, 1995).*

14. Ibid.

15. Dr. J. Robert Clinton and Dr. Richard W. Clinton, *Ultimate Contribution. (Barnabas Publishers, 1990).*

16. Bobby Clinton, "Three Articles on Finishing Well," http://www.bobbyclinton.com/articles/downloads/3FinishWellArticles.pdf.

17. www.bobbyclinton.com; jrclintoninstitute.com.

Chapter 3: The Jesus Blueprint

1. Richard Foster, *Celebration of Discipline* (San Franciso: Harper, 1988), 192.

2. G. Campbell Morgan, *Inspired by Tozer,* (Ventura, CA: Regal, 2011), 185.

3. Lauren Barlow, *Inspired by Tozer,* (Ventura, CA: Regal, 2011), 185.

4. David M. Rhoads and Kari Syreeni, *Characterization in the Gospels: Reconceiving Narrative Criticism* (New York: Continuum International Publishing Group, 2004), 155–156.

5. Dr. Jon Ruthven, *What's Wrong with Protestant Theology: Religious Tradition vs. Biblical Emphasis* (Tulsa, OK: Word and Spirit Press, 2012), 243–244.

6. Bill Hull, *The Complete Book of Discipleship: On Being and Making Followers of Christ* (Colorado Springs, CO: NavPress, 2006), 63–67.

7. Rabbi Jason Sobel, www.fusionglobal.org.

8. Dr. Jon Ruthven, *What's Wrong with Protestant Theology: Religious Tradition vs. Biblical Emphasis* (Tulsa, OK: Word and Spirit Press, 2012), 242–243.

9. Hans Weder, "Disciple, Discipleship," *The Anchor Bible Dictionary*, ed. David Freedman, vol. 2 (New York: Doubleday, 1992) 209.

10. Dr. Jon Ruthven, *What's Wrong with Protestant Theology: Religious Tradition vs. Biblical Emphasis* (Tulsa, OK: Word and Spirit Press, 2012), 241–242.

11. www.biblicaltheology.com/Research/WallaceQ01.html. Note Endnotes.

12. Gary W. Kuhne, http://sites.younglife.org/sites/ChesapeakeBayRegion/Shared%20Documents/Discipleship%20Quotes.pdf.

Chapter 4: What Are You Reproducing?

1. Dr. Henry Blackaby, *Conversations with Fathers of the Faith DVD Series* (Franklin: Lionshare Leadership Group, 2009).

2. Darrow L. Miller, *LifeWork: A Biblical Theology for What You Do Every Day* (Seattle, WA: YWAM Publishing, 2009), 40.

3. Henry Blackaby, *Experiencing God: Knowing and Doing the Will of God* (Nashville: LifeWay Press, 1993).

4. Steve Fry, *Thy Kingdom Come*, http://stevenfry.myshopify.com/collections/cds.

5. Leith Anderson, *A Church for the 21st Century* (Minneapolis: Bethany House Publishers, 1992).

Chapter 5: Disciple-Making and the Dozen Domains

1. www10.gencat.cat/pres_casa_llengues/AppJava/frontend/llengues_detall.jsp?id=288&idioma=5.

2. www.jesusfilm.org.

3. http://www.thefreedictionary.com/domain.

4. Facts on Noah's Ark and the Flood, http://ldolphin.org/cisflood.html.

5. O. E. Feucht, *Everyone a Minister* (St. Louis: Concordia, 1979), 80.

271

6. Jack Hayford, *Conversations with Fathers of the Faith* (Franklin: Lion-share Leadership Group, 2009).

7. Martin Luther, Henry Eyster Jacobs, Adolph Spaeth, *Works of Martin Luther* (A.J. Holman Company, 1915).

8. Gene Edward Veith (1999), "The Doctrine of Vocation: How God Hides Himself in Human Work," *Modern Reformation*, May/June 1999, Vol: 8, Num: 3.

9. William Perkins, *Treatise of the Vocations or Callings of Men* (John Legat, Printer to the University of Cambridge, 1605).

10. Gene Edward Veith (1999), "The Doctrine of Vocation: How God Hides Himself in Human Work," *Modern Reformation,* May/June 1999, Vol: 8, Num: 3.

11. Ibid.

12. Ibid.

13. Ibid.

14. Winkey Pratney, "Finding 35 Major Vocations Given by God Rooted in His Nature," http://www.crossrhythms.co.uk/articles/life/Winkie_Pratney_Finding_35_major_vocations_given_by_God_rooted_in_his_nature/37162/p1/.

15. Dr. Glenn R. Martin, *Biblical Christian Education: Liberation for Leadership*, www.biblicalchristianworldview.net/HomePage/biblicalChristianLeadershipGlennMartin.pdf, page 7.

16. Winkie Pratney, *Revolutionary Faith*, www.winkiepratney.com/_files/pdf/tracts/RevolutionaryFaith.pdf, page 1.

17. Robert J. Banks, R. Paul Stevens, *The Marketplace Ministry Handbook: A Manual for Work, Money and Business* (Regent College Publishing, 2005).

18. Hans Schwarz, *True Faith in the True God: An Introduction to Luther's Life and Thought* (Minneapolis: Augsburg Books, 1996), page 24.

19. Elizabeth O'Conner, *Eighth Day of Creation* (Washington D.C.: Potters House Book Service), 14–15.

20. Martin Luther, *Collected Works*, vol. 5, p. 102

21. Timothy Cardinal Dolan, *The O'Reilly Factor*, March 28, 2012.

Chapter 6: Dozen Domain Snapshots 1

1. Robert E. Coleman, *The Master Plan of Evangelism* (Grand Rapids, MI: Revell, 1963).

2. David Padfield, "God and Government," www.padfield.com/acrobat/sermons/civil_government.pdf.

3. Ibid.

4. https://www.dmdc.osd.mil/appj/dwp/index.jsp

5. www.nleomf.com.

6. Tim Elmore, *Generation iY: Our Last Chance to Save Their Future* (Poet Gardener Publishing, 2010).

Chapter 7: Dozen Domain Snapshots 2

1. http://newsroom.fb.com/content/default.aspx?NewsAreaId=22.

2. http://socialmediahive.com/about-us.

3. http://twitter.com/about.

4. http://www.youtube.com/t/press_statistics.

5. https://www.msu.edu/~jdowell/135/factoids.html.

6. Laurie Beth Jones, *Jesus CEO: Using Ancient Wisdom for Visionary Leadership* (New York, NY: Hyperion, 1996).

7. http://ezinearticles.com/?Faith-in-the-Workplace&id=155896.

8. http://adsabs.harvard.edu/full/1985gamf.conf...75P, page 90.

9. http://www.christianity.co.nz/science4.htm.

10. Ibid.

11. Ibid.

12. www.itpro.co.uk/612913/man-on-the-moon-technology-then-and-now.

Chapter 8: Dozen Domain Snapshots 3

1. www.worldhunger.org/articles/Learn/world%20hunger%20facts%202002.htm.

2. http://nccs.urban.org/statistics/quickfacts.cfm.

3. Ibid. http://nccs.urban.org/statistics/quickfacts.cfm.

Chapter 9: Cultivating Disciple-Making Communities

1. Dr. John Perkins, *Conversations With Fathers of the Faith DVD Series* (Franklin: Lionshare Leadership Group, 2009).

2. Bill Hull, *The Complete Book of Discipleship: On Being and Making Followers of Christ* (Colorado Springs: NavPress, 2006), 24, 26.

3. Dr. Lloyd Ogilvie, *Conversations With Fathers of the Faith DVD Series* (Franklin: Lionshare Leadership Group, 2009).

4. Jack Hayford, *Conversations With Fathers of the Faith DVD Series* (Franklin: Lionshare Leadership Group, 2009).

5. Robert E. Coleman, *The Master Plan of Evangelism* (Grand Rapids, MI: Revell, 1963).

6. Martin Luther King, Jr.; *A Knock at Midnight Sermon*, June 11, 1967, http://mlk-kpp01.stanford.edu/index.php/encyclopedia/documentsentry/doc_a_knock_at_midnight.

7. Dave Buehring, *A Discipleship Journey* (HigherLife Publishing, 2004/2011), 247.

8. John Tolson, www.highimpactlife.com.

9. www.quickmba.com/marketing/product/diffusion.

Chapter 10: Making Disciple-Makers

1. Dietrich Bonhoeffer, *The Cost of Discipleship* (New York: Touchstone, 1995).

2. Greg Ogden, *Transforming Discipleship: Making Disciples a Few at a Time* (InterVarsity Press Books, 2003).

3. Grant Edwards, First Steps, www.disciplinganother.net.

4. LeRoy Eims, *The Lost Art of Disciple-Making* (Grand Rapids: Zondervan, 1978), 45-46.

5. Robert E. Coleman, *The Master Plan of Evangelism* (Grand Rapids: Revell, 1963).

6. http://en.wikipedia.org/wiki/World_population_estimates.

7. Dallas Willard, *The Great Omission* (New York, NY: HarperOne, 2006).

18. Dr. J. Robert Clinton and Dr. Richard W. Clinton, *The Life Cycle of a Leader. (Barnabas Publishers, 1995)*

8. NetDMC, www.lionshare.org.

9. http://christianquotes.org/tag/cat/18/58.

ENDNOTES

IF YOU'RE A FAN OF THIS BOOK, PLEASE TELL OTHERS:

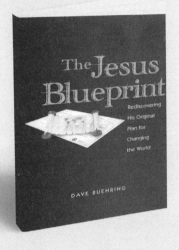

- Write about *The Jesus Blueprint* on your blog, Twitter, MySpace, and Facebook page.

- Suggest *The Jesus Blueprint* to friends.

- When you're in a bookstore, ask them if they carry the book. The book is available through all major distributors, so any bookstore that does not have *The Jesus Blueprint* in stock can easily order it.

- Write a positive review of *The Jesus Blueprint* on www.amazon.com.

- Send my publisher, HigherLife Publishing, suggestions on Web sites, conferences, and events you know of where this book could be offered at media@ahigherlife.com.

- Purchase additional copies to give away as gifts.

NOW THAT YOU ARE ENVISIONED FOR DISCIPLE-MAKING—HERE'S HOW YOU CAN BE EQUIPPED TO DO IT:

A Discipleship Journey (ADJ) is a Scripturally sound, proven and practical resource to aid individuals, leaders and churches in obeying Jesus' command to "make disciples". It provides you with a deliberate one-year formational journey which can result in real life transformation when used as a tool to apply Scripture, walking in relationship with others and obeying what the Holy Spirit is revealing. And, in the end, it equips you with the ability to reproduce disciple-makers for the rest of your life!

ADJ can be ordered in three distinct formats:

1. **Small Group Resource** *(Includes a leader's guide, 10 ADJ manuals and 48 video segments)*
2. **Mobile App** *(features all the video segments, the entire ADJ manual and more)*
3. **ADJ Manual**

> To order ADJ in any format, simply go to our website at:
> www.lionshare.org or email us at: info@lionshare.org.

ENGAGE:

There's a growing network of disciple-makers who like you are passionate about returning to God's original plan to change the world in the domains of societal influence where they already are. It's an ever-expanding network of disciple-makers called NetDMC. Our shared decade-long '2020 Vision' is teaming to reproduce one million disciple-makers as catalysts in domain transformation locally and globally. If you'd like to learn more or get involved with NetDMC and our 2020 Vision visit www.lionshare.org.

YOU CAN ATTEND OR HOST A JESUS BLUEPRINT WORKSHOP:

Imagine for a moment the impact, if every follower of Jesus was deliberately discipled around His character, ways and mission and reproduced the same in others. Imagine if that was the norm – like Jesus intended it to be. How might that change the way you live your life? How could that change how your church functions? How would that transform your city and society?

Dave Buehring, is facilitating one-day regional workshops throughout the country for pastors, godly societal leaders, and their teams. Would you be interested in teaming with Dave to host a workshop in your region? If so, contact him and his team at info@lionshare.org / 615-377-4688.

CONNECT WITH US:

Lionshare
7065 Moores Lane, Ste 200
Brentwood, TN 37027
Phone: (615) 377-4688
Email: info@lionshare.org
www.lionshare.org

The Disciple-Maker:

If you'd like to sign up to receive *The Disciple-Maker*, a weekly blog from Dave and disciple-makers serving the Dozen Domains, visit www.lionshare.org today.